INTO THE FIELD

INTO THE
FIELD

A FOREIGN
CORRESPONDENT'S
NOTEBOOK

TRACY DAHLBY

UNIVERSITY OF TEXAS PRESS
AUSTIN

Requests for permission to reproduce material
from this work should be sent to:
 Permissions
 University of Texas Press
 P.O. Box 7819
 Austin, TX 78713-7819
 http://utpress.utexas.edu/index.php/rp-form

The paper used in this book meets the minimum
requirements of ANSI/NISO Z39.48-1992 (R1997)
(Permanence of Paper). ∞

LIBRARY OF CONGRESS CATALOGING-IN-PUBLICATION DATA
Dahlby, Tracy.
 Into the field : a foreign correspondent's notebook /
Tracy Dahlby. — First edition.
  pages cm
 Summary: "In this lively memoir of covering the Asian Pacific Rim, a veteran reporter for *National Geographic* and *Newsweek* tells "the stories behind
the stories" that reveal the hard work, skill, and luck it takes to be a successful
foreign correspondent. His real-world advice about everything from successful
travel planning, to finding a great local fixer, to dealing with circumstances that
can range from friendly to formidable makes this book a practical how-to guide
for aspiring journalists"—Provided by publisher.
 ISBN 978-0-292-72913-1 (hardback)
 1. Journalism—East Asia. 2. Journalism—Pacific Area. 3. Dahlby, Tracy.
 4. Journalists—East Asia—Biography. 5. Journalists—Pacific Area—Biography.
 6. Americans—East Asia—Biography. 7. Americans—Pacific Area—Biography.
 I. Title.
 PN5630.D34 2014
 079'.5—dc23

                                                           2014012770

doi:10.7560/729131

For my first teachers, my parents, Hugh and Joan Dahlby—
and my students, who continue to educate me every day

Traveler, there is no path.
The path is made by walking.

———

ANTONIO MACHADO

CONTENTS

On assignment for Newsweek,
Iwo Jima, 1985.

SOMETHING LIKE
A CALLING

1

One Sunday night in the winter of 1969 or thereabouts, I fell prey
to a mental hijacking from which, as the record herein will plainly
show, I've yet to fully recover.

An overly groomed college kid, I was sitting on my bed in my
boyhood home in Seattle's working-class South End tuning a radio
the size of a shoebox. Sunk in the doldrums of early adulthood, I
was looking for a tune, a beat, a message, something to fire up the
internal dynamo and yank me outside of myself. It was, in short,
one of those pain-in-the-ass times in life when you yearn for adventure, would do anything for a taste of it, but adventure isn't returning its messages.

My mother thought I was being absurd. "What on God's green
earth do you have to be unhappy about?" she'd demand, as I skulked
around the house, bemoaning the cruel twist of fate that had seed-
ed in me the urge to travel the world, scale its peaks and explore its
oceans, only to trap me in the horizontal terrain of the shopping
mall that leads nowhere and to nothing.

Melodrama aside, I knew my mother was right: I did have it
good. *Too good.* I had a tidy room in our daylight basement with a
blue-and-white chenille bedspread and matching curtains on a window that overlooked a soggy patch of lawn where my friends and
I played badminton in the summers. I had a comfortable chair for
reading, my own TV set, and a refrigerator not a half-dozen paces
away in our furnace room that was larded with enough milk, cold
cuts, and homemade desserts to sate a pasha.

To my mother, who had grown up a grocer's daughter during the Great Depression and read desperation across the counter in her neighbors' eyes, it was a sin to take such riches for granted. As she was fond of reminding me: "You should get down on your knees and thank your lucky stars, Mister."

But I didn't feel lucky. I felt smothered. So there I sat, tuning the big radio, when I heard a plumy, authoritative voice say the word, "China." I stopped tuning. Something about that vast, mysterious country had long since caught my fancy, and now there was some exciting news. The studio host was talking about developments in the Great Proletarian Cultural Revolution that was bedeviling the Communist giant. He said the whole country was in an uproar.

I wasn't completely naïve. I'd heard about this real-life drama at school from my professors. China's maximum leader, Chairman Mao Zedong, had unleashed millions of student Red Guards to help him consolidate his grip on power. Roaming the countryside, they looted schools and temples, forced writers, artists, teachers, and "capitalist roaders" to clean toilets and pigsties, and generally smashed or sacked anything smacking of the Four Olds that were alleged to be holding China back from realizing a pure Communist state—old customs, old culture, old habits, and old ideas. It was a wave of violence that made America's rowdy youth rebellion of the day look like a beach party by comparison.

And now, events in China had taken a bloody new turn. Chairman Mao, having egged on the Red Guards in the name of revolution, had called in his People's Liberation Army to restore public order *by eliminating the Red Guards*, and the life-and-death struggle for China's soul entered a new phase. Heightening the mystery was the fact that Western travelers were rare in China at the time and Western journalists even rarer. In a way that's hard to fathom in today's world, where pictures snapped by smart phones can go viral and travel the world in nanoseconds, China was a black box virtually impossible for ordinary Americans to see into.

I don't remember the radio broadcast verbatim, but the narration for a popular 1967 TV documentary, *The Roots of Madness*, captures the overheated mood of the time: "There are 700 million Chinese today, one quarter of the human race, and they are taught to hate. Their growing power is the world's greatest threat to peace and light."

Such bulletins were heady stuff, even for somebody cocooned behind chenille curtains half a world away from the action. And so, I was listening closely to what the man on the radio had to say for clues to the mayhem in Red China when the program cut away for an on-scene report from the British colony of Hong Kong, the Free World's great listening post in Asia. Suddenly there was a new voice in the room.

In contrast to the muted, scholarly tones of the host, this new voice spoke in a brisk, manly baritone betraying what in south Seattle was regarded as the height of savoir faire, an English accent. In dramatic cadence, the Voice described a bumper crop of corpses that had come sluicing down the Pearl River from China, testifying to intensifying political upheaval. Snagged by fishing boats and police cruisers in Hong Kong waters, it intoned, some of the bodies looked suspiciously like they had recently belonged to the beleaguered Red Guards.

The report lasted no more than a minute or two, yet somehow, by adding in the presence of the professional eyewitness, the story came alive in a way that made the goings-on in far Hong Kong as easy to picture as a Hollywood spy thriller. I imagined the Voice as a rakishly handsome James Bond figure and saw him clear as day: Dressed in a white tropical suit, he stood on a patch of pavement shimmering with sun and heat, as a jostling Eastern crowd broke around him like waves around a lighthouse. Meanwhile, at the back of the frame, the green hills of giant China whispered signals of political intrigue and derring-do.

Well, we all need a fairy tale to drive us toward the reality of our lives, and that radio spot pretty much did it for me. In the blinking of an eye, that magical Voice, so canny and urbane, the voice of high adventure itself, had traveled the airwaves into my bedroom and swept me away to an enigmatic world of floating corpses and bloodthirsty commissars. I was not yet twenty, but from that point on, I knew that more than anything in the world I wanted to become a foreign correspondent.

It was an unusual dream for somebody with my qualifications. Excepting a single trip to exotic California to visit relatives, I'd never been more than a couple hundred miles from home, mostly on campouts with the Boy Scouts. I occasionally read the newspaper beyond the comics but found the news of the wider world as numbing as novocaine. The Vietnam War was raging, Uncle Sam was sending friends I'd grown up with to fight the Communists there, and if my number came up in the new draft lottery, I could be joining them. Yet my ignorance was so thick I had trouble telling America's allies from its enemies, and the foreign-sounding battlefields—Bien Hoa, Hue, Ia Drang, or Khe Sanh—were little more to me than a confusing alphabet soup.

Not that I yearned to see the face of war—I didn't. But somewhere the world was burning with energy and excitement, and I kicked myself for not being close enough to the flames to toast a marshmallow.

But miracles do happen. As that eternal student of the human mind, Carl Jung, wrote, "The unexpected and the incredible belong in this world," and something incredible happened to me. How else could you explain it?

Five or six years after listening to the radio at home in Seattle, I was out in Asia working for an Englishman who had actually broadcast such stories on the Cultural Revolution with the dashing sign-off, "From Hong Kong . . . *this* is Ian Dunbar." Bulky and rumpled, he looked nothing at all like James Bond—and Ian Dunbar was an alias, not his real name, for reasons we'll get to in a minute. But the central fact remains: Against all odds and reason, my long-ago hijacking by radio started a process that was to pull me out of my parents' basement and into a world where I discovered my impossible dream of becoming a foreign correspondent was one from which a life could actually step. And I thank my lucky stars that it did.

2

This book is my attempt to share with readers the joys of a hard-to-describe career. Today, being a foreign correspondent can mean a number of things. A relatively few intrepid souls risk all to tell the story of war or revolution in places like Afghanistan, Syria, or Egypt, from the inside out. More often, workers in international news find themselves firing a computer terminal in London or Tokyo or Beijing, crunching numbers and pronouncing on the health of global markets. Meanwhile, the brisk decline of newspapers, news magazines, and the broadcast news business has shuttered costly foreign bureaus as advertisers and readers head for the digital hills. One day soon, the invention of a digital reporting drone could make the globe-girdling, eyeballs-on-the-ground foreign correspondent as rare a sighting as the pterodactyl.

Thankfully, we're not there yet. I say that because it is precisely the rare individual who goes out into the world on a mission to make visible what for most people is largely invisible about their lives and times, in a way that informs, educates, or honestly entertains, that fits my definition of a foreign correspondent. Good foreign reporting is mainly the result of hard digging and nimble, prodigious footwork in the field. Much of it goes on behind the scenes in ways the audience never hears about—jousting with an immigration official to get into or out of a country, talking your way into a far place or out of a tight spot, or finding the ship, train, plane, or helicopter that will get you to your story and back. If that still sounds a little gauzy, I've made my point: It's easier to explain if you, the reader, come along and join me in the field.

To that end, this book centers on the travel and reporting I did for a half-dozen pieces that ran in *National Geographic* during the decade I regularly contributed to the magazine. Part 1 looks at a broad swath of Asia, the South China Sea, at a time when China's growing power and influence began rattling teacups in the neighborhood and shaking America's sense of itself as the world's one true superpower. Like other interested parties, I'm convinced that apart from learning how to accommodate Islam as a cultural and political reality in the world, America's greatest challenge in the years ahead lies in understanding the rise of China and how it will shape American lives and the lives of people in places we barely know.

Part 2 takes on Japan, where I lived for a dozen years during that country's economic heyday in the 1970s and 1980s while serving as a reporter for the *Far Eastern Economic Review*, a Hong Kong–based newsweekly, and then the *Washington Post* and *Newsweek* magazine, and where the *Geographic* allowed me to return years later to find a people struggling through a collective midlife crisis in a risen but rudderless industrial state. Part 3 deals with two Southeast Asian countries, Vietnam and Indonesia, which I belatedly discovered and learned to love. Although the American news media have virtually ignored them, they have much to teach us about the past, the present, and ourselves.

Why these particular stories?

The answer, in a word, is luxury. My editors at the *Geographic*, particularly the late Bill Graves, the magazine's former editor-in-chief, and Bob Poole, its then-executive editor, bestowed a rare gift on their writers and photographers—the luxury to travel the world in pursuit of a story while the magazine generously footed the bill. (I always loved the way the official *Geographic* expense booklet listed "Hired Aircraft/Watercraft" as a standard line item, though in fact I only chartered an airplane a single time, and perhaps for good reason—it crashed.) The ultimate luxury was freedom; released from the rigors of tight news deadlines, I was free to report exactly where my nose led me and without adult supervision of any kind. It was a gift of such magnitude that it confused me at first, and I naively asked one of my editors how long I'd have to spend in the field. The man looked puzzled and said, "Come back when you're finished reporting."

The point is it takes so much time to cook an omelet, as the saying goes, and a good job can't be rushed. Bill and Bob understood that and, while the products displayed herein may undershoot the

LOCATION:		DATE May 15				REMARKS
Vou. No.	DAILY EXPENDITURES	Cash Expenditures		Corporate Card Charges		(To indicate business purpose of expenditures, list exchange rates, record guests & their business relationship, etc.)
	Hotel (Room & Taxes)					
	Meals (including tips): Breakfast					
	Lunch					
	Dinner					
	Entertainment—Other than meals (identify guests under remarks)					
	Tips (Other than meals)					
	Taxis					
	Telephone					
	Guides/Interpreters/Assistants					
	Auto-Rental Fees (Gas, etc.)					
	Air or Rail Travel					
1-36 B	Hired Aircraft/Watercraft →→	1168	500			C BOAT 2nd CLASS + UPGRADE FOR. C DAHLBY, WIBOWO * TANYA ALWI
	Equip. & Supplies (describe)					
1-37	Supplies for boat trip	118	500			BOTTLED WATER + SNACKS.
	Laundry					
	Research Material (Newspapers, Books, etc.)					
	Miscellaneous (describe)					
1-38	uuuuuuuuuuu	4000	000			PARTIAL PAYMENT FOR AIR CHARTER. (REDUCED FROM $1000.00 DUE
	Page Total—prevailing currency	5287	000	No Totals Required		AIR MISHAP + ONE-WAY
	Converted to U. S. dollars (if applicable)			for		UTILIZATION ONLY.)
				Corporate Charges		

(1)

NATIONAL GEOGRAPHIC SOCIETY

EXPENSE ACCOUNT

of

TRACY S. DAHLBY

NEW YORK, NY 10017

NAME

INDONESIA

ASSIGNMENT
(Project title or business purpose of trip)

Dates of Assignment:

From 05-01-00

To 05-18-00

Signature of Traveler

14 DAYS

Expense report, Indonesia,
May 2000.

virtuosity I was after or the editors were looking for, the opportunity to shed light on far places was an unqualified blessing.

I have only one serious complaint. You do all that work—spend weeks or months in the field while you cruise the outback, pick dead flies out of the fried rice, tax the hospitality of farmers, fishermen, and oil-rig workers, and fly in airplanes not infrequently in hair-raising states of disrepair. Back home, you devote endless hours to distilling notebooks into reams of typed notes, and then into a mere twenty or so double-spaced pages of story—fewer words than you'll find on the daily editorial pages of the *New York Times* or a hyperactive blogger extrudes in a few hours.

Suffice it to say a lot gets left out. Accordingly, what I've tried to do in these pages is to place each of my published stories in a greater depth of field, offering just enough of the original to set the scene so I can then step out of the frame and explain the stories behind the story—the bits of background that show how it all came together. Think of it as a how-to book for observing the world that is wrapped in a memoir of a reporting career. So if current events and political analysis are what you're after, stop reading here; on the other hand, if you're looking for clues as to how a professional observer goes about trying to navigate the world and make sense of it, then this book really is for you.

Just a few more things to keep in mind: Original passages from the *Geographic* have endured a minimum of tampering but have been abridged, in some cases, to fit more happily with their new format and purpose. The new stuff, the stories behind the stories, meanwhile, is mainly based on notes I took during my field reporting. For anecdotes from my boyhood or young adulthood, I've relied on what was once called "a reporter's finest tool"—his memory—while bearing in mind that even a trained observer's memory is still a human one. You do the best you can.

My goal in all this is twofold: For one thing, I want to provide a better sense of what it's been like to be at least one kind of foreign correspondent. But I'm also out to inflict on the reader this personal article of faith: It behooves all of us, I think, to develop a highly individualized stance from which to observe and act in this hard-to-parse, idiosyncratic world of ours. Because we understand the world through the "reporting" we do, and ultimately from the stories we tell ourselves about our experiences, it stands to reason that our approach needs to take into account our individual tics, tastes, and judgments or it won't take us very far. In short, the better storytellers we become, the more others are likely to get out of our stories.

My friend Christina helped plant that idea in my brain. An artist working in recovered materials, she was creating marvelous *tableaux* from things she'd find in streets, alleys, or along the railroad tracks. When she phoned to welcome me back home from tramping around the South China Sea, she said, "I can't wait to hear the story."

Still jet-lagged, and already feeling the hot breath of my writing deadline, I misinterpreted her message as a friendly injunction to stop dogging it and get to work.

Oh, no, Christina said, "I don't mean the story you're *writing.*" What appeared in print was okay, she conceded. What she really liked, though, was the way I *talked* about where I'd been and what I'd seen with a kind of preacher's passion—in other words, the stuff that rarely had a prayer of making it into print. Those were the stories that were really interesting!

How could I argue? Truth be told, I've always felt that way too. And so, I very much hope you'll agree, as we go off together into the field for a look at the delights, the trials and tedium, and the eccentric treasures of one long-distance reporter.

PART
ONE

NAVIGATING THE CHINA SEAS

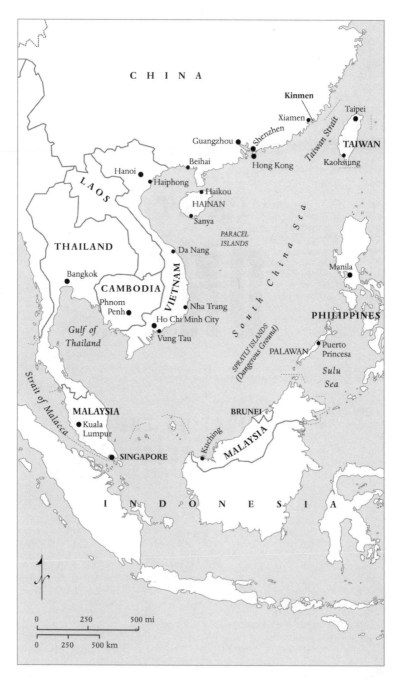

The South China Sea.

WORKING
THE COAST

1

"A man begins every stage of his life as a novice." That's how the French writer Nicolas Chamfort famously put it, and I think he was onto something.

In early 1997, I had been a foreign correspondent, off and on, for over twenty years. Like other tradesmen of a certain age—plumber, doctor, or computer technician—I felt reasonably competent at what I did while resigning myself to the likelihood that dreams I'd chased as a younger man might now never come true—taking up ballroom dancing, for example, or writing the Great American Novel, or becoming a cowboy.

On a personal level, though, the previous twelve months had been fraught with midlife growing pains. A documentary film project in Toronto had turned into a hornet's nest of conflicting personalities. Disease had reared its head. My father had died of prostate or bladder cancer, it wasn't clear which, the previous June in Seattle. Meanwhile the prostate cancer gene was making its rounds in my family and, in October of 1996, it was my turn; a biopsy came back positive, and just after New Year's Day 1997 my surgeon at New York Hospital carved out the offending walnut-sized gland.

I was feeling cursed and tender when Bob Poole phoned me from *National Geographic* headquarters in Washington, DC, with some rare good news. On July 1, 1997, after marathon talks between London and Beijing, Britain would return its 156-year-old crown colony of Hong Kong to China. It was a big, symbolic event. After what the Chinese called their "century of humiliation"—the foreign meddling that began with the First Opium War in 1839 and ended with Mao Zedong's triumphant Communist revolution in 1949—the "Handover," as it was being called, would mark China's rise as a burgeoning global power.

Bob said the editors had approved a pitch I'd made for covering the event and asked me if I was available for duty. "Yes!" I said, and my spirits soared at what promised to be the assignment of a lifetime.

As Bob and I worked it out, I would start with the Handover in Hong Kong and then just keep going. I'd travel down along Asia's curved belly and around Southeast Asia asking diplomats, business tycoons, cab drivers, fishermen, shell pickers, farmers, merchant sailors, and whomever else I could find what they thought about China's growing reach. And since this was a *Geographic* story, and dealt with the natural drama contained by the perimeters of the South China Sea, one of the globe's most strategic waterways, I'd travel by sea wherever possible to get a gull's-eye view of the territory.

For my "hook," or central metaphor, Bob suggested I think of the South China Sea as an arena in which people and nations had vied over the centuries for limited resources and the power and wealth that went with them. In the past the prizes had been spices, gold, and religious converts; nowadays, it was the lure of a possible king's ransom in oil and undersea minerals. China had become a key player in the region and the South China Sea, long considered the American superpower's lake, was gradually becoming a Chinese one, a change that worried China's closest neighbors. That, in turn, raised a fundamental question: Would the waking dragon show its claws or its finesse as its power grew?

Ever the gifted editor, Bob provided me such a brilliant summation of what I ought to be doing that I wished I'd thought of it myself. But there it was, the South China Sea, the ultimate gladiator's ring in which, over the centuries, the rough-and-tumble of life had shoved forward winners and losers, poetry and strife, dire poverty and unfathomable wealth, the freedom to dream big dreams and the ever-present threat of enslavement to ambition, ideology, and

**NATIONAL
GEOGRAPHIC
SOCIETY**

ROBERT M. POOLE
Associate Editor
NATIONAL GEOGRAPHIC MAGAZINE

May 15, 1997

TO WHOM IT MAY CONCERN:

This letter will introduce Mr. Tracy Dahlby, a writer on assignment in your country for the **National Geographic Society.**

The **National Geographic** has assigned Mr. Dahlby to write an article on the South China Sea to appear in a forthcoming issue of the **National Geographic** Magazine.

The **National Geographic** assumes full responsibility for Mr. Dahlby. He has been provided with adequate funds to carry out this assignment. He will obey all laws and regulations of your country.

We appreciate any assistance or cooperation you extend to Mr. Dahlby while he is working on this assignment.

If you have any questions about Mr. Dahlby or his assignment for **National Geographic**, please call me (collect) at ███████ ███.

Thank you.

Sincerely,

[signature]

1145 17th Street N.W., Washington, D.C. 20036-4688   Telephone: ██████   Fax: ██████
♻ Recycled-content paper

Letter of passage, 1997.

political power. All that exotic churning had, in the minds of Westerners at least, made this corner of the world's oceans a place of romance and danger, and that raised a second big question: Would—could—the West abandon its antiquated illusions to come to grips with the new realities in Asia?

Speaking for myself, and after my private *annus horribilis*, I was past due for a little romance, and I couldn't wait to get back into the field, which to me represents true freedom. Making a documentary film can be great fun, but it's journalism by committee—to do the job right you need film editors, video shooters, sound technicians, and a small army of support staff. In the field, all I would need was a stack of fresh notebooks, a fistful of reliable pens, and my reporter's nose to guide me to the story.

Optimistic and raring to go, I planned to travel for eight weeks. (Since I misjudged the distances involved, it would take me eleven weeks.) Then, as Bob had decreed, I would wrap up Asia's new gestalt in an article of no more than six thousand words. That worked out to something less than one hundred words per reporting day in the field; not exactly heavy lifting, I thought, and besides the whole thing sounded as dashing as an old Clark Gable movie. (Here, I should point out that I suffer from a chronic but fairly typical case of occupational amnesia that prevents me from remembering the trials and tribulations of actually reporting and writing a demanding story.)

As the weeks rolled by, however, I began to wonder if I hadn't bitten off more than I could chew. Trying to find vessels to fetch me from place to place, I faxed and emailed letters of introduction to commercial shipping agencies and learned that, in spite of my own illusions about the romance of the sea, seaborne commerce wasn't made for adolescent adventure; it is a cutthroat business in which owners must ruthlessly control costs to turn a profit. Few titans of shipping, it seemed, wanted a nosy reporter hanging around to take up space, add to insurance bills, and ask irritating questions about the smuggling and piracy for which the South China Sea was notorious.

By late spring, with departure only a few weeks away, I was getting cold feet. My wife, Toshiko, and I were back in New York now, living in our old apartment on Forty-Ninth Street just up First Avenue from the United Nations. My recovery from surgery hadn't been as complete as I had hoped and, to top matters off, Tammy, our pet sheltie, a loyal family member for sixteen years, was dying of old age and going downhill fast. How could I possibly leave home at such a critical time?

I put that exact question to Toshiko one afternoon when she was standing at the kitchen sink peeling carrots for dinner. She stopped peeling, smiled sympathetically, and then let the soul of her samurai upbringing in Japan give it to me straight: "You can't chicken out now," she said.

Well, it was hardly a matter of chickening out, I spluttered. I, I, I . . .

"You might not get a chance like this again," Toshiko said flatly, and she didn't have to spell out that part. "Just pretend you're young again and seeing Asia for the first time." Tammy rolled her eyeballs and thumped her tail, as if in agreement. They were right, of course. If you're not prepared to be lucky then to hell with you, I thought; you have no business taking the field. I got to work.

2

When you get right down to it, a correspondent is a multifunctional traveler, and by now I had most of my bases covered. I'd picked out my library—a single dog-eared volume of Joseph Conrad's stories of the sea—all I could fit into my duffel bag in those unenlightened, pre-e-reader days. My travel agency came in the form of a wad of air tickets from Ann Judge at the *Geographic* travel office. My bank was a thicker wad of traveler's checks, ten crisp hundred-dollar bills, and two credit cards. A primitive, brick-like mobile phone constituted the communications department. Everything had its place in my "office"—a ratty leather shoulder bag that also housed a laptop.

Ever helpful, the *Geographic* shipped me a medical kit that would put a small hospital to shame. It contained an arm sling, sterile syringes in airtight plastic wrappers, and one of those epinephrine injectors you jam into your thigh if you find yourself lapsing into anaphylactic shock. There were bandages, regular and butterfly; water purification tablets; light and heavy-duty painkillers; Lomotil for diarrhea and Cipro for whatever Lomotil couldn't stop; a salve for insect bites, two anti-malarial medicines, and two types of industrial-strength mosquito spray, one for the skin and the other for clothing and mosquito netting. Given my recent adventure in the land of the medicos, I studied each piece of paraphernalia with great interest—and then left half of it in a cardboard box in the hall closet to make room for the provisioning of other departments.

Establishing contacts remained a challenge. On the theory that the long-distance reporter who doesn't check on real-time conditions is asking for trouble, I fired off e-mails and faxes to old friends and pros in Hong Kong, Bangkok, and ports of call around the rim of Asia who could fill me in on current events and introduce me to people in places where I didn't know a soul. Ever mindful of Louis Pasteur's routinely ignored dictum, "Fortune favors the prepared mind," I am a stickler for elaborate, nit-picking preparation, and while sainted friends and a few absolute strangers did come forward with offers of help, the lack of a well-worked agenda made me nervous.

Well, you plan when you can and you don't when you can't, and at a certain point you indulge what the self-help gurus refer to as "acceptance." As a final act of preparation, and a little melodramatically, I'll admit, I ordered my barber to scalp me in the manner of a Buddhist monk setting out on a religious pilgrimage.

So there I was, the adventurer at age forty-seven. The glamorous self-image of the foreign correspondent only slightly diminished by postsurgical bladder-control issues, I headed for JFK airport. In due course, the game was afoot, and I found myself on a military transport plane, ponderous as a pregnant guppy, its hold filled with heavily armed Filipino marines and a dangerously shifting load of bedsprings, as we lumbered over the region's most remote geopolitical bull's-eye. And so began my story in the pages of the *National Geographic*:

> *After a long flight over the southeasterly reaches of the South China Sea, the C-130 transport plane banged down on Pagasa atoll in the middle of the Spratly Islands. Getting out to stretch my legs on the crushed coral runway, I could see a clump of spindly trees, a mossy concrete pillbox or two, and then nothing for 360 degrees but dazzling, jet-blue sea.*
>
> *"This is Armageddon?" I thought, chuckling to myself, as 50 Filipino troops, armed with rifles, sauntered smilingly toward the tree line.*
>
> *Not that there is anything funny about the Spratlys. Sporadic shooting sprees have left dozens of sailors and fishermen from neighboring countries dead or wounded as their governments vie for control of this scattered rosary of coral specks and sandbars. Officials in both Washington and Beijing peg the Spratlys as a possible trigger for a showdown between the United States and China.*
>
> *But from Pagasa, a Philippine military encampment since the early 1970s, the Spratlys appeared to me less to augur the end of the world than to occupy it. From atop its battered concrete observation tower the island looked deceptively small, a disk of land that seemed no bigger around than Yankee Stadium, with a sparkling lagoon where huge brains of mottled coral communicated with a shallow bottom. Watching surf pound the thin reef wall separating the turquoise pool from the wild indigo sea, I felt my heart sink a little at the beauty of it all. How could any place this remote be the source of so much trouble?*
>
> *The answer, in a word, is location. The Spratlys lie along one of the most strategic shipping routes in the world, a deepwater slot that zigzags up the middle of the South China Sea for 1,700 miles from the Strait of Malacca in the southwest to Hong Kong in the north. Each day some 200 merchant vessels haul oil from the Middle East (including 80 percent of Japan's total supply) and*

thousands of other riches. Shrimp come from Thailand, rice from Vietnam, Nike sneakers from Indonesia—much of it to stock store shelves in the West. What's more, the Spratlys could harbor sizable untapped oil reserves.

The delicate job of keeping this strategic ocean artery open for business ranks high on the U.S. list of global security concerns. But what keeps its big gray-hulled warships on permanent patrol there may increase the risk of a collision among major geopolitical interests. When and if a newly robust China, which claims historical deed to the entire sea, acquires the naval weaponry to enforce its ambitions, will the U.S. be forced to get tough?

Publicly American officials downplay the potential danger, but privately they worry. "I just hope they don't find oil in the Spratlys," a Navy officer told me.

And after laying out what journalists will recognize as the lede and context for the story, I served up a smattering of historical background before driving on to the overall point—the way the area's age-old rivalries had renewed themselves in a sharp-elbowed competition for territory, wealth, and national self-esteem:

For 2,500 years the South China Sea has seen one scramble after another for its limited and valuable resources. Early navigators— Malays, Chinese—braved its murderous typhoons, soul-numbing calms, and mysterious monsoon currents.* They chased the lure of sandalwood and silk, teas and spices, over a no-man's-land of reefs and shoals, establishing its first trading routes. Beginning in the 1500s, European—and eventually American—fortune hunters sailed in, pursuing visions of God, gold, and glory. They were spellbound, as Joseph Conrad put it, by "dark islands on a blue reef-scarred sea." Pragmatic colonial powers meanwhile set up elaborate

---

* Mention of early navigators should also properly include Indians, Arabs, and Persians, and the "maritime silk road" that linked China, through the South China Sea and the Indian Ocean, with India, the East Coast of Africa and, via the Red Sea, with Europe.

engines for pumping tin, antimony, rubber, nutmeg, gold, and other natural treasures to the outside world.

Today the old, semi-enclosed sea is more vital to the global economy than ever. Shaped like a hammerhead shark with a weight problem, the 1.4-million-square-mile body of water carries roughly a third of the planet's shipping and could harbor trillions of dollars in undersea deposits of oil and natural gas.

With so much up for grabs, the ten Asian nations that crowd the sea's coastline view these waters and its prizes as a source of national pride—and survival. Exactly what China intends is anybody's guess, but there is little doubt about how most Chinese feel when it comes to questions of ownership. During my travels I stood on the bridge of a pitching cargo ship while the Chinese second officer hovered over a nautical chart to give me a geography lesson.

"China owns all of this." His finger looped around the entire sea, including territory also claimed by Vietnam, Malaysia, the Philippines, Brunei, Indonesia, Taiwan, and possibly Thailand and Cambodia.

"What belongs to China's neighbors?" I asked.

"It's China! All China!" he said. His finger marched from the Paracel Islands in the northwest through the Spratlys in the southeast. It paused over a jot of land near Luzon in the Philippines. "This might belong to the Philippines," he mused. "But probably China!"

3

Making sense out of chaos, for yourself and others, is the long-distance reporter's stock in trade. It's like Ralph Ellison says in that great line from *Invisible Man*: ". . . the mind that has conceived a plan of living must never lose sight of the chaos against which that pattern was conceived."

In Hong Kong the commotion was unavoidable. About to be flung back into Beijing's embrace, the colony seemed caught between excitement and dread. Over the years, Hong Kong had made China less poor but China had made Hong Kong filthy rich, and the place was flashing with cash and bling. It was all very soigné, with the Rolls-Royces and Bentleys pulling up to the curb at the city's dazzling hotels, the sleek, self-assured men in their Italian-style silk suits, and the women dripping jewelry from shapely necks and elegant wrists. Yet not a soul, from street sweeper to grandee, could guarantee what was about to happen.

Mind you, few thoughtful observers believed China would purposefully shoot itself in the foot by destroying the vitality of the great entrepôt on which plans for developing its economy depended. Instead, the prudent worry was that ham-fisted apparatchiks from the mainland, lacking modern managerial experience, might do the job inadvertently. A more proximate cause for the colony's case of nerves was China's titillating decision to move an advance unit of People's Liberation Army troops to the border with tanks and armored personnel carriers set to roll across the line after midnight on July 1. Then what?

Reactions on the Chinese motherland were mixed as well. Undocumented mainlanders poured into Hong Kong on rumors that amnesty awaited individuals, particularly children, in place by the July 1 deadline. In Beijing, top officials worried about the possibility of terrorist attacks that would mar Handover events and humiliate China on its historic day. In Hong Kong, wild bits of gossip, circulated mainly by visiting journalists, had workers in the Shenzhen industrial zone, twenty miles north, fleeing factories to escape the outbreak of an imagined Asian Armageddon—a last great showdown between China and Perfidious Albion in which the British colonial masters would go out with gunboat cannons blazing.

To get a proper measure of the place I had flown into Hong Kong a week before Handover. It was late evening when my plane touched down, and I was instantly delighted to be back in a city that was as dramatically vertical as I remembered, its skyscrapers growing out of the hillside like glass-and-steel thistles, their neon signs radiating electric colors. Checking into a room the *Geographic* travel office had booked me on an upper floor of a five-star hotel, I stood at the wraparound window enjoying the spectacle of the nighttime harbor. In the middle distance, two late ferries on the Hong Kong–Kowloon run crossed paths halfway, their wakes bisected by ubiquitous tugboats and darting catamarans. In the foreground, the Royal Yacht *Britannia*, in port for Handover, was moored so vertiginously close I wondered if a good softball heave might not carry the distance.

But the city's edgy mood was never far away. The hotel staff seemed disgruntled and combative. Earlier, at the airport, I had been snubbed by a local cop. Tall and smart in khaki, he sneered when I asked for simple directions and turned his back. Well, all the more reason for me to relax, I thought, and so I settled in with a stack of newspapers to get on with my homework. This was in strict compliance with Personal Reporting Rule No. 1: Give yourself time to catch your breath before going into the clinch with reality.

I found one piece of news particularly alarming. In addition to Hong Kong's general population swelling by as much as one-third as people flooded in to witness the Handover festivities, press reports said some eighty-four hundred journalists would be on hand to cover the story. Terrible at fighting my way forward in a mob, I thanked my lucky stars I wasn't going to be expected to report the "tick-tock," or the blow-by-blow of events. Luckily, my editors at the *Geographic* wanted something different—meditated prose and time-steeped reporting in which people and events illustrated larger issues, not the other way around. The magazine boasted a circulation just shy of nine million at that point, with readers ranging in age from grade-schoolers to über-seniors, not only in America but also around the world. Stories had to be intelligent, human, and broadly accessible to ordinary thoughtful readers while not talking down to them. They also had to have a shelf life that would hold up not for hours or days but for months and years.

It was a unique mandate and sometimes misinterpreted. A fellow writer, an alleged friend, once remarked publicly in Manhattan that he had to hand it to me because I had "mastered the eighth-grade style of writing" the *Geographic* favored. I did not take offense but simply noted the gross misunderstanding of the magazine's mission, which is to make visible for the many what without the effort would remain visible only to the relative few. That's why I've always loved the Geographic Society's mission statement, as limned by that original great communicator and founding member, Alexander Graham Bell: "THE WORLD AND ALL THAT IS IN IT is our theme, and if we can't find anything to interest ordinary people in that subject we better shut up shop . . ."

In the way I thought of it, the magazine wanted us to create documentary films printed on paper, the dynamism supplied by photographs produced by some of the world's finest photographers and by informed, energetic writing. As a result I worked with an old screenwriter's trick in mind: Inject your story with themes as big and smart as you can muster—and then do your damnedest to hide them inside a human tale lest they take over and club your audience senseless with boredom.

For this particular assignment, therefore, my job lay not in Hong Kong at all but farther south, where the South China Sea wraps in the islands and peninsulas of Southeast Asia and connects through the Strait of Malacca with the Indian Ocean. And so, I vowed to avoid the journalistic herd like the plague. What I couldn't avoid were the false starts that inevitably accompany any long-distance reporting trip.

4

On my first afternoon in Hong Kong I felt invigorated and ready to work, and so I bounded forth from the hotel like a frisky teenager, sucked the tangy sea air off Victory Harbor into my lungs, and went to find a taxi. Determined to get my reporting off on the right note, I'd arranged for my very first interview to talk with a group of local sea captains steeped in the ways of the South China Sea. I couldn't wait to ask them how the romance of local seafaring traditions stacked up against the day-to-day realities of the trade and what effect China's rise might have on all that going forward.

But the taxi queue was infernally long—all those damned journalists and Handover tourists, I thought—and after a slow crawl to the head of the line, I slipped into the backseat of a cab. The driver spoke no English but nodded confidently when I showed him the directions for the harbor-side offices of Merchant Navy Officers' Guild. Off we roared.

Thirty minutes later we were back exactly where we'd started, in the hotel driveway, the driver demanding a premium on the metered fare for having failed to deliver me to my destination. Studying the cabbie study me in the rearview mirror, I entertained dark thoughts. Rather than throw a tantrum, however, I responded with saintly patience and unimpeachable self-control. I was bearing in mind Rule No. 2: Never pick a fight with a taxi driver or shout at a person at a wheel. The simple truth is that it's bad karma: Someday you'll need a vehicle to extract you from a tight spot or get you to an airport on time, and the gods of transport have long memories.

And so I smiled and nodded, and paid the driver his ridiculously inflated fare. Wilting from jet lag now and feeling completely demoralized, I wanted to go home to New York. Instead, I got back in the long taxi queue and waited my turn, now following Rule No. 3: Never give up, even when the sweat has laminated your undershorts to your trousers and your trousers to the leatherette seats. Tell yourself, confidently, heroically, that things will get better.

I was an hour late for my appointment at the Merchant Navy Officers' Guild—but in plenty of time to remind myself of how making the best efforts to do your homework in advance of taking the field (which really ought to be Rule No. 1) can still leave you totally at odds with reality. Accordingly, I had allowed myself to picture the Guild as a clubby enclave of dark wood paneling and threadbare easy chairs where nautical men with brushy beards and twinkling eyes reminisced about the sea over gin and tonics.

In reality, the Guild's offices were decorated with institutional ceramic tile suggesting the interior of a veterinary hospital. Three or four Chinese clerks shuffled around in house slippers or sat list-lessly tapping at boxy computers amid the faint tang of boiled meat. Ushered into a narrow conference room, I suddenly found myself face-to-face with a half-dozen brusque, wary men—the local skippers.

Why had I come? demanded the grizzled sea dog at the head of the table, eyeing me suspiciously. What was it I wanted to know? He spoke a decibel short of a yell, appearing to think I was hard of hearing. I said I simply wanted to hear what it was like to work on the South China Sea. Admittedly, it was a fuzz-ball question, poorly asked, and I got what I deserved.

"That question is too broad!" a second captain jumped in. When I tried to explain, I was struck by how pathetically sophomoric I sounded. I'd read about the South China Sea's famous hazards to navigation, including a large area of reefs and shoals tantalizingly called "The Dangerous Ground" on maritime charts. What was it like to navigate such a tricky stretch of water? I asked.

"You mean pirates!" shouted the first man.

Well, yes, that was part of it, I replied.

"That's an old story. You're a latecomer! There's smuggling be-tween the U.S. and Canada. Why don't you go cover that?" Transla-tion: Why don't you mind your own business and go home where you belong?

A third, somewhat friendlier man chimed in at one point to ask, incongruously, whether I thought the Americans were justified to have fought a war in Vietnam. A nervous assistant fiddled with an old-fashioned reel-to-feel tape recorder to log our conversation. As the stand-up comics say, I was playing a tough room, and I had completely lost control of our conversation.

Don't get me wrong: These were fine, tough men seated around the table, and I respected that. It also occurred to me, however, that they didn't think very highly of the press and likely didn't have much experience dealing with it successfully. So I did what I nor-mally do in such situations: I closed my notebook and tried to re-assure them that I was not out to write an exposé or dive into the company books; I simply needed help. To write about the South China Sea, I had to hear from the experts about its fickle weather and whatever else gave the sea its churlish reputation. Nine times out of ten, appealing to the wisdom and generosity of your sources is all it takes to get them talking—but not with these wily mariners.

In spite of the image of British "spit and polish" its name had conjured up, the Guild, its captains bluntly informed me, was in reality a local trade union. The captains, all union men, got together to discuss practical issues—cost-of-living and insurance benefits, for instance, and the damage land reclamation was doing to Hong Kong harbor, forcing ships to anchor farther and farther to the west, exposing them to harsh weather and crews to longer rides in a tender to get ashore. If it was romantic tales of the sea I was after, I was in the wrong place. Feeling like a total fool, I nonetheless did my best to invoke Rule No. 4: Try to make every interview pay off, no matter how challenging the circumstances, as you may not pass this way again.

I asked the captains whether young people were as keen on going to sea nowadays as the captains had been when they were starting out. The barking man at the head of the table stared at me as if I were a lunatic. "Nobody wants to spend six months on shipboard to make the same money they can make on shore!" he bellowed.

I kicked myself again. I could easily have avoided this screw-up by checking out the Guild's organizational profile in advance; being on time might have helped. But the captains were generally in a kicking mood too. As I wondered how to extricate myself from this reporterly disaster, one of them exclaimed, "London gave you bad advice!"

London?

That brings me to Rule No. 5: False starts go with the territory—they are Nature's way of testing the purity of our resolve—and no matter what your line of work, you just have to take it.

You don't have to like it, though. After just a couple of days in that hotel room with the stunning harbor view, management saw fit to give me the boot to make way for an American TV network, and I moved, grumbling unheeded complaints, to a moldering mansion embedded in the green hillside of Victoria Peak. It was there one night I asked the duty manager for the loan of a telephone book. My first real correspondent's job was at the *Far Eastern Economic Review*, and I'd heard my old mentor there, Ian Dunbar, was in town. I absolutely had to track him down, but the young man was unhelpful. His face rising from behind the desk like a pale moonflower on a narrow stalk, he shot me an insolent look and said, "Wait in your room!"

"But . . . but . . ." I stammered.

"Wait in your room," he repeated dismissively, his patience wearing thin with a pushy guest, who did not appear to understand English. *"W-a-i-t in your room!"*

I did as instructed. Nothing is more important than to listen to what your story is trying to tell you and the message seemed to be that everybody, desk clerks included, was feeling that nervous-making edge of change. We could all afford to take a chill pill, I thought magnanimously, as I rode the clanking elevator. In my room, I waited patiently for a telephone book that never arrived, and was left to silently root for the swift rise of the brutal commissar.

5

Before we strike out for new adventures, it's good luck, or so I tell myself, to pay our respects to the road so far traveled, and so I made my pilgrimage to the reporter's sanctum sanctorum, the Foreign Correspondents' Club. Established in China in the years before World War II, it later occupied a mansion on the Peak that doubled as a hospital set for the classic 1955 film *Love Is a Many Splendored Thing*—the story of an affair between a dashing American correspondent and a beautiful Eurasian doctor that teases out against the backdrop of revolution in China. The movie, based on a novel by Han Suyin, launched dreams in many a young person's head, from Paramus to Perth, about becoming a long-distance reporter.

At Handover, the FCC had reincarnated itself in a gentrified former ice factory on, fittingly, Ice House Street, where in anticipation of the big event the ground-floor barroom was mobbed. Hands were being strenuously wrung, backs slapped, shoulders embraced. Men and women of a certain age rested drooping bodies against the horseshoe bar, hands gesticulating in misremembered tales of youth. It looked for all the world like a stage set for a Last Supper for Old Hacks, and I couldn't think of any place I'd rather be.

Today you can tap a few keys and your e-tablet becomes a font of information on China. But back in the days when China was viewed as an inscrutable puzzle, Hong Kong was the place where journalists, scholars, and spies, all three occasionally inhabiting the same person, came to listen for muffled signals from the mainland in the hope of decoding its mysteries. At their best, these China hands, as members of this company of men and women were called, displayed a detective's nose for clues, a four-year-old's curiosity about what made the world tick, and a psychologist's understanding of human nature, all wrapped into an adventurer's soul.

It was from Ian Dunbar and other august denizens of the FCCs in Hong Kong and Tokyo that I learned many useful things about the world—how to think like a journalist, how to drink like a journalist, and how to punish truculent and demanding editors back in the newsroom by writing stories that were hell to edit, all the while running up the expense account with diabolical intent. (I knew I was making progress on my expenses when an editor at the *Far Eastern Review* challenged my spending on taxis with the tart observation that I must be hailing cabs for trips to the men's room.) In those days, meaning the mid-1970s, I'd have happily sacrificed my writing hand to the knuckles to be talked about as a member of that quick-thinking, hard-drinking, irreverent crowd.

Helene Cooper of the *New York Times* captured the spirit of the *Review* and the people I worked with there in an appreciation she wrote after the magazine ceased publication in 2004: "For someone who grew up dreaming about swashbuckling journalists reporting from far-flung places, there was no greater model than the

Far Eastern Economic Review, a weekly founded in Shanghai in 1946 and put out by a raffish staff of adventurers."

In my case, when I had achieved my dubious professional goals fingers intact, I recognized my next challenge was to survive it. Thus I'd given up both drinking and smoking in 1985 when the Lutheran gods of my ancestors would permit no more tomfoolery without inflicting lethal consequences. The glamour of barrooms was for me, I hoped, a thing of the past.

But the past is a tricky piece of real estate. A red-faced man sat hunched over the bar top, puffing on a French-looking cigarette and staring into space. "Dahlby," he muttered, as if searching his memory for some indictable offense, "I remember that name." A few steps further on, a man with owlish features and a too-familiar smile approached, saying, "I've been hearing stories about you for years." I gulped inwardly as he paused—menacingly, I thought—before adding, with a newsman's irony and a laugh, "Mostly good."

It sounded like a compliment, but I wasn't taking any chances. I headed for the door, in compliance with hard-won Rule No. 6: Don't let the night be the enemy of the day. Now all I wanted was to return to my hotel room for a dish of strawberry ice cream and an early night. *Sic transit gloria mundi*, as an old colleague put it, "Thus passes the glory of the world."

6

Handover arrived. On the morning of June 30 Mike Yamashita, the photojournalist assigned to our *Geographic* story, and one of the best in the magazine's highly competitive stable, hired a helicopter to shoot aerial photos of the British naval squadron's farewell turn around Hong Kong Island and invited me along for the ride. After getting beyond a British soldier guarding access to the harbor-side helipad, which was also being used by visiting dignitaries ("Fook you, mate. I got me orders, don't I?"), we lifted off in time to see three frigates slice through the choppy blue-green waters of Victoria Harbor. Built like a rugby player and brave, Mike hung precariously from the open door to snap his photos, his mane of salt-and-pepper hair flying. It was a thrilling scene, at a variety of altitudes.

At 4:30 p.m. I was back in my hotel room looking down into the garden of Government House when a military band struck up "Auld Lang Syne," and Chris Patten, last of the British colonial governors, prepared to leave the premises for the last time. I watched the pomp and circumstance for as long as I dared and then rushed downstairs to the taxi I'd hired, so I could tail Patten's Rolls Royce as it wound down the Peak. Taxi karma paid off beautifully. With perfect timing, my driver pulled in behind Patten's entourage, and we followed the switch-backing roads all the way to the harbor as crowds of Chinese Hong Kongers waved flags and clapped.

That evening Mike and I attended one of the big Handover parties at a grand harborside hotel where we rubbed elbows with a collection of Hong Kong glitterati, roving fleets of weepy Brits clutching open champagne bottles by the neck, and B-list celebrities from Hollywood. At midnight TV monitors in the echoing lobby broadcast official ceremonies at which Britain's Prince Charles marked the transition with a courtly, ironic nod. The tearful Brits sang a rousing chorus of "God Save the Queen." Muscular Chinese men pounded lion drums in honor of Hong Kong's new ownership, and an adjacent press platform collapsed, sending photographers and TV cameramen sprawling. Sometime in the early hours of July 1 PLA troops rolled their tanks and APCs over the border—and, in an anticlimax for the worrywarts and fearmongers, went straight to their barracks. The party was over.

Or very nearly. The next day I huffed and puffed my way up the Peak to privately celebrate Handover by having brunch with Ian Dunbar, the man who, under his real name of Russell Spurr, had hired me for my job at the *Review* in 1976. Now retired and living in Sydney, Australia, Russell and his wife, Rosemary, had returned for the big event and were staying in an elegant flat belonging to their son Stephan, who was now a wheel with a Hong Kong investment house.

"Fantastic!" said Russell, screeching in welcome. "Good on ya, mate!" Well into his seventies now, he had suffered a stroke and walked using a pair of canes. Long gone were the days when he so ferociously moonlighted for rival news outlets in support of his family that he'd been forced to concoct the devil-may-care pseudonym Ian Dunbar to keep his regular employers from giving him the sack. His spirit was still remarkably unchanged, however. He and Rosemary had recently traveled all over China, before his stroke struck but just after he'd freshly broken his shoulder and Rosemary her wrist.

Russell said it was one bloody thing after another, as he winked and roared with laughter, and called me "matey," like in the old pirate movies, and I remembered how much I loved him—and had learned from him too. Russell was a member of a special subfraternity of China hands known as "old friends of China," meaning foreigners the Chinese trusted and favored with access. Some interpreted this, in Russell's case, as code for trading information with the Chinese intelligence service, the CIA, or both, but the gossip was unfounded. (As it turned out, it was our former mutual boss, Derek Davies, longtime editor-in-chief of the *Review*, who had been the bona fide spook, having once worked for MI6, the British spy agency, in Hanoi and Saigon, something the British press reported after his death in France in 2002.) Yet it's true that Russell was well connected for a foreigner during China's anti-foreign period, and he introduced me to some fascinating characters.

Topping the list was General Wu, the military attaché at the Chinese embassy in Tokyo, who was rumored to run its intelligence operation. According to Russell, the general, who was so flinty he looked as if he might use sandpaper as an aftershave, had been assigned to supervise the reeducation of the Red Guards during the reverse course of the Cultural Revolution. Wu displayed perhaps his most surprising talent during a dinner party at our home in Nishi Azabu one night. After lubricating his pipes with a banana daiquiri or three, he launched into a repertoire of Japanese military songs from a time when the Imperial Army had run roughshod over China before and during World War II. His voice sounded like a semi-melodious cement mixer operating at medium speed. When I asked him if by any chance he had been a prisoner of the Japanese (how else would he know such songs?) he glared at me with such withering intensity that I thanked my lucky stars I hadn't been a Red Guard scheduled for reeducation. Ah, the good old days!

Long story short, I owed Russell a lot and I was feeling suitably nostalgic, when, over our quiche and salad, I noticed that Rosemary, in contrast to the warmth of yesteryear, was fixing me with an obsidian stare. Trying to remember what ancient crime she might be holding against me, I smarmily asked, "Tell me, Rosemary, how do you like living in Sydney?"

"Boring as bat shit!" Rosemary shot back, her eyes narrowing with suspicion.

As the conversation rolled mercifully on, Russell recapped for me the death of an old colleague—"the longest-running suicide in Hong Kong history." The lovely and talented man of whom he spoke had succumbed to years of excessive drink but not before a Chinese fortuneteller on one of Hong Kong's outer islands had eerily foretold his passing to the "astral plane." When talk turned to happier memories of wayward old colleagues, I was delighted to see Rosemary's face light up with a smile, as if she were savoring historic images of the flamboyant, the quixotic, and the foolhardy. Knitting her brows, she asked, pensively, "Do you remember Tracy Dahlby?"—he had been such a nice boy.

Russell stopped his screeching in mid-crescendo, and when it was explained to Rosemary, who had apparently been dealing with memory issues, that the graying man in front of her was that very boy, her eyes widened with surprise. Appearing very pleased with herself for having caused a stir, she looked at me as if I had suddenly materialized out of thin air, and we all had a good laugh, as if the years did not matter.

7

The time had come to leave Hong Kong. I'd booked Mike Yamashita and me on a cruise ship that catered to the Cantonese gaming bug, and skirted local prohibitions, by shuttling its passengers into international waters. There they could gamble their heads off legally and excuse it diplomatically with a brief tourist stop on Hainan, the big island that sits like a teardrop between the Gulf of Tonkin and the South China Sea, and marks China's southernmost compass point. As I summed it up for the *Geographic* audience:

> *It began one steamy evening as the sun dropped behind the green cone of Hong Kong's Victoria Peak and I hauled my duffel bag along the dock toward a boxy cruise liner called the* Star Pisces . . .

There was just one further hitch. Mike and I nearly missed our sailing time when our taxi driver insisted on taking us to the airport instead of the Ocean Terminal based on the not unreasonable assumption that all foreigners with luggage go to the airport. When we'd finally pulled onto the pier, it was well past boarding time.

The driver waggled his hand and ducked his head in apology. But New Jersey, Mike's home turf, wasn't buying it. "You are an idiot, sir!"

"Sorry, sorry."

"Don't say you're sorry," Mike said. "I don't want to discuss sorry!"

There was a lot riding on Mike and me getting on that ship and, as I said before, we were all a little on edge. But Mike's imprecations only deepened the driver's frenzy. Wide-eyed and unhinged, he zoomed up the wrong ramp for an extended tour of the bowels of a cavernous parking garage. When he finally deposited us quayside, several decks below the gangway, he insisted on wildly overcharging us.

Out of saintly consideration for the man's pain and suffering, but mostly because of my dread of taxi karma, I offered to double his take to 200 Hong Kong dollars, or about 25 bucks. But he was truly a thickheaded lout. He demanded the 200 plus 120 more.

"Screw you," I snapped (or words to that effect), stuffing the bills back into my pocket, as the driver stamped his feet and cursed blue heaven.

Human nature is a terrible thing, and I confess to having savored this moment of triumph over the unhappy, sweating cabbie. But in my experience taxi karma is typically repaid quickly and in kind, and as angelic Filipina crew members sang us on board with an energetic rendition of "You Are My Sunshine," I knew I'd soon have cause to regret my unsporting behavior. When it came to the writing I would set the scene like this:

On the bridge Captain Peder Nilsson, blond and gruff, looked radioactive in the gilt-edged twilight as he eased the stern away from the Ocean Terminal. Freighters, hydrofoils, water taxis, ships of every size and type moved in all directions at once. Below him the decks of the Pisces throbbed with nervous energy.

To unwind, the passengers headed for the casinos. In a big L-shaped room furious with sound and motion, they elbowed for space at crap tables, baccarat tables, and tables for games I did not know, slapping down big Hong Kong notes as they went.

"Aiya!" cried a bespectacled matron, smacking her forehead as a blackjack dealer drew 21 to her 18. Undaunted, she inched her last chip forward—then turned up a winning hand.

Such gutsiness paid off for her and struck me as symbolic too. While for 1.2 billion mainlanders the British handover was a source of soaring nationalistic pride, the 6.5 million Chinese residents of Hong Kong, who had prospered over the years precisely by not being in China, viewed events with mixed emotions. "When I saw the new flag go up," a Hong Kong businesswoman in her late thirties told me, recalling the ceremonies on TV, "I felt this intense fear deep inside."

Would the new China, now freed from its colonial past, prove a political heavy or an enlightened landlord? Since it was too early to tell, she suggested a strategy: Keep the upper lip stiff, in the British tradition, and a shrewd eye peeled for new commercial opportunity.

8

For the long-distance reporter, learning to listen is important, and conversations like that last one boggled my mind. Only a few years earlier the suggestion that China would be capable of taking on management responsibilities for thriving Hong Kong, or anything else for that matter, would have seemed too ludicrous for words. The basic problem was that China's future was very hard to see.

In the early 1980s, when I served as Northeast Asia bureau chief for the *Washington Post*, China had started to tread the road to a market economy thanks to its pragmatic new leader, Deng Xiaoping. A historical giant who stood four-feet-eleven, Deng was a very tough nut, indeed. Twice purged from Communist party leadership during the Cultural Revolution, he had displayed an impressive knack for fighting his way back to the top. After Chairman Mao died in 1976 and the Cultural Revolution entered its last fizzling days, Deng set out to methodically cast decades of Mao's self-willed economic disasters onto the ash heap of history. (Reliable estimates say at least forty million people died as the result of Mao's Great Leap Forward campaign in the 1950s; you can probably add at least thirty million more deaths for the Cultural Revolution, many again from hunger.) Elbowing Communist dogma from the driver's seat, Deng exhorted his countrymen "to seek truth from facts" and ditch ideology wherever it got in the way of pushing the economy forward. "It doesn't matter whether a cat is black or white, as long as it catches mice," he said famously. The approach was not unlike the Madison Avenue ad campaigns in the 1950s that encouraged frugal, Depression Era-minded Americans that there was no sin in making money and spending it, and Deng worked to liberate the Chinese from their corresponding dogma.

He had his work cut out for him. The simple truth is that, in the early 1980s, nothing in China worked very well. The massive, lumbering, resource-poor economy was obliged to make the most of facilities that were decrepit when the Communists took power in 1949, including factories that rolled out brand-new trucks with the big ballooning fenders that were all the rage in the 1930s. All that old stuff was only fit to produce more old-type stuff, of course, and in any event everything seemed to be falling apart, sprocket and screw. One colleague joked that, at any given time, roughly three-quarters of Chinese workers, undernourished and arbitrarily employed, were asleep on the back of a clapped-out truck somewhere in the service of the unattainable goals of the latest vaguely understood five-year economic plan, and the scenario didn't seem all that far-fetched.

The absurdity of China's economic development plans was highlighted for me in 1983, when the Chinese government invited the American playwright Arthur Miller to Beijing to stage his play *Death of a Salesman*. The most prominent theatrical exchange with America since the Cultural Revolution, it was a very big deal for Beijing's cloistered correspondents, and as luck would have it I managed to score a hotly contested interview with Miller. We met over a couple of big bottles of Chinese beer at his hotel and, as we sat and talked, I was awestruck by the great man's avuncular genius. I was equally flabbergasted, however, when he insisted that China, including all those workers snoozing on the back of trucks, would one day become the leader of the world economy.

I asked him why he thought so. An avid woodworker, Miller said he loved to putter around his home workshop in Roxbury, Connecticut, and had recently purchased a carpenter's vice made in China. I should see this thing, he said, smiling rhapsodically, and went on to describe in loving detail the workings of this minor marvel of engineering, the way its moving parts moved, and so on and so forth.

What on earth did a carpenter's vice have to do with China conquering the world? I wondered. I could only assume the Chinese propaganda machine had done a number on Miller. There was a lot of loose talk back then about the country's potential for leapfrogging the traditional stages of economic development. Advances in telecommunications, for example, would allow China to skip the costly business of laying old-fashioned telephone lines everywhere, substituting microwave technology instead.

That was an intriguing theory, but stacked up against realities on the ground I regarded it as little more than wishful thinking. China still rattled and banged like one of those big new-old trucks with the balloon fenders, and you couldn't transform an arthritic industrial base into an industrial powerhouse with a technological snap of the fingers. To think that a fourth-rate economy like China could best the United States of America at anything was preposterous.

My basic problem in those days was that I thought I was pretty hot stuff in the reporting department and still wasn't listening closely enough to what people were trying to tell me. A really good reporter is always on guard against ego, which stops up the ears and makes you think you know better than your sources. Instead, with the future on its way but blinded by the present, I thought smugly: "This guy may know a lot about writing plays but he doesn't know beans about China."

Then the further delicious thought occurred: "Hey, I'm smarter than the guy who married Marilyn Monroe!"

Lo and behold, when I returned to China to report the Handover story for the *Geographic* a decade and a half later, the mixture of manufacturing skill, economic self-interest, and growing confidence of which Miller had spoken was dramatically on display. Between 1979 and 1997, China's GDP grew on average at a high-octane 9.95 percent a year—a pace it would keep up for the thirty-three years through 2012. That trajectory not only proved me wrong but also marked what my friend, fellow correspondent and China hand Robert Delfs, calls "unquestionably the biggest and fastest jump in wealth and living standards for the people of one country or region of significant scale in human history."

And nowhere was the energy behind that juggernaut more rambunctiously on display in microcosm than on Hainan Island, China's gateway to the South China Sea.

9

The sun was boiling in a high, hazy sky when Mike and I tramped down the *Star Pisces'* gangway in Hainan's main city, Haikou, with the Hong Kong gamblers. Ahead on the pier, I could see a man dressed in a luminous orange shirt bouncing on the balls of his feet and frantically waving his arms to get our attention.

"Mike, Mike! Tracy, Tracy!" yelled the man as he bobbed and weaved toward us through the crowd. With his sharp features and prominent cowlick, he looked to me like a friendly bird of prey.

"Ah, there's Li," said Mike, waving at the man who by now I'd guessed was Li Hubing, our government-appointed translator and guide. Working on a long project in China required a journalist's visa, and that meant accepting a fixer from the All-China Journalists Association—typically a mixed blessing. Right off the bat, Li signaled that he was going to be a piece of work. He fought Mike for the privilege of carrying his camera equipment and bulled his way through the crowd. Shooing us toward a nondescript Toyota van, he vented his unhappiness about a bureaucratic snag that had prevented a better parking spot.

"Red tape, red tape!" Li protested in what, in the coming days, would become a familiar lament about China's inefficiencies: "China is changing. . . . it's changing . . . but too slowly!"

Inside the car, a handsome young man sat sprawled behind the wheel sucking on a toothpick like a Hainanese James Dean. (Let's call him Driver Wang, the Chinese equivalent of Smith, since it's possible he survived his own driving and should not, in any case, be unduly held to account for the routine lapses of youth.)

When I smiled and introduced myself, Wang said, in English, "I speak no English," a fact of which he seemed inordinately proud. He then stepped on the gas and roared down an access road, hell-bent for the freeway and our destination, the resort town of Sanya at the island's southern end. One reason for visiting Hainan, apart from the opportunity to tag along with the gamblers, was to get a closer look at one of China's free-market testing grounds. Under Deng's reforms, Hainan had been designated a Special Economic Zone in 1988 and, while not on a par with booming Shenzhen or other large-scale economic experiments, it nonetheless provided a yardstick to measure the pluses and minuses of laissez-faire investment. As I wrote in my finished article:

> With few rules to regulate commerce, the island attracted freebooting investors, mainly from Hong Kong and Taiwan, who pumped cash into real estate and even planned a Club Med. But when the speculation had run its course, ornate but unsellable resort condos littered the palm-fanned coastline, and Hainan was hit by bankruptcies, unemployment, and rising crime.

The heady mixture of elements had proved too rich and volatile for their container, and now, in spite of Driver Wang's apparent attempt to set a new land-speed record, the evidence was everywhere to be seen. From a distance, Haikou . . .

> . . . appeared as a gleaming, elongated cluster of big buildings splashed with turquoise and silver light that reminded me of the Emerald City in The Wizard of Oz. But I saw that many of the structures were weirdly empty—gray skeletons of rusting steel and crumbling concrete, with no glass in the windows.

Local officials later told me I was looking at the wrong thing. All would be well, they assured me, as soon as China, the pestering counterclaims of its neighbors notwithstanding, regained its historical ownership of *Nanhai* or the South China Sea. Hainan, now the country's smallest province, would automatically become its largest, growing rich on the added bounty of undersea oil and natural gas, and marine products. As I noted for readers, the fact that

China's neighbors thought its sea claims to be total baloney "cut little ice in China," where nationalist propaganda referred to *Nanhai* as a key to the future of a billion-plus people.

On our way to Sanya, though, I was less interested in geopolitics than in sizing up our new fixer. First impressions can mean everything to a traveling man, and it's vital for a correspondent to evaluate the local staff as quickly and brutally as possible. Think about it for a second: Your ability to get your job done, and not infrequently your personal safety, possibly even your life, will depend on these complete strangers. Although Mike had worked with Li on a previous assignment, I didn't know him from Adam, and so I zeroed in.

My first reaction was one of alarm. Li talked a blue streak, nearly as fast as Driver Wang drove, which was hair-raisingly fast. As we hurtled south, he sounded like a CNN analyst on fast-forward:

"Look, look, look! Mike and Tracy! This highway is brand new," Li said, his finger waggling excitedly at the clean, smooth ribbon of concrete that curved into the middle distance amid vibrant green rubber plantations and gashes construction had left behind in the blood-red topsoil.

"Look, look, look! Local developers are in trouble due to the overheated economy!" he cried, sweeping his arm toward lush hillsides dotted with abandoned luxury condos, as he dilated on Hainan's dismal real estate bust.

In another microsecond, Li might focus on the inordinate number of luxury sedans traveling this stretch of rural highway. "Ooh, look! Another Mercedes sedan!" he shouted as the tenth such vehicle zipped past in the space of a few minutes. Good Lord, I thought, the man barely stops to draw a breath.

Ordinarily, all that chatter would have driven me crazy. But somehow, Li's machine-gun patter, backed as it was by the force of an obviously curious and energetic mind, beguiled me. For one thing, it was clear that Li was no motor-mouthed airhead. He'd done his homework, was blisteringly smart, and seemed impatient with a world that moved too slowly for him—all excellent traits I hold in the highest esteem.

Driver Wang, on the other hand, was in a different category altogether. It wasn't so much his perpetual sneer, or the fact he seemed incapable of driving at speeds of less than a hundred miles an hour. The fundamental problem was that, in the technical parlance of the field, he appeared to be something of an asshole.

Blasting down that near-empty highway, Wang delighted in pulling up behind slower-moving vehicles, laying on his horn, and—his pièce de résistance—trying to pass them on a curve. When he drew alongside a rusted-out pickup truck and prepared to make its pilot, a toothy, grinning farmer, eat his exhaust, the farmer wasn't having it. He yanked his wheel, swerving to the left, and forced us to drop behind him. Wang responded by doing the level-headed thing, which was to pull up within inches of the maniac's rear bumper and ride his tailgate at sixty miles an hour.

I said, "Li, we're not going to get past the guy if he doesn't want us to. Tell the driver to slow down."

Li fired a torrent of Mandarin at Wang and, sneeringly, he backed off—but only long enough to reposition our van and barrel past the pickup on the right-hand shoulder. As he did, the unhinged pickup driver tried to ram us again.

"Jesus Christ," said Mike, stating the gruesomely obvious, "this driver is going to get us killed."

Li ordered Wang to pull over and both men jumped out. Hopping on the balls of his feet, finger waggling at top speed, Li proceeded to give Wang what I would come to think of as "the treatment." He lectured him on the importance of road safety especially while carrying important foreign guests. He also made a technical point at Mike's behest: If a driver drove too fast for the photographer's eye to keep up with the surrounding visual opportunities, Mike was likely to miss something important.

Wang did not take instruction well. Back in the van, he sulked, playing jazzy pop tunes on the car cassette player while he crooned the lyrics under his breath and beat time on the dashboard. Incredible. By the time Wang careened into our beachside hotel's circular drive in Sanya, souvenirs sellers darting from our path, I believe it's fair to say we all wished him dead.

Later that evening I was in my room, getting ready for bed and pondering the wages of taxi karma that had led to our bad luck with Driver Wang, when there came a knock at the door. When I opened up, I saw Li Hubing standing there in his parti-colored shorts and looking fierce in his natural plumage.

"He's on the phone all the time!" Li said, complaining about the driver with whom he was sharing a room. "Can I use your phone?"

"Be my guest," I said, and I couldn't help but feel surprised. In the old days in China, meaning in my case the early 1980s, a government handler would never in a million years have entered a client's room, let alone complain openly about a Chinese coworker. I was warming to the idea of Deng's new China and especially to this man called Li.

10

You've guessed by now that the local fixer is the unsung hero of long-distance reporting, and for a correspondent there is absolutely nobody on earth more important. This jack-of-all-trades translates your interviews and important documents, keeps you up to speed on developments in the local media, and arranges travel on the ships, boats, trains, and planes necessary to get you from one place to another. It's the fixer's job to zero in on the best sources, the best hotels at the lowest prices, and locate a good meal in the least promising of circumstances. If a fixer is good he or she deserves at least half the credit for a story; if bad—conniving or just dim-witted—well, heaven help you.

Luckily, my instincts about Li Hubing were right on. He was a fixer of the very first rank, a fine example of what veteran journalists have called "full-body reporting" or perhaps in this case full-body fixing. Forever hustling, Li rushed to carry the heaviest bag or ferreted out the most obscure location in his tenacious, no-nonsense way, often while simultaneously chewing out a cab driver, hotel clerk, government functionary, or whomever he thought needed guidance at the moment. I kid you not: I loved to watch him work.

Li was especially good at projecting you into the thick of things. Hollywood profiles of swashbuckling correspondents notwithstanding, success in reporting across cultures not infrequently depends vastly more on being a fly on the wall, observing the scene without drawing attention to yourself, than in being obstreperous or demanding. That's easy to say, of course, but hard to put into practice if, like me, you happen to be six and a half feet tall and stick out everywhere you go like the proverbial sore thumb. With Li running culturally appropriate interference while I stayed in the background, however, we made a first-rate team.

On our first morning in Sanya, Li, Mike, and I piled into the van of death with the daredevil Wang behind the wheel and were soon flying down the narrow streets at the speed of light. Turning a corner on two wheels, or so it seemed, we zoomed past a large outdoor café where men with full bellies leaned back in their chairs, toothpicks waggling, while they cast furtive glances at our dangerously speeding bullet. When the road ended abruptly at a big, open fish market on the harbor, even Wang recognized he had no choice but to apply the brakes, and we got out to take a look.

The market was the size of a football field with the violent energy to match. People swarmed around in astonishing numbers, yelling at the top of their lungs in the local dialect as if a civil war had broken out. Fishmongers in pajamas and straw hats loudly presided over boxes of squids, clams, and snappers while equally vociferous customers and wholesalers assessed the *fruits de mer* with thick, horny fingers. Carpeted with a fetid mash of rotting vegetables and fish parts, the arena gave off indescribably pungent odors that drilled into your nostrils from the ground up. When a fistfight broke out nearby, Mike smiled from ear to ear. "China, man, you gotta love it," he said before he turned to melt into the crowd.

That was the moment in a nutshell, and for people like Mike and me it was the thing we have lived for throughout our careers—to be mooching around for a story almost as an excuse to be exactly where we were now, in the middle of something so alive and vibrating with energy, so unfamiliar in a familiar, organically human kind of way, that it makes you curious as hell about distilling mean-ing from what William James called "the blooming, buzzing confu-sion" of the world.

On this particular morning, I was eager to find out what I could about Hainan's reputation for being the redoubtable smuggler's cove of southern China. In particular, I was remembering a story I'd tried to report a few years earlier about an ingenious interna-tional car-smuggling ring in which Hainan was the alleged pivot point for supplying customers on the Chinese mainland with lux-ury vehicles that had been stolen in California and secreted across the Pacific in cargo containers. So I had suggested to Li that we see what the locals might have to say on the QT about smuggling and piracy.

And this is where Li showed his true colors. In earlier times, such a request would have caused a guide in China to blanch and stare at his shoes. Not Li. He marched authoritatively around heaps of garbage and decomposing cardboard until he'd delivered us to the office of the local harbor police and demanded an audience. I admired Li's gumption tremendously but based on my experiences with Chinese officials, I had serious doubts about going straight to the police, especially since security officers had been implicated in the area's smuggling activities.

"For godsakes, Li," I said, "the police are never going to tell us about their problems."

Li reared back, looking at me with the expression of a bird that has just been stunned with a pebble. "This is the new China," he scolded, finger wagging and cowlick aflutter. "You can ask anybody anything you want."

That was not technically true of course. The authorities in China were then and remain today notoriously uncooperative with the news media. On the other hand, Li's enthusiasm was so infec-tious that I said to hell with it and followed him up the stone steps and into the small stationhouse. As we entered, two young cops looked up, staring in amazement as if Mao Zedong and Madonna had just walked through the door arm in arm.

"Good morning," Li announced and, as if he were speaking through a megaphone, stated our intention of probing local anti-smuggling efforts.

The young policemen traded nervous looks but were exceedingly cordial. One of them, barefoot and wearing a uniform shirt the color of key lime pie, invited us to have a seat. Bottles of water were passed around while the man tried phoning his superior officer who he said could best address our concerns. In that moment I knew the boss would never show up or give his approval, and I would learn absolutely nothing I didn't already know about smuggling. On the other hand (another helpful rule), when approaching a stone wall it's best to remain flexible and look for fresh openings. And so, I decided to take advantage of a first-class opportunity to learn a little about life in a semi-rural police outpost on a typical, humid Sunday morning.

From where I sat, I could look out the big windows over the harbor and size up the approach to the station. The entrance was framed by elephant-eared palm trees, and some yards farther on boat taxis and dilapidated junks passed to and fro across a surface that was bright with the blue-green sheen of motor oil. Looking the other way, I could see into an interior courtyard where the cops' perspiring young wives tended a pack of kids amid jerry-rigged clotheslines slumped with uniform shirts and undergarments pinned upside down. There were kids everywhere.

I was scribbling notes (". . . walls decorated with maps of harbor area . . . mug shots of officers assigned to this office . . . complaint box with three big red characters, "Complaint Box" . . . gray metal safe . . . desktop computer draped with a red velvet cover") when hospitality or embarrassment compelled the second cop to speak up. "In our station we have over sixty guards," he said, adding emphatically: "And we think we are doing a good job." Then really climbing out on a limb, he said, "Our main job is patrolling the inner sea area!" I smiled inwardly when I noticed his T-shirt said, "Frogs Win Over Crocodiles—Super Match," and made another note. There was talk of overlapping police jurisdictions, which I found impossible to understand.

At length the key-lime man apologized for the holdup. "Mei wenti, mei wenti," Li said, waving him off. "No worries, no worries."

Li was now in overdrive, talking a mile a minute, the sophisticated northerner drowning the southern rubes in a sea of words. Having long ago lost the thread of the conversation, I suggested that Li not stand on ceremony—as my translator, he could tell me what they were saying any time now.

Li looked at me, startled by my naiveté. "I don't understand this local dialect at all—not one word!" he said before plunging back into the verbal scrum without losing a beat.

When the cop finally succeeded in getting his boss on the line, it was as I had predicted. Frowning, he covered the mouthpiece with his hand and said, apologetically, "It will take time for him to come. He has guests."

At eight o'clock in the morning? That is a scandalously late hour in nonmetropolitan China, I'll grant you, but the head cop was never going to show and everybody knew it. In Asia you never step on somebody's face unless you have a very good reason for doing so, though. Consequently, I thanked the friendly young cops for their hospitality and we all shook hands and smiled, and Li and I set off to board a small ferry whose single deck was jammed with people. Unless I'm mistaken, our fellow passengers got a big kick out of the sight of the animated man in the colorful shorts gesticulating at a giant foreigner whom he appeared to be leading by the nose. Two young girls under a single parasol giggled uncontrollably while a pixie-faced young stud leaned against the gunwale, shrewdly assessing my Rolex wristwatch while he ate a banana.

Okay, from the reporting standpoint, the morning shed absolutely no new light on smuggling. On the other hand, things could have been worse. How often do you get the chance to fill your notebook with jottings on the life in a Chinese border patrol station? The truth of reporting is this: You rarely know with certainty what material is going to wind up in your final story, and the reporter who isn't pretty much constantly taking notes, trying to hoover it all in, isn't really doing his or her job.

11

Li continued to be a happy warrior on my behalf. In earlier times, as I've suggested, government-appointed news assistants were warned from on high to keep their distance from foreigners lest they open themselves to "spiritual pollution," the subversion of Chinese values by Western wantonness, or just unwanted complications. But Li prided himself on being a man of the evolving China of freer markets and slowly expanding economic and personal freedoms. As such, he took China's inefficiencies as a personal affront. Woe to the unsuspecting hotel clerk who, clad in a slick blazer with a badge boasting an adopted nickname, like "Kathy" or "George" or "Ken," made the mistake of ignoring Li's complaint about lackluster service. That kind of lofty, bureaucratic disdain put Li over the edge. Though he may not have looked the part, dressed in his crazy-quilt shorts and a T-shirt, Li was a senior bureaucrat himself and, if you wanted to get technical about it, a division chief, who outranked your average counterperson in the national pecking order several times over.

"You are humiliating a foreign guest," Li shouted one morning in the crowded lobby of a big hotel in Guangzhou when a cashier balked at cashing my traveler's checks while displaying an administrative hauteur that was old when Marco Polo hit China in the thirteenth century. As people stopped to stare, Li continued: "That is not good! You should not question a trustworthy person!" And when he had everybody's undivided attention, which included members of a girls' volleyball team from Kent, Washington, he cocked his head to one side, as if inspecting the lobby floor for health code violations, wagged his finger in the air, and lectured the offending parties about the wages of arrogance and moral turpitude until he had them whining for mercy.

"This hotel looks good but the software is very bad," said Li, making his point—and in the process finally joining Mike and me in that special moment I refer to as blowing one's cork. It's that precise juncture when the stresses and strains of life on the road, indignities little and big, build up to a point where even a relatively minor snag can send you over the edge. On a challenging assignment, I've calculated, I go ballistic once every ten days to two weeks, like clockwork. As far as I was concerned, Li's relatively mild freak-out represented a great leap forward in China-U.S. relations.

Li turned out to be such a marvelous minder that I really had only one serious reservation about working with him. Based on past experience, I knew that a headstrong fixer, left unchecked, could lead to confusion about who was ultimately running the show and to what end. In such cases, I've learned to keep said fixer on his or her toes, and lines of command crystal clear, by devising a series of cheap tricks to keep things just slightly off balance.

In dealing with Li, I had a brainstorm. The two of us were very nearly the same age, which meant that Li had come up during the Cultural Revolution when Chinese youth were required to fill their brains with the propaganda slogans Chairman Mao used to fuel the creation of his revolutionary New China. Having read *Quotations from Chairman Mao Tse-Tung* and assorted aphorisms as an armchair ideologue in college, I too had committed a number of Mao's maxims to memory. Now I realized I could use them to engage Li in a kind of trivia contest in which, for instance, I might throw down the beginning of a random line . . .

"Dig tunnels deep, store grain everywhere . . ."

And Li would finish it off . . .

"Never seek hegemony!"

Or, I might say: "The guerrilla must move among the people . . ."

And Li would respond: ". . . as a fish swims in the sea."

It worked like a charm. Li and I reconnoitered Deng's latest version of the new China, quoting retro propaganda sayings and getting along like a house afire. I even took to calling Li the "Iron

Man," after a propaganda hero from the 1960s called Iron Man Wang, a sort of Marxist-Leninist Paul Bunyan who according to the myth had helped break China's dependence on foreign oil by doing everything to boost domestic production but suck it from the ground through a straw. Li protested at first but from the way he later puffed out his chest and smiled, I could tell he loved it.

At the same time, I discovered this man who had done so well in Deng's more open China was still at heart a terrible Maoist prude. One morning in Sanya we were negotiating a narrow pedestrian tunnel that was leeching water through its crumbling brick façade when I spied a scandal. It was a poster for a movie or perhaps a pot-boiler novel and depicted a young woman nude from the waist up, her haunches retracted in a steamy pose. Absent from China for more than a decade, I was gobsmacked. Mao's old New China would never have countenanced such a public display of wantonness.

"Look, Li," I said, pointing. "Pornography!"

Li quickly examined the poster and then averted his eyes. With a dismissive wave of his hand, he sniffed, "Not pornography!" and kept on walking toward the flare of light at the end of the little passage.

I was incredulous. "But it's right there, Li," I said, standing my ground. "A nude lady!"

"Pornography is illegal in China," Li said, as he primly refused to turn his head to reconsider the offending poster.

"Okay, if it isn't pornography," I asked, "What do you call it?"

"It's illegal," Li said, haughtily defending the Socialist advance, and I thought, "Ah-hah!" A man of such Spockian logic as Li would be the first to acknowledge that for something to be illegal it had to exist. I had him. But as much as I enjoyed giving Li the business and keeping him off-kilter, I also recognized the importance of providing a face-saving way out.

To break the escalating shirtiness, I suggested we simply agree to call it "spiritual pollution," that party slogan Comrade Deng Xiaoping had used to warn of the cultural side-effects of opening China to the outside world. Had not Deng himself famously pointed out, "If you open the window for fresh air, you have to expect some flies to blow in."

Li turned and flashed a smile. "Yes, *you know*," he said, nodding his head appreciatively. "Spiritual pollution!" Thus did Li and I happily surmount our first ideological struggle.

Our karmic driver, Wang, meanwhile, remained a source of chronic irritation. When he wasn't driving too fast he was at table with us in a restaurant, invariably slumped in his chair, working his gums with a toothpick, while he undressed the female waitstaff with his eyes. After he'd picked a fight with one of our local contacts, a sweet-tempered fellow who was helping us find our way to a local marine park, Mike and I told Li we thought Wang should get the sack. But firing somebody in a Communist country wasn't that easy. Li suggested we suffer through with Mr. Pigheaded-Driver-Who-Has-Used-Up-All-Patience, and see if things came to a head.

We didn't have long to wait. It was early evening when Mike, Li, and I climbed into the van to head back up island to Haikou for a couple of nights. We'd all been working hard and, tired and hungry, were eager to arrive in the big city and find a decent restaurant. When Wang suddenly pulled off the highway in the middle of nowhere and into a filling station, Mike asked tartly, "Why are we stopping here?"

"The driver says we're nearly out of gas," said Li, gingerly, his cowlick alert to the sudden tension in the car.

Thus had we arrived, under the ghostly fluorescent lights illuminating the gas pumps, at a magnificent moment of full-scale cork blowing, and this time it was the usually imperturbable Mike who did the honors. (Someday I'll meet the saintly person who is immune to occasional bouts of cork-blowing, but it hasn't happened yet.)

"Well, you can tell the driver he's a fucking idiot," yelled Mike. Why didn't he fill up in Sanya before we left? "He's the driver, *that's* his job!"

Wang, who had made it a point to remind us he understood no English whatsoever, nonetheless recognized the famous four-letter word used in its role as a present participle and nursed a slow burn all the way up the highway to Haikou. When we finally swerved into our hotel's circular drive at a million miles an hour, Wang jumped out of the van, flung open its back hatch, and let one of Mike's expensive telephoto lenses fall to the ground with a thud. (Here's another important rule to keep in mind: Never, ever, mess with a world-class photographer's camera gear unless you want a fight on your hands.)

"You idiot!" screamed Mike, running around the end of the van like a tackle homing in on a running back. Wang stepped back and threw a shoulder-high but badly aimed gung-fu kick that nearly put him on his rear. Before the two men could come to blows, courageous Li stepped in to separate them, while the turbaned doorman, gussied up in a uniform reminiscent of the British Raj, looked on, as if he might have swallowed one too many crumpets.

Li gave Driver Wang his walking papers that night. But not before we had been sized up for our commercial potential by the prostitutes flashing goo-goo eyes from round, wrongly rouged farm-girl faces; had wolfed down an unsatisfying meal—insipid spaghetti Bolognese for me—in the hotel restaurant; and poor Li had endured Wang's shrieking complaints about Mike's use of the infamous four-letter English word and the insufferable demands of all foreigners. Whatever happened to that fine old propaganda slogan, "Serve the People," I wanted to know. But for the time being, Li wasn't playing the trivia game—he was too busy trying to iron out what Mao had called "contradictions among the people."

12

The next afternoon Mike, Li, and I set off by taxi for Haikou's ferry dock and the overnight run to Beihai, a leafy port city on China's under-coast. Our boat, a big flat-bottomed rust bucket, sat at the far edge of an expanse of broken pavement, its open maw swallowing up a line of trucks carrying staples for the mainland, things like coconuts, pineapples, cashews, sugarcane, coffee, and palm oil.

As we climbed from the taxi I asked Li if he had our tickets, knowing that comfortable accommodations on public conveyances in China have a way of filling up fast. To my chagrin, Li shook his head, replying snootily, "There are always rooms available on these boats. You just have to know how to negotiate!"

That's just great, I thought, shooting Li a dirty look as I pictured myself trying to sleep standing up for the entire twelve-hour voyage. I found something else to obsess over when Li and I schlepped our bags up the narrow stairway to the main deck and took a look inside the public lavatory. A stickler for basic hygiene, I routinely carry out a painstaking inspection before committing myself to any kind of accommodation on land or sea, and I was appalled. The common toilet was horrifyingly filthy, the bowls backed up and stinking to high heaven.

Topside, and realizing his street cred was on the line, the Iron Man shouted to a young woman who was stuffing stewed chicken feet into Styrofoam boxes in the ship's galley. "Younger Sister," Li said, in his authoritative manner, "we need your help!" and asked her what accommodations might be available.

Attractive in a no-nonsense, girl-next-door kind of way, the woman smiled, wiped her hands on her apron, and told us we were in luck. We followed her pumping elbows forward to a cabin where the door swung back on a room with dirt-streaked windows and four short, grubby bunk beds that struck me as lodgings suited for a third-rate acrobatic troupe. "Li, this room is filthy," I said.

"Yes, filthy," he agreed, simultaneously turning on our guide and unleashing a high-pitched complaint in Mandarin, his hands loose and flying, as if to say, "This is the best you've got? How do you expect this big man here to fit into that tiny bunk?" Unfazed, Younger Sister spoke softly, as if calming a lunatic. Hold your horses, she said, there were other rooms available, and her elbows led us below decks to a windowless cabin the size of a college dorm room.

"Not bad," Li said under his breath. "This girl must share this room with other women on the boat," he marveled. "Look how clean it is." Indeed, it was spotless, and charmingly threadbare.

Faded cotton blankets featured scenes involving bunnies and other nursery rhyme animals. Feeling uncharacteristically gallant, I said, "But Li, if we take this cabin, where will the ladies sleep?"

Li shushed me. I was spoiling his timing. "Okay," he said to Younger Sister. "How much?"

"Two hundred yuan," she said, brightly—about twenty-five dollars.

Li was thunderstruck. Spluttering and stammering, he said, "Two hundred! That's impossible! For two hundred we should get *two* rooms. Just look at this big man here," said Li, tapping my chest with a forefinger. "He's a writer! He has to *write!* How do you expect him to get any work done in a cramped place like this?!"

While Li was giving Younger Sister the business, I fell into my role as the good cop. Stretching out on one of the bunks, I put my hands behind my head and smiled serenely, as if to say, "Now, this is living!" Younger Sister looked over and laughed—she was onto our cheap tricks by now but seemed to enjoy the show. Meanwhile Mike, knowing a good thing when he saw it, jumped in to say he and Li would take the room.

What about the big man? Li asked Younger Sister.

"There is another room," she said coyly, and again her elbows led us down the corridor and through a door marked in Chinese characters: "First Officer." Now this was more like it, I thought. The cabin had all the modern conveniences: a desk, a chair, upper and lower bunks, a TV, VCR, refrigerator, and a fire extinguisher in the form of a pail of water with sodden cigarette butts floating on top.

Li said to Younger Sister, "I'll take both rooms for 200 yuan."

"Three hundred," she said.

"Okay, okay," Li shot back, fussing as if he'd fallen prey to the biggest swindle in history. Secretly, of course, he was delighted with himself. Only a gifted fixer could have taken us from zero to two reasonably clean, comfortable cabins in fifteen minutes' time.

There was even some noteworthy reading matter included in the bargain. A magazine on top of the first officer's desk featured on its cover a swarthy miscreant ripping at the skin-tight blouse of a buxom young woman as she writhed in an ecstasy of agony, inches from a dangling noose.

"Li, look at this, more spiritual pollution," I said.

Li smiled sheepishly, as I pushed it toward him. "What's the title say?"

The Iron Man studied the picture clinically. "'Young Girl Under the Noose,'" he said.

"I gathered it wasn't 'China Reconstructs,'" I said. "What's it about?"

"It's the story of a crackdown on crime," said Li with a straight face.

"Yeah, I'll bet it's a real blistering exposé."

When Li chuckled sarcastically, I told him in journalism in the States we called that "piggy-backing"—using a high moral issue to retail trash and titillate the reading public.

"Yes, maybe," he said, but in China, he speculated, adopting a law-and-order story line was also a way of avoiding the censor's noose. "Anyway, China is a big country," said Li, equivocally, and I took him to mean the government couldn't possibly make every publisher toe the line.

It wasn't until the Iron Man left me alone to get settled that I discovered my accommodations had one major drawback. The ventilation system consisted of two movable ceiling fixtures that looked like inverted miniature foghorns; they appeared to suck air directly from the engine room and kept the cabin swirling with a rich mixture of diesel fumes. Feeling semi-delirious, I headed above decks for some breathable air.

The ferry was just getting underway, gliding slowly through the clutter of Haikou's port, the setting sun bathing its junks and rusting hulks in a buttery glow. A dozen or so people were leaning against the railings looking expectantly out to sea when Li showed up with our dinner—a pair each of Styrofoam boxes, one containing steamed white rice, the other filled to the brim with Younger Sister's stewed chicken feet and sautéed green peppers. The foot of the chicken is not normally my first dinner choice, but when that's all that's on the menu, that's all I eat. And so I ate with relish while my fellow passengers enjoyed the spectacle of a foreigner eating chicken feet on a Chinese ferry. It was a memorable experience all around.

As we moved out into the channel, the sea got rougher, twilight deepened into night, and Li left me alone, saying he wanted to explore the ship, while the other passengers wandered aft to stake out the pew-like deck seats on which to sleep. All passengers, as I noted in my *Geographic* story, but one . . .

> *After 50 years of communist rule, old ways of defining survival are themselves undergoing revolutionary change. I discovered this on board the* Zhong Hai No. 3, *Hainan's overnight ferry to the old coastal city of Beihai. Next to me at the rail was a grinning young man in a flamboyant sport shirt.*
>
> *"I like Hollywood movies!" he volunteered. "I like Arnold Schwarzenegger!"*

Eating chicken feet with Li Hubing, Zhonghai No. 3 to Beihai, 1997.
Photo by Michael Yamashita.

I regretted having had to condense our conversation to make it fit the published article because it struck me as a reasonable inkblot test of Chinese fears, resentments, and aspirations at the time. My new friend wanted to know, "Do you know Bill Gates?" Not personally, I said, but I'd heard of him of course.

"Are there many people like Bill Gates in America?" the man asked, and then, without waiting for me to reply, he said, "I want to go to America!"

"Did many people lose their jobs in America because of the information economy?" he asked, by which he meant the bursting of the recent dot.com bubble. Then, out of the blue:

"I hate the Japanese. . . . The Japanese they *creet* nothing. . . . *Amelican creet*. . . . Japanese make few changes. That's all." This was matched, at an earlier point, with, "I hate the British . . . for what they did to Hong Kong."

My friend told me he'd spent six months training for a computer job in West Germany. "I very much regretted coming back to China," he said. "China is progressing too slowly. We have few freedoms."

He went on to complain about history. There was too much of it in China, he said, and the Chinese were "always looking to the past," whereas, he ventured, "Americans always look to the future."

I suggested that ignorance of history was a problem for Americans—maybe one of China's strengths was its long traditions and cultural cohesiveness. My friend nodded. Yes, our countries may have something to learn from one another, he allowed. But he was no pushover, saying moodily:

> "America has two big oceans! That is unfair!" As if in agreement, the South China Seas walloped the creaky hull, dousing us with spume.
>
> "China was a great country but became weak," the man plunged on. "We need money! We need Taiwan! We should take it!"

But when I raised my eyebrows (it was little more than a year since China had lobbed missiles toward Taiwan in military exercises suspiciously coinciding with presidential elections there and putting U.S. Navy aircraft carriers on alert), he added, "But it won't happen."

Looking out over the darkening waters, where a string of illuminated squid boats began to flash in the night, my friend grew gloomy. "I hate the communists!" he said.

Having reported from China in darker times, I looked over my shoulder to see if anyone was eavesdropping. But few people seemed concerned about the party line. In the new China citizens were wheeling and dealing with the gutsiness I saw earlier in Hong Kong. Another young passenger explained how she had gone from selling black-market gasoline to selling sea snakes. She bought them in Beihai and sold them in Haikou for a tidy profit.

I thought of this passenger as the Snake Lady and, I must say, she was really something. Small and tightly coiled, she had intense dark eyes, jet-black hair tied back in a severe bun, and a shy way of talking tough. I made her acquaintance when I went aft looking for Li and found him eating a ripe mango she'd given him.

"Li!" I said, feigning shock. "What are you doing?!"

Li jumped up, the juice dripping from his fingers, and stammered an introduction to the Snake Lady. He acted as guiltily as if I'd just opened a hatch and found the two of them stealing a smooch. It was clear the Snake Lady had charmed Li like a pet cobra and he was totally mesmerized.

"How did you ever learn about snakes?" I asked.

She said it wasn't that complicated: "There are two kinds of sea snakes, the poisonous ones and the nonpoisonous ones. I sell the nonpoisonous ones."

Which ones taste better?

The poisonous ones, of course, the Snake Lady said: "The more poisonous the better they taste and the better they are for your health."

When I complimented her on her ingenuity, she shrugged and said, "There are a lot of women like me. I'm just trying to survive. Every family is in business now."

The Snake Lady's personality was a combination of the introverted and the feral, and she made me just a bit uneasy. So I praised her again, telling her she seemed to be going about things the right way. "It's not a matter of right," she said flatly, "it's a matter of being realistic. If you're in business you have to deal with reality!"

Look, she said, "I'm twenty-five. I haven't found anybody I want to marry. So I concentrate on my business. . . . When I was a girl, all the boys got to go out fishing or do the interesting things. I finished school when I was thirteen. So I've been in business for myself ever since." And now, she was thinking about expanding . . .

Her dream was to get ahead of intensifying local competition by marketing Nanhai products in Beijing. Something as exotic as sea snakes, I suggested, might make a splash in the faraway capital.

"Do you think so?" Her face illuminated in stages, like a three-way lightbulb. "Or coconuts!" Click. "Or mangoes!" Click, click.

The Snake Lady's real name was Ms. Mai, and I was delighted to find a place for her in my story. Later, though, I felt I'd made her sound too Pollyannaish, which was at odds with the reality. When Li had innocently sat down on the wooden bench next to her, and before she seduced him with a mango, Mai intoned menacingly, "You're sitting on my bed," and threatened to cut him a new one.

13

We arrived in Beihai at dawn. The leggy prostitute who had spent a noisy night with some gentlemen in the cabin next to mine walked awkwardly away from the ship on ultra-high heels, smiling sleepily and with her false eyelashes askew. Suffering from eating too many late-night candy bars in my diesel-choked room, I felt as fragile as she looked. It was time to invoke the foreign correspondent's rule (which number, I've lost track) that goes like this: When the going gets tough, the tough look for the best hotel in town.

I asked the Iron Man where we might find such a place at such an hour in this fine city. "The Shang-gorilla," Li said without hesitation, meaning in fact the Shangri-La, which belonged to a large Hong Kong-owned chain with a good reputation.

"Then the Shang-gorilla it is," I said, and soon I was checking into a comfortable room with an unimpeded view of a sun newly risen over goopy brown mudflats.

Beihai turned out to be a surprisingly pleasant place, with its clean, tree-lined streets and long, curving stretches of attractive beachfront. We spent the next several days there, the happy captives of a group of genial boosters from the town office. Eager to please, they took me out to a sequestered cove for a glimpse at the *Anna Sierra*, a ship pirated for its $5 million cargo of sugar that now lay grounded on the muddy bottom, its hull listing hard to one side, with some of the cargo still on board and at risk of turning to syrup. (The foreign owners blamed the Chinese authorities for the ship's plight and the Chinese authorities blamed the owners for refusing to pay the costs incurred in handling the hijacked ship.) Meanwhile, a local TV crew followed Mike and me around, chronicling our historic visit to the local government fisheries office where the deputy director spoke soporifically of rising coral production and fish catches and the cultivation of the mystical-sounding blue pearl.

Then there were the sandworms. "Watch out for the worms," an old friend in Hong Kong had warned me when I told him I was going to Beihai. The locals considered them a delicacy, he said, which "makes them hard to avoid if you're there for very long." Alive, the tubular creatures looked like night crawlers on steroids, a foot in length and fat. Boiled, they easily passed for limp rigatoni. Deep-fried, they were dead ringers for spears of batter-fried zucchini. Until you tasted them, of course, when they all tasted like mud.

I prided myself on having successfully avoided the worms when, over a lunch with our hosts, Li demonstrated the new relationship between fixers and foreign friends by playing a lowdown trick on me. When our server plunked down a large platter of sandworms on the oilcloth in front of Li, he talked on and on about their virtues. He sounded like a food critic extolling a rare form of foie gras, before preposterously concluding, "I myself prefer them to duck intestines," another Chinese delicacy.

Li was such a faker. A fastidious man from Beijing, I knew for a fact he liked the idea of eating worms even less than I did. Without taking a single integument, he passed the plate to me and said, loudly, "Try some."

I recall pausing to remove a fish scale from my sunglasses, but there was no ducking the challenge. All eyes were on the foreigner and toothpicks hung from mouths waggling expectantly. I grabbed a length of worm in my chopsticks and set my jaws to working.

"Delicious," I lied, staring daggers at Li, who found the whole scene highly amusing. That evening, our last in Beihai, the boosters threw us a send-off dinner at a fancy floating restaurant, where the ubiquitous worms were dipped in batter and lightly fried. Mistaking them for something edible, I chopsticked a pile onto my plate and then realized my error too late. It may have been the sound of mild gagging that caught the attention of Mr. Liao, one of our nice hosts. "A *real* native," he said, "eats them raw, with a little mustard." I was grateful to him for helping me draw a new culinary line in the sand.

I was going to sorely miss the Iron Man. We had worked together for no more than ten days, but elapsed time isn't the measure of the fixer-reporter relationship. Because of the concentrated and demanding nature of the work, you may be worn out and tired of dealing with your fixer and your fixer with you after just a few days, but here's the remarkable thing: If you haven't come to blows, and your personalities have clicked, you know that, deep down, you've formed a bond that will last for a long, long time, whether or not you ever lay eyes on said fixer again. And so, every time the word "Shang-gorilla" comes to mind, which it occasionally does, I smile and think of my friend and colleague, Iron Man Li.

14

From China, I planned to travel down Vietnam's coastline, which sweeps south in elegant curves like those of a giant sea horse—by ferry, fishing boat, or whatever manner of seaworthy vessel I could arrange, arriving in due course at the oil fields off Vung Tau in the south. I'd eventually set it up for *Geographic* readers, in the limited space available, by playing Vietnam's aspirations off against its rivalry with its huge northern neighbor:

> *Farther south, Vietnam has equally big economic dreams. Things would go much more smoothly there if only Bien Dong, or the East Sea, as the Vietnamese call it, would yield more oil. Disputes with China over offshore drilling rights have hampered Vietnam's efforts to turn its communist past into a more open-market future.*

But sometimes, forced to turn a tight corner, the writer can undershoot a key point, and that's what I did here. While the Vietnamese chafed (and still do) at the large swath of coastal seas China claimed for itself, which one source called the "buffalo's tongue" for the way it rasped uncomfortably up against local geographical sensibilities, the bigger challenge to Vietnam's future was Vietnam itself.

I'd spent enough time in the country to know that unlike big China, where there could be hell to pay for local officials defying the central government or the party, Vietnam often operated like a collection of separate fiefdoms where the writ of the central authority not infrequently meant very little. What that meant for me was this: Getting what I needed from my foreign ministry–assigned fixer, a shy, scholarly man we'll call Minh to protect his privacy, was like pulling teeth.

Wherever we happened to be, in Haiphong in the north or Nha Trang three-quarters of the way down the coast, Minh would dutifully deliver my requests for sea travel to local panjandrums so they could automatically deny them on grounds of national or local "security." If the Chinese were subliminally preoccupied with "spiritual pollution" from the West, Vietnamese officials could be downright paranoid about it. One Canadian traveler named Marisha told me a typical story. She and her boyfriend were on a tourist boat near Nha Trang one day when the cops boarded and filmed everybody with a video camera. "The police wanted to know why there were so many foreigners on the boat," she said. When it was explained to them that it was, after all, a tourist boat, the cops wanted to know why the foreigners were swimming so far from the vessel. Ultimately, they took their bribe and left.

The sad truth was that Vietnam wasn't ready to produce the Iron Man Li–type of fixer. With its much smaller economy, the country was spinning off neither the degree of buoyancy nor confidence evident among the Chinese. It was, to me, a much tighter, darker place, where people tended to look over their shoulders as much as they looked forward. Living and working in such an Orwellian system, my man Minh had little incentive to push the envelope for a foreigner. Suffice it to say, I'd have enjoyed knowing him under any other circumstances. He was a sensitive, well-educated man, with a charming, melancholic smile. But Minh was as inert as a bivalve when it came to getting the job done, with the result that I got relatively little of use for my story.

That's not to say the trip didn't have its moments. In Haiphong, Minh inadvertently booked Mike and me into a brothel where the staff members were mean as snakes but thankfully ignored us. (Well, it may only have been a seedy hotel with brothel-like features, but in any event here's a travel tip: Avoid any place of lodging in Vietnam whose signage proclaims, in English, "Sauna and Massage," which was code for sex for pay.) We spent a pleasant day on a tourist boat put-putting through Halong Bay, a gorgeous World Heritage site consisting of thousands of karst limestone islands formed over millions of years. According to legend, the islands were jewels and pieces of jade spit into the ocean by a family of dragons in order to create a barrier against foreign invaders. In fact, these magical islands were the setting for several real-life historic naval battles. In one, in 1228, a Vietnamese admiral successfully repelled a major invasion by placing steel-tipped stakes in the Bach Dang River at high tide, sinking the encroaching Mongol fleet.

Apart from the tourist boat, however, the closest I got to water was in my morning shower. I eventually blew my cork. "I'm not here to write a travel brochure," I told Minh brutally. I needed access to places and people. "I like you, I like traveling with you, I've had a pleasant time," I said. "But that's different from journalism. As a journalist, I'm not getting what I need."

Minh looked misty eyed, poor guy, but nothing changed because nothing could change. I pined for Iron Man Li, which was wrong of me, I know; my bad behavior wouldn't have been tolerated for a minute down at the writer's cooperative. But when you're reporting from the road, burning up the miles and the money, and getting precious little in return, I'm not the only correspondent I've known who would say to hell with unfair. I could have canned Minh outright of course, but in a place like Vietnam that risked either a long delay while bureaucrats in Hanoi found a replacement or simply canceled my visa. In other words, I was stuck. Mine had become an overland "voyage" by default.

My psyche appeared to be working overtime to resolve my inner turmoil. One night I dreamed I was a passenger on a big ship slowly sinking in the middle of Hong Kong harbor. Afraid of drowning and knowing myself to be a poor swimmer, I set out flailing for the distant shore. Buoyed by an overwhelming feeling of the depth beneath and supporting me, however, I made the trip with surprisingly little effort. Well, one way or another, the work gets done.

Over dinner at the aforementioned Haiphong brothel, or whatever it was, Mike was explaining to me why Vietnam had, for him, become the "armpit" of our journey. We were sitting in the empty dining room eating mystery meat in a gooey brown sauce when the electricity failed and the air conditioner went on the fritz. "What a bunch of jive," Mike muttered, as we sweated it out in total darkness.

When the power was restored and the lights came up, Mike was looking at me dejectedly from across the table, perspiration droplets beading his forehead. But nothing ever seemed to get the irrepressible Mike down for long. Ever the scrappy traveler, he cracked a wry smile and started humming that theme song from those *National Geographic* adventure programs on TV: "Dah-dah-DAH-dah, dah dah DAH DAH dah dah . . ."

You had to have been there, I guess, but under the circumstances it was pretty funny. Immediately, I joined Mike in song, and our fractured notes echoed through the empty canteen, much to the annoyance of the scowling waitresses who observed us from behind the counter. So let it be noted: We are all pilgrims on the road, and there is nothing as priceless on the face of the earth as having a solid and companionable traveling companion.

15

In Vietnam, for the reasons described, reporting victories were few and far between, and so I was relieved to make it to Vung Tau at long last, where we met up with Quang Le, Mobil Oil's chief in-country representative. As I pointed out in my story, expensive years of searching had yielded "exasperatingly little oil," but Quang was nonetheless happy to take us out over the rolling sea, in this case to a Mobil oil platform, for a look at the company's drilling operations.

> "It all boils down to luck, luck, luck," said Quang, as we rode a helicopter out into the south Con Son Basin, 190 miles southeast of Vung Tau. On the drilling deck men in hard hats and greasy overalls wrangled lengths of pipe down the drill shaft amid a noise that sounded like prehistoric animals fighting for turf.
>
> When a gusher of mud blurted out, the men danced away, laughing and shouting. After only four days of drilling, Quang explained, they were 2,600 feet below the seabed, with 10,400 to go

and 56 days left on an 11-million-dollar drilling contract to get there. "It's once down, once to the side," said Quang. "Find out what we have and we're out."

The rig had a fantasy-camp wildness about it that appealed to me. The crew—mainly the Europeans and the Filipinos—wore fantastical walrus mustaches, tattoos, and flowing, shoulder-length hair. When I asked what attracted them to life on the rigs, they said that it was the good wages and the adventure. "The economy in Vung Tau goes up a few notches when we hit the bars and open our wallets," said an Australian with a gap-toothed smile.

What a blessing it was to visit that oil rig! After the frustrations of traveling in Vietnam, the company of plain-speaking men was as bracing as a good protein shake. Perhaps a little too bracing. I was standing inside the rig's superstructure chatting with the "tail-pusher," or driver supervisor, John Adin, a robust, barrel-chested New Zealander. He was filling me in on operations, when a man with a severely lopsided gait swung down the corridor and stopped in front me. He had a bent, twisted-around appearance, as if his head and shoulders had fused into a single unit. From the way he glared up at me, he appeared to be very angry.

"Who's Tracy?" he demanded.

"That would be me," I said.

Well, hissed the man, he just wanted me to know, "You disappointed a lot of people, mate." I must say I found the charge totally stupefying. I'd never laid eyes on this man in my life. I'd been on the rig maybe an hour. How could I have possibly disappointed anybody?

The man sniffed and told me that his fellow roustabouts had been expecting a *woman* reporter named Tracy. And suddenly the penny dropped. It was clear my churlish friend had been looking forward to the moment when a glamorous reporter on assignment from the glamorous *National Geographic* would climb out of the chopper, showing a little leg perhaps. Instead, they got me.

"Story of my life," I said with a shrug.

"Yeah, you fooled a lot of people," the man snarled, "but you didn't fuckin' fool me!" And then, smiling sardonically, he turned and loped off down the corridor. Later I learned the whole thing had been the man's idea of a joke but, in keeping with the theme, he could have fooled me.

The rest of the crew did a better job of hiding their disappointment. Steve Minter, a former photocopier salesman from Melbourne, invited me to join him in the "control shack" on deck where he operated the platform's ROV, or Remotely Operated Vehicle, the expensive multifunction robot that trained a camera on the seabed eighty-four meters down so the drillers could see what they were doing.

"We're the eyes of the whole operation," said Steve, which is why he'd had his hands full earlier that day when a ripping current had caught the ROV, with its seven Shiva-like "function" arms and two "camera" arms, at a bad angle. Twisting the contraption around, the undertow had snapped connections and made the cameras go dark.

It took six hours to fix but the problem was solved. Steve admitted that apart from "a little drama on the high seas" now and then, life on the rig could be witheringly dull. That helped explain the tape he popped into the VCR. It was entitled "Seafood Cocktail."

The video screen suddenly flashed silver as clouds of krill floated by, chased by a large, hungry squid. (I failed to note down the soundtrack but, if I remember rightly, it was the Rolling Stones.) Next a lionfish swam center stage, showing off its spikey prehistoric frills in a variety of brilliant reds. "We call her 'Rosemary,'" said Steve admiringly, adding by way of thoughtful observation: "There are some weird-looking things down there."

He explained that the ROV "makes a perfect natural aquarium," seeing as how the heat generated by drilling for oil attracted all kinds of curious fish and the ROV cage provided them a respite from strong ocean currents. And that created ideal conditions for a film study. The title "747" floated across the screen followed by the bullet-shaped body of a giant grouper. The behemoth swam up to the camera until all that was visible was a pair of huge, bony lips. "He camped out in the ROV and resisted all efforts to dislodge him," Steve told me with a laugh. The curious fish were no problem, he said, "as long as they don't try to mate with the rig."

I very much liked the idea of the oil-riggers, disappointed with the nonappearance of Tracy, the journalist femme fatale, amusing themselves by chronicling their peculiar corner of the ocean on videotape. The plain fact of the matter is that life, even in the most exotic locales, is made up mainly of humdrum routine occasionally interrupted by enlivening crisis, and I greatly admired Steve's capacity to wring a little romance from a tedious job. To me, that's real talent—and one of life's great secrets.

16

After Vietnam, Mike decided to take a break and flew home to New Jersey. That meant from Ho Chi Minh City onward, I would travel alone, circling and crisscrossing the South China Sea, hopping back and forth from one far-flung venue to the next. To capture a sense of that in the writing of my story, and fighting that infernally tight six-thousand-word budget, I would stoop to inserting yet another cheesy transition paragraph, trying to tag the bases and push the narrative forward:

Despite difficulties in the search for fossil fuels, plenty of dreams do pan out in the South China Sea. In Singapore I met Dorian Ball, a South African salvage diver, whose tortuous six-year search for sunken treasure on the Diana, *a British sailing ship that went down near the mouth of the Strait of Malacca in 1817, nearly wrecked his personal life and finances, until he finally found the ship and its 3.5-million-dollar cargo of Chinese porcelain. In the Philippines I met Richard Gordon, a local politician, whose vision turned the abandoned U.S. Navy base at Subic Bay—once famous for brothels and clip joints—into a burgeoning special economic zone that has generated thousands of jobs, a billion dollars in foreign investment, and enough public acclaim that, when we spoke in Manila, Gordon was considering a bid for the country's presidency.*

In the meantime, back in the field, my reporting plans hit another serious snag. In doing a story on the South China Sea, any journalist worth his or her salt has no choice but to address the contentious issue of the Spratly Islands. Those remote specks of coral, invisible sandbanks, and half-hidden shoals lying to the west of scimitar-shaped Palawan Island in the Philippines have been embroiled in long-running ownership disputes between and among at least six countries (China, Vietnam, Taiwan, Malaysia, the Philippines, and Brunei) because of the belief—shared by many, substantiated only piecemeal or not at all—that the area sits atop more oil than Kuwait.

At the time, as I ultimately pointed out in my story's lede (the one that begins this part of the book), such tensions had come to a head between Beijing and Manila over a godforsaken chunk of coral called Mischief Reef. To stake their claim, the Chinese navy had built structures that from aerial photos looked like a cluster of backyard tree houses or maybe earthbound UFOs, and the Filipinos were up in arms. That, in turn, had reignited concern about what the experts call the "militarization" of the South China Sea, tensions that have only escalated with China's rise.

Of course you could try to fudge that part of the story, yielding to yet another bit of boilerplate exposition, the reporter saying he'd been on a ship that had steamed close by the disputed territory— or she'd talked to policy types who were troubled about all the saber-rattling—and try to stake a claim for writing about the topic by proxy. But frankly, any numbskull could do that. If you were on assignment for the *National Geographic* you really had no choice but to fly into the bull's-eye for a firsthand look.

But how to get out there? None of the countries with skin in the game easily granted journalists access to the area because of national security concerns. The only government I thought might be remotely cooperative was the Philippines, where I was headed next. Over a dinner of shrimp and avocado salad in Manila, a well-connected friend of friends said traveling to Mischief Reef wasn't in the cards—still too sensitive. But she thought I had a good shot at setting foot somewhere in Freedomland, or Kalayaan, which is what the Filipinos called their eight-island claim in the Spratlys.

I talked with senior government officials who I was given to believe would talk to other senior officials who would, in turn, authorize the local base commander on Palawan Island, the jumping-off place for the Spratlys, to put me on a military plane bound for the disputed islands. While I hung around Manila, waiting for a word, I learned a little about the passions the issue stirred up. A high-ranking military man I met decried the Chinese for destroying the delicate coral structures on Mischief Reef to build their ugly tree houses.

"That young island, rising from the deep with its delicate crown . . ." he said, stopping in midsentence, apoplectic. "It's an offense to the rest of humanity!"

The officer's protect-the-environment argument struck me as somewhat contradictory, seeing as how he'd had a role in commando operations that tried to demolish a Chinese placement elsewhere in the Spratlys. Ultimately, he admitted that playing the environmental card was a good way to win international support for a country whose poorly equipped military didn't have a prayer of defeating the Chinese toe-to-toe on the open sea.

Permission to enter the Spratlys still hadn't come when I decided to force the issue and flew out to Puerto Princesa, Palawan's biggest city and the home of the Philippine military's Western Command. After checking into a large, tropically gothic hotel decorated in pitted, oily hardwoods that made the place seem as oppressive as a horror movie set, I hailed a tuk-tuk (no taxis on Palawan) to take me to the WesCom base. That kicked off a long, complicated afternoon in which the bureaucracy seemed dead set on preventing me from doing my job.

The driver threaded us along the island's wet, winding jungle roads until we came to a gate enclosing WesCom, a collection of clapboard buildings under a canopy of coconut palms hard by a turquoise bay. In a sweltering administration office the size of a Quonset hut where no one had the slightest idea as to who I was or why I was there, I was told to wait, for what I wasn't exactly sure. To kill time, I went outdoors and found a cool spot under the sheltering palms from which to get a good look at the Sulu Sea.

The Sulu Sea! Growing up in Seattle, I'd spent rainy Saturday mornings poring over a world atlas, telepathically transporting myself to places with the most exotic names I could find, and the Sulu Sea was on that list. Now, here I was taking in the amazing scene—a long stretch of coffee-colored tidal flats, followed by a narrow paring of white sand that was succeeded, in turn, by a band of turquoise sea that levitated under a sky of hazy blue all the way to the horizon. With all the various layers of color and texture, it reminded me of a vast, delectable parfait.

That moment of geographical bliss was followed by more bureaucratic dyspepsia, when a fresh-faced young captain smiled and said, "I'm sorry to tell you that we cannot allocate air assets to or allow a foreign national to travel in a secured area without a directive from General Headquarters."

"So you're telling me I've come all this way for nothing," I said.

"I'm sorry, sir, but we cannot allocate air assets . . ."

I may have pushed the truth a bit when I told him I'd been assured that the defense secretary himself had given his approval and General Reyes, the base commander, was handling the matter personally.

"General Reyes is in Manila," said the skeptical officer, still smiling. "He will return by the Philippine Airlines flight at five o'clock." He suggested that I go to the front gate and try to hail a tuk-tuk—in other words, that I get lost.

Deeply annoyed at being given the bureaucratic bum's rush, I muttered an unpleasant thanks-for-nothing and slunk back to the hotel. While I waited to call my contact in Manila—the trunk line was busy, I was told, and my cell phone wasn't cooperating—I sat glumly on my bed watching a torrential rain lash a primeval garden. I looked at an old Humphrey Bogart movie on hotel

TV. I battled a large, evil-looking insect with a hooked snout that emerged from the bathroom to patrol the pockmarked mahogany floors and dispute my occupation of his territory.

Desperate, I tried phoning the mayor, a friend of a journalist friend in Hong Kong who told me the man could really pull the local strings. But the unfriendly woman who answered said the mayor wasn't at home. When would he return?

"Negative knowledge, sir," she said.

Negative knowledge? I thought she had to be pulling my leg. It was as if everybody on Palawan had been coached in military-style doublespeak.

"Yes, negative knowledge, sir." Click.

It was time for the direct approach. When the clock struck five, I headed back to WesCom determined to find the general. At the gate a guard pointed me to his residence, a small nondescript pre-fab, and I walked over and banged on the door. When a young adjutant opened up, I said, "I'd like to see General Reyes, please," and in a minute or two a handsome man in his late fifties stepped onto the porch and shot me a cloudy look. The general. Business-like but polite, he invited me to sit with him on his patio overlooking the water. He then told me bluntly how much he disliked the press.

I had arrived at what some long-distance hacks refer to as the jump point, and I told myself, Okay, Tracy, here you are on the edge of the Sulu Sea with one shot and one shot only of getting out to the Spratlys, and it all depends on persuading a man who hates the press to see things your way. I told Reyes I appreciated his candor but I also wanted to make it clear I wasn't after some seedy exposé. My job was to rope the immensity of the South China Sea into a single article that could be seen by millions of people, and I needed his help. I was laying my bet on appealing to this cultivated man's spirit of enterprise.

Part of our patio conversation was not for publication, but I can say I took it as a very good sign that when it was over Reyes invited me to stay for dinner, and I followed him inside the little house. In the narrow kitchen, we sat down at a Formica table while the general's adjutant served one succulent dish after another. There was a sweet-and-sour soup made from milky-looking cow innards; a delicious seaweed and onion salad; a broiled whole fish, possibly a bonito; Spanish dried beef; steamed rice; and a sweet fresh mango for dessert.

Reyes apologized for the quality of the meal, but everything was delicious. I must say I've never had such tender, sweet-tasting seaweed before or since—its long pale green stalks supported knots of tiny polyps that popped in your mouth to release a fluid that tasted like honey. While we ate and talked, I sidestepped my burning desire to visit the Spratlys—I knew high-pressure tactics would only confirm the general's feelings about press trickiness. Forbearance paid off. When we'd finished our meal, Reyes told me there was a transport plane leaving the following day for Pagasa atoll, one of the islands in Freedomland, and he'd hold a place for me—provided the proper authorization came through from Manila. My dispute with the horned beetles inhabiting my hotel room notwithstanding, I was elated.

Just how or by whom I was cleared for travel remains a mystery, but the next morning I found myself riding through a hot, wet rain to the military airstrip where I boarded a guppy-like C-130 transport for the ninety-minute flight. The plane's cargo hold, which smelled of damp cardboard, was occupied from deck to ceiling with a Matterhorn of steel bedsprings and mattresses around which were randomly arranged sacks of potatoes and hairy-noggined coconuts, big, nubbly truck tires, crooning chickens in bamboo cages, and a yapping, tethered puppy or two.

My guide, a tall, smiling colonel in an olive-green flight suit, who didn't want me to use his name, found me a seat, which I shared with another man, on a large toolbox outfitted with an inconveniently placed handle. I sat down. Meanwhile a contingent of marines, taut in camouflage gear, squatted crab-like in the crevasses of "Mount E-Z Rest," their rifles sticking out at precarious angles. Not an inch of space went unoccupied.

Then came the moment of truth. The pilot rolled the grossly overloaded plane slowly down the tarmac, preparing to defy gravity. The bedsprings did what bedsprings do in such circumstances—they bounced and shifted. Men yelped and twisted to avoid being pinched or pinned. And then suddenly, halfway down the rain-slick tarmac, the pilot slammed on the brakes and "Mount E-Z Rest" slid ominously forward. Fighting to keep my balance, I inadvertently grabbed the man seated next to me on the toolbox and pulled both of us forward, as if attempting a wrestling takedown. Around us the marines traded nervous, oh-shit smiles or hurriedly made the sign of the cross.

Personally speaking, I thanked my lucky stars for the aborted takeoff, assuming, in an absurd flight of wishful thinking, the pilot would now call it quits. Instead, he wheeled the plane around to the top of the apron to try again, and we rattled and banged down the runway, the plane sounding as if it would fall to pieces at any second. And then—I repeat, miracles do happen—we somehow clawed our way into the heavy, humid air, clearing the tall coconut palms at the end of the runway with what seemed like inches to spare.

I had no idea at the time that my trip to Pagasa atoll would become the anecdote to lead my South China Sea story. After the usual indecision, and trying and abandoning various openings, though, I realized the contest over the far Spratlys was by far the best current example of the rivalries that had historically bestirred the South China Sea. I had nothing else in my notebooks to match it.

On Pagasa I met a weathered construction worker in a floppy sun hat who told me he had first visited the island in 1977, half a dozen years after the Marcos government sent troops in to occupy it. What was it like back then? I asked.

"It was very peaceful here," the man said, wistfully, as he swiveled his head to take in the less-than-breakneck activity on the runway apron, which was empty but for a jeep and a battered yellow tractor, neither of which was moving at the time.

Not exactly Grand Central Station now, I said to myself, though my guides, the debonair colonel in the flight suit and a jovial junior officer, informed me that Pagasa was in fact a voting precinct of Palawan province with a detailed urban development plan. They had to admit, however, that the "municipal housing" area was yet to house a civilian community. Even Pagasa's mayor lived back on Palawan. An "ice factory" produced no ice; the runway was too short to fly in the proper machines.

We were literally standing on almost nothing in the middle of almost nowhere, and in my notes I jotted down the address: 11° N. LAT., 114° E. LONG, 540 nautical miles from Hainan Island, 700 from Taiwan, 300 from the southern tip of Vietnam, and 275 from Puerto Princesa. Yet it happened to be a nowhere in which the American intelligence community was actively interested. After I returned to New York I would receive a phone call from a gentleman who said he was an analyst with the CIA. Would I care to come to the Washington area for a conversation with him and his colleagues? I didn't attend, but the offer confirmed that if you talk your way out to an interesting place to which few ever go, people of intelligence will be interested in what you have to say.

What was exciting from afar, however, was a lonely business up close. Standing on that small jot of coral with the deep blue sea raging all around, I asked the men I encountered what on earth they did on Pagasa to keep from going stir-crazy. The popular answer seemed to be that they had plenty of work to keep them busy, thank you.

Yes, but what about free time?

"We fish," said one officer matter-of-factly as he nodded toward the nearby lagoon. "There is fishing and we fish."

And then what? I asked another man.

Well, he said, after a pregnant pause, "and then there is the fishing."

They were humorists, after all, these sturdy men at the end of the world, which, not unlike Steve Minter and the men on the Con Son Basin oil rig, I suppose, helped them no end in carrying out their assignments.

17

There comes a time in every long-distance reporting trip when inevitably you find yourself sitting on the edge of a bunk, often in a broken-down dive of a hotel someplace, the hoped-for glory of the expedition having long since evaporated and, like Dante's pilgrim, you wonder what on earth you were thinking when you got yourself involved. Or as I would write in my story:

> *Every solitary sojourner hits a low point, when the fabric of romance refuses to stretch over the day-to-day realities of travel. Mine arrived in mid-journey, in Bangkok. A ship that would have fetched me to Singapore had burnt to the waterline and sunk. Lead gray and car-infarcted, the city, its infamous bars decorated with Christmas lights in July, held little glamour for a marooned, middle-aged hack.*
>
> *I decided to hire a fishing boat to take me down the Chao Phraya River where it empties into the Gulf of Thailand. Maybe I could find the spot where the captain in* The Shadow-Line, *my favorite Conrad tale, his ship fatefully becalmed, falls prey to deadly currents that move, mysteriously, "with a stealthy power made manifest by the changing vistas of the islands fringing the east shore of the Gulf."*

The fishing boat was a good idea, but actually hiring one can be harder than it sounds. Unless you're fluent in the local language, you first have to find the person who can find the boat—that is to say, a fixer. But in Bangkok I discovered that journalist friends who lived there and offered to help orient me had all decamped to reporting trips or holidays, and I was rowing my dinghy alone. In desperation, I rode the elevator up to my hotel's executive business center. Such places can be a waste of time for the traveling hack, catering as they do to routine chores like filling out customs forms for visiting businesspeople that, frankly, don't take a lot of initiative.

But I lucked out. I connected with two eager-beaver college students and put them to work immediately. There was Pop, bright-eyed and effervescent, and Pit, a bulky young man with a face-splitting Cheshire Cat grin that made him look as if he'd escaped from the stage set of an "Alice in Wonderland" revival. Presto!—I had an editorial team, and life and art took on new hope.

I assigned Pit the task of finding the boat. I told him I wanted to make absolutely sure "we get out to bar." I meant, of course, the sandbar marking the maritime boundary between the Chao Phraya River that flows through Bangkok and the Gulf of Thailand. Pit misunderstood.

"The bar, sir?"

Yes, I told him, the one at the end of the river.

"Yes, sir?"

Heaven knows what flickered through his mind just then, this dutiful son of devout Muslim parents. For an uncomfortable moment, he may have entertained awful visions of being ensnared in some seamy foreign escapade in the city's legendary tenderloin district. I clarified.

"Pit, do you know what bar I'm talking about?"

"Not really, sir," he said, flashing his marvelous grin.

"I'm talking about the place where the river flows into the sea," I said. Pit's eyes lit up and, visibly relieved, he quickly, if belatedly, grasped the point of the exercise. You could see the mental wheels turning. His father, he said, was a retired ship mechanic; maybe he had a connection to somebody with a boat. I was impressed with the reporterly way he put two and two together and told him to let me know when he'd come up with options.

The following evening I enjoyed a delightful meal at a fine Thai restaurant with my friends Edwin Aye Tut, a Burmese émigré and veteran ship's master, and his wife, Tammy, and returned to my hotel for an early night. I was staying in a cozy junior suite with a stone Buddha's head smiling serenely from a plinth and was just drifting off to sleep when the bedside phone rang. It was Pit. He was tremendously excited: "I've found a boat, sir!"

"Good going, Pit," I croaked.

"Yes," he said. "And do not worry, sir. It's a very good boat, sir. A fishing boat, sir!"

"Sounds dandy, Pit."

"Yes, sir, will it be okay, sir?"

"You bet, Pit. Perfect. Couldn't be better. Good night, Pit."

"Good night, sir!"

Pit was such a good kid. Large and round-shouldered, with his hair parted down the middle and sweeping into his eyes, he told me his dream was to go to Switzerland to study hotel management, though he appeared to have already completed Heel Clicking 101 with flying colors. I tried to get him to ease off on the "sir" business, to which he invariably responded: "Yes, sir, very good, sir!"

The next morning Pit picked me up at the hotel in his shiny black Isuzu four-wheel-drive pickup with its serious stereo system. "Where's Pop?" I asked.

"Oh, yes, sir, she is not coming, sir. She really wanted to come, sir, but her parents said no. They did not want her going out on the boat, sir. They thought it was too dangerous, sir."

I told Pit that was perfectly understandable, and not to worry one bit.

"Yes, sir," he said.

Pop-less but undeterred, we drove through Bangkok's tangled streets to a quiet residential neighborhood. Turning down a bumpy gravel road toward the river, we found our boat, a dilapidated thirty-footer, tethered to an arthritic wooden dock next to an ice factory. As we walked up, the skipper poked his head out of the wheelhouse, grinning from ear to ear, and shouted something at Pit in Thai. He had a sunburned face, long hair streaked with silver, and shrewd, squinting eyes. The only way he could have looked more the part would have been to affect an eye-patch and have a dagger clenched in his teeth. This is how I served it up for *Geographic* readers:

As if from central casting, my skipper, Somsak, steered his
crumbling red-and-white craft down the Chao Phraya. He sat

cross-legged on the engine cowling, a gnarled big toe—its nail
opaque as a shrimp cracker—turning the wheel.

I was feeling very good now, and why not? I sat out on the engine cowling, headed downriver, the wind kicking up an enlivening fuss while I thumbed my disintegrating, much-traveled copy of the complete Conrad, gripping it tightly to keep whole sections from flying away. I was trying to match the scenery rolling past us with descriptions from the old master:

> *To my delight the clutter of factory chimneys, cargo cranes, and*
> *steel-hulled warships riding at anchor opened to reveal glimpses of*
> *the "great gilt pagoda" at Paknam and other landmarks from the*
> *time Conrad knew the river a hundred years ago.*
> *"Ah, the romance," I thought, my mood soaring.*

It really was quite a scene. Seabirds and gulls shot overhead, making for the open sea. Above them, the sun was burning holes through a blanket of high, slate-gray clouds, opening up little patches of blue over headlands that stuck out on either side of the Chao Phraya and signaled our approach to the bar. It was then I discovered an exciting anomaly that I couldn't wait to share with Pit.

"Look here," I said, shouting over the wind. "Conrad says his captain can see the Paknam pagoda from the bar, from the head of the Gulf. But here we are and you can't see it at all!" (In a discovery that made Conrad seem more human, I also learned he had made an amateurish geographical mistake, common among foreigners at the time, of calling the Chao Phraya "the Meinam," which is, in fact, the generic Thai word for river.)

Pit had never read Conrad, and had no earthly need to, but he was familiar with literary license. "Maybe he compress, sir," he said, thoughtfully.

In my excitement, I'd neglected to notice the river growing choppier and choppier as we drew nearer the bar, and I could see that Pit was looking decidedly green around the gills.

"Are you okay, Pit?"

"Yes, sir, no problem, sir."

Just then a big wave washed over the bow, splattering my notebook and causing my pen to malfunction. "Time to go inside," I shouted, gesturing toward the wheelhouse. Pit smiled and nodded eagerly.

I got the impression Pit hadn't spent a lot of time on boats, so I led the way, showing him how to inch along the narrow ledge, grab the structural supports and slide his body into the hatch while the vessel pitched and rolled. Inside, Somsak greeted us with a crafty grin, ducking and flinching from the jets of spray that were shooting into the wheelhouse through the side hatches and cracks in the windshield.

"I've been fishing here for thirteen years," the skipper said, as Pit translated. "The fish used to almost jump into your boat. Now . . ." and a dismissive sweep of the hand said the rest. Rampant pollution was killing off the coral reefs and the fish that relied on them all over the South China Sea.

It was right about then that Pit interrupted the interview, swinging his large body out of the wheelhouse and emptying the contents of his stomach into the churning, mealy water. In the process he demonstrated his unfamiliarity with a first rule of seamanship: Don't spit, or whatever, into the wind. The captain, meanwhile, made a beeline for a large fishing vessel several hundred yards ahead . . .

Somsak, who didn't know Joseph Conrad from Conan the Barbarian, alerted me to a special buying opportunity: His friend, right around the next bend, just happened to have a catch of fresh lobsters for sale.

"No lobsters," I said.

Somsak chuckled piratically at my refusal as the wind kicked up and we juddered through mud-colored waves like an eggbeater in a bowl of gravy. Minutes later, he pointed a finger, alluvial with grime, toward pincer-like headlands that crimped the channel, shouting, "That is the outer bar!"

With a sidelong glance Somsak said, "The lobsters are very delicious."

"No lobsters," I said.

But I couldn't blame him. In his late 40s, he had spent his life fishing in the gulf. Now too many fishing boats and toxic runoff from factories and shrimp farms have depleted what was, until only recently, one of the world's most abundant fisheries.

To survive, Thai fishermen venture farther and farther out, into waters claimed by Vietnam, Indonesia, and Burma. Some have died in shoot-outs with border patrols, and many more languish in jails around the region.

Somsak, too, had harbored dreams of filling his boat with Vietnamese fish. "We got within 50 miles of the coast when we got caught in radar," he said, recalling his brush with a border patrol there several years ago. "We tried to get away, but our engines overheated. So we took ice off the fish and threw it on the engines to cool them down!"

How had he escaped? Somsak tapped his temple. "We steered for a slower boat, and the Vietnamese caught them instead!"

So it was I managed to wrap into my story both my pursuit of Conrad and the grim realities of fishing in the Gulf of Thailand. I see from reviewing my notes, however, that I underplayed Somsak's real worry, which had persuaded him to retire from long-distance fishing. He had lived in fear, he said, that his men, hopped up from the drugs in widespread use among the fishing crews in those southern waters, "might murder me and steal my boat when we were out of sight of land."

All in all, our trip had been a big success, and the sun was dancing on the septic waters of the Chao Phraya when we arrived safely back at the dock near the ice factory. On dry land once again, released from the curse of *mal de mer*, Pit was smiling up a storm.

"I hope it was all right, sir," he said.

All right? Pit was my hero. His energy had rescued me from my dreadful, becalmed state of mind. He'd engineered our voyage with the wily Captain Somsak all the way to the bar and back again.

"Pit, we've been to sea together. We're friends now."

"I hope so, sir. If you ever come back to Bangkok and you have some problem, please call me."

"Pit, I will call you, even if I don't have a problem."

Pit beamed, his face splitting with another enormous grin.

"Yes, sir!"

Next stop was Singapore where I had an important rendezvous in store. While still bucketing down the coast in Vietnam, and before heading for Bangkok, I'd received some very good news from Arthur Bowring, managing director of the Hong Kong Shipowners Association. Bowring was the cousin of an ancient friend from *Far Eastern Economic Review* days, and had promised to do his best to arrange passage for me on a Chinese merchant vessel traveling the Singapore-to-Hong Kong run.

"You're in luck, mate!" Arthur had said into the telephone. A fifty-thousand-ton bulk cargo carrier, meaning a big one, was presently taking on a load of steel bars in Richards Bay, South Africa. Typically, it had Hong Kong owners, flew a Liberian flag, and shipped an all-Chinese crew. It would pass through the Singapore Strait in late July and slow down long enough for me to hop on board. Interested?

Absolutely, I said.

"Brilliant!" said Arthur.

I asked him what the ship was called.

"The *Pacific Mercury*," Arthur said, and I kid you not, my heart skipped a beat.

PLYING THE
WATERS

1

"Good morning, sir!" I was standing in the ocean terminal in Singapore, day-trippers and ferryboat commuters eddying around me, when the skipper of the *Sea Wren*, the harbor launch that would take me out to the *Pacific Mercury*, approached and saluted. Reed-thin and smiling a luminous smile, he heaved my duffel bag to his shoulder, crumpled a little under its weight, and asked, "Sir, excuse me, sir. Are you the captain of the *Mercury*, or the chief engineer?"

It was a perfectly logical question—why else would he be obliged to deliver a shambling American of a certain age to a merchant vessel as it made its way through the Singapore Strait? Yet I suddenly felt an absurd rush of juvenile pride. Here I was leaving behind the global shopping mall, which means pretty much everywhere nowadays, and not for some pedestrian ferryboat jaunt. I was going to sea! On a real ship! Bound for an exotic port of call!

The *Wren*'s roomy passenger cabin was decorated in the style of an old-time mechanics garage, with nude calendars from rival shipping agencies tacked to the bulkheads. Up front, near the wheel, a young acne-faced attendant occupied a jump seat vigorously reading some kind of religious pamphlet, his head bobbing and his lips moving, as if trying to keep himself chaste in unchaste surroundings. Farther aft, a plump, fussy-looking character in a rumpled business suit flopped down on a cushioned bench and immediately fell asleep. Next to him, his skinny, cat-faced partner feigned sleep but in a way I found unnerving kept a bloodshot eye blinking in

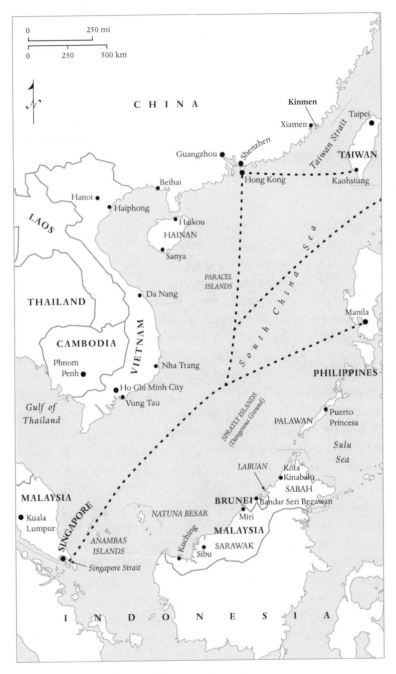

South China Sea shipping routes.

my direction. Him I pegged as some kind of dangerous maritime criminal.

Quickly enough, the smiling skipper took the wheel, threw the *Sea Wren*'s engines into gear, and we cruised slowly into the sun-spangled inner harbor. An old-fashioned lighthouse glided by, its white tower surrounded by a clutch of palms, green and shaggy above the turquoise waters—a bit of the old-time romance amid the sci-fi ductwork of the oil and gas storage tanks that crowded the general area. And then, the Strait, as Conrad says somewhere of the eastern oceans, opened to us "like the sea of a dream."

Riding at anchor or steaming majestically through the indigo waters were the behemoths of seaborne trade—oil and natural gas tankers, container ships and super-size bulk carriers—that transported products to help keep the inhabitants of the globe fed and clothed and their homes and factories fueled and lighted. At one point I counted twenty-two vessels to port and twenty-four to star-board. It really was like watching the modern world come to life in the pages of a beloved old novel.

I was thoroughly absorbed in the scene and jotting notes when from the back of the cabin a voice demanded, "When do we board the *Pacific Mercury*?" It was the plump, fussy guy, who had just woken up from his nap. "At this rate, we won't get back to Singa-pore until eight o'clock tonight."

"The *Mercury*'s cut her engines but she's still drifting," replied the skipper, who had been monitoring the radio chatter, which indi-cated the ship would be approaching us from the south-southwest. "As you know, she has to come to a complete stop before we can approach her."

The skipper was remarkably courteous, but for the life of me I couldn't fathom what business the chunky complainer could pos-sibly have out in the Strait. Then suddenly the rich, creamy voice of the harbormaster emerged from the crackle and pop of the *Sea Wren*'s radio: "*Pacific Mercury, Pacific Mercury . . .* Come in, please."

I was straining to hear the *Mercury*'s reply when the complain-er's crafty-looking partner, slid to the edge of his seat, at attention, as somebody pointed and said, "There she is!" And sure enough, the ship hove into view. It reminded me of a vision from the pages of Conrad's novel *The Shadow-Line*, in which a young, untried captain beholds the glory of his first command. The *Mercury* was long, sleek, and graceful for something so very big. Her main deck, dominated by four towering cranes, seemed to roll forever forward from a multistoried deckhouse in the rear. Hooray for the romance of the sea!

But my thrill was short-lived. When the voice of the *Mercury* had broken through the radio static, it said, "Zeez eez zah pah-shee-fee-kuh mah-kuh-rhee. Gooh maw-ning . . ."

Good Lord, I thought. The English was so fractured I could barely make out the simplest greeting. Since I spoke no more than a dozen words of Mandarin, I had specifically asked the shipping agent in Singapore if the officers and men of the *Mercury* spoke good English—"Yes, yes, have to, you see," he said, mumbling something about English being the language of global commerce. But now my reporterly antennae were fully extended. Traveling fixer-less, how the devil could I get my story if I wasn't able to communicate?

I was pondering this unwelcome complication when the skipper made a beeline for the *Mercury*, bouncing out across the choppy waters at top speed. Just before we smacked into the big ship broadside, he cut engines and deftly spun the wheel to bring the *Wren's* stern within a few yards of the bigger ship's near-perpendicular hull. When it was time to board, I followed the cat-like man and his dyspeptic friend out on deck where, to keep from being pitched headlong overboard, I found myself performing a kind of involuntary clog dance, my feet slapping the deck in goofy rhythm. Meanwhile, up, up, up on the *Mercury's* main deck a stick figure lowered a long wobbly ladder down, down, down the side. I froze.

To this day I don't have a clue as to how I got my bad basketball knees up that flimsy-looking contraption without a terrible mishap. But when you have no choice but humiliating retreat, you do your best, and so I snatched at the ladder's loose polystyrene hand lines and started climbing. I missed my footing on the first or second rung and felt my leg plunge toward the wild, inky deep. Then, lucky stars be thanked, I recovered my balance, got into a kind of rhythm with the swing and bounce, and trudged my way to the top. The next thing I knew an acrobatic seaman had fetched my duffel bag from the *Sea Wren* and was leading me into the deck-house. Up three flights of stairs, he stopped at a door on the upper bridge marked "Pilot," tossed my belongings onto a small purple couch, and made his silent retreat.

Taking stock of my accommodations, I felt encouraged for the first time. Lucking into the pilot's cabin produced another silly shiver of adolescent pride as I remembered *Heart of Darkness* and Conrad's description of the Director of Companies: "He resem-bled a pilot, which to a seaman is trustworthiness personified." Mainly, though, I was feeling a sense of grateful relief. In contrast to what friends in Hong Kong had led me to expect on a Chinese ship, my quarters were exceedingly homey and shipshape. There was a metal desk with a freshly laundered towel on top and a new bar of soap on top of the towel. To my left was a single bunk over which a porthole looked out on the main deck and the big cranes. Just inside the door a fiberglass module containing a toilet, shower, and sink sparkled like a TV commercial for bathroom cleanser.

"You're lucky," said a voice from the corridor behind me. "This ship is almost new so they haven't had time to screw it up yet." I turned to see the suspicious-looking man from the *Sea Wren*, ex-tending his hand with a cordial smile. "My name's Iqbal," he said, explaining that he was the bunkering agent, the person in charge of tallying up the volume of oil the fuel boats pumped into the ship's tanks so a bill could be sent to the *Mercury*'s owners. He was so friendly and helpful I felt ashamed of myself for having mistaken him for a pirate.

Speaking into his walkie-talkie, Iqbal said, "Hello, Captain. I see you've got a new pilot," to which I could hear a disembodied voice reply, distractedly: "Yes, yes."

"The old man is down from the bridge now," Iqbal told me, and led me the way down the passage to the captain's office.

But for two portholes the size of dinner plates, the room could have belonged to an insurance broker in a suburban strip mall somewhere. There was a desk stacked with papers and manuals and a low boomerang-shaped coffee table behind which, hunkered against the bulkhead, sat the querulous complainer from the *Sea Wren.*

"This unhappy man is the boarding agent," Iqbal said, with a quick laugh, meaning he represented the ship's owners. Looking up from his papers, the agent smirked a greeting. The only other man in the room, meanwhile, was a nervous young Chinese steward with sharp features and a head of thistly black hair who flitted between desk and table fetching soft drinks and cigarettes for the captain's guests. Watching me watch this comic figure, Iqbal smiled, as if savoring a private joke, and said, "And this is the *old man.*"

I was astonished. The fellow looked barely old enough to be out in public without adult supervision, let alone the master of a lordly cargo vessel on the China seas. While the agent completed his paperwork, the captain sat on the settee as if suffering from an advanced case of ants-in-the-pants-itis. He pulled on his cigarette in quick, nervous puffs, and tapped his feet on the deck in quick, nervous taps.

What a fix, I thought. Here I was, bound for Hong Kong, the only non-Chinese on a ship with thirty-three mainlanders, very likely non-English speakers to a man, while my Mandarin consisted mainly of "Hello," "Good-bye," and "I don't understand," and the whole show was to be presided over by a man who looked like a panicky teenager? Meanwhile, ever helpful, the boarding agent took grim pleasure in briefing me on just how fast the local sea robbers, mainly Indonesian, he said, could overtake a big, slow-moving ship like the *Mercury.* As I noted in my story:

> "There was a vessel just like this one off Singapore six months ago," said the agent in hushed tones.
> "We finished bunkering her in the evening, just about this time," he said, giving me a searching look. Two hours later, he said, "she was boarded by pirates.

"That ship was going to Hong Kong too."

When that stirred no reaction, he said: "You know, pirates like these big carriers when they're fully loaded because they're so low in the water" and easy to board.

Captain Lu, a steely product of the China ports, raised his head from his paperwork. "Meiyou!—No pirates!" he said, with a sweep of his hand. "If anybody tries to board, we'll hose 'em off!"

Good for Captain Lu, I thought—and good for me! He might have resembled a skittish assistant, but the captain was tougher than he looked. And although Lu had been speaking in Mandarin, I also got the impression he spoke some basic English too, though I quickly learned how limited. When I asked him to tell me a little about himself, the question seemed to puzzle him. When he finally spoke up, he said—I'm almost sure—that he was forty-one, had been at sea seventeen years, and in command of the *Mercury* for three months. With the aid of a notepad he communicated the important news that breakfast was served in the ship's mess promptly at 0745 hours, lunch at 1155, and dinner at 1645.

"Dawn fah-ghet!" ordered the captain. And then with a generous sweep of his arm, he invited me to "Gah anah-whar," which I interpreted to mean I had the run of the ship or I was to get lost, or both, it wasn't entirely clear. Rarely had I felt more isolated or gloomy. As the only outsider on a ship manned exclusively by sailors from the People's Republic of China, how was I ever going to break the ice?

2

When we sailed that night in near-total darkness, Singapore was a wafer of light on the far horizon. On the bridge the big radar screen emitted a greenish glow, reflecting the face of the Pacific Mercury's watchful master. Fore and aft, spectral plumes of water looped over the side—the fire hoses going full throttle to keep pirates at bay . . .

One of the most important skills in the long-distance reporting game is to try to be happy where you are and not wish to be somewhere else. And so, in spite of my communication challenges, I left the wheelhouse for the outer bridge to get a better look at the star-filled night, and what a spectacular view it was. The jet-black sky pulsated with pinpoints of light, the scene punctuated at irregular intervals by flaming orange cinders that would shoot from the ship's funnel with little crackling sounds. Underneath me I could feel the giant hull roll pleasantly forward while, up ahead, the big deck cranes looked otherworldly now, like massive stone totems gliding mutely into the blackness of the open sea.

The overwhelming power of my surroundings—the world just being itself without the slightest concern for my petty cares—proved therapeutic and, after a few minutes, I was ready to get on with my reporting duties.

Stepping back inside the wheelhouse, I was observing the officers of the watch go about their tasks in monkish silence when the ship's radio suddenly squawked into action: *"Eeeeeeeeee! Eeeeeeeeee! The monkey wants a banana."* The voice was amused and fruity, and belonged to a Singaporean of Malay extraction, unless I missed my guess. *"Maawn-ka-eee want a ba-na-nah!"*

I couldn't help but laugh. Somebody out there in the black, teeming strait was trying to take the edge off the boredom of routine duty by having a little fun. But not everybody on the wavelength thought it was funny. A gruff second voice, also betraying a Malay lilt, was soon shouting: "Hey, you, monkey boy, get the fuck off this channel and stop fucking around!"

Monkey Boy shot back, angrily: "Hey, fuck you yourself, fucker. Go fuck yourself."

"Who's telling me to go fuck myself, you fucker . . ."

And so it went, inconclusively, for a minute or so. All the while, Captain Lu and his officers, mute as clams, appeared either not to get the joke or not to be interested. Either way, it was shaping up as a long, humorless run up to Hong Kong on board the *Pacific Mercury*. To lift my spirits, I went below and focused on the boredom-busting prospects of a pirate attack . . .

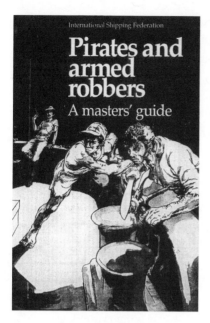

International Shipping Federation

Pirates and armed robbers
A masters' guide

A mariner's primer on piracy.

Locking myself in my cabin, I consulted my copy of Pirates and Armed Robbers: A Masters' Guide. *Sure enough, fire hoses were an approved but not foolproof antipiracy precaution. If pirates did manage to board, the manual advised: "Don't be heroic—[they] may be armed."*

The night passed without heroism becoming an issue, but next morning . . .

The next morning, I didn't have the guts, quite literally, to face the ship's galley. When I'd reported there for dinner the previous day, as Captain Lu had instructed, the ship's steward set before me an oval platter piled high with sautéed Chinese greens and white radish, glistening pieces of fried chicken, and two fried eggs. The only item that hadn't been dipped in salt and fried to oily saturation was a large overturned mixing bowl of white rice so huge I dubbed it Mount Ricemore.

Famished, I had wolfed the whole thing down in big, airy gulps and now, in the pale light of early morning, my stomach felt as if it might explode. So I skipped breakfast and made myself a cup of instant coffee from private stores the canny correspondent stashes away for a rainy day. In this case I'd brought along a mild European cheese encased in wax, a tin or two of goose-liver pâté, and a selection of gourmet crackers and fancy chocolate bars. Battling chronic, salt-induced thirst, however, I kicked myself for not including any fresh fruit. Mainly, though, I continued to fret about my total isolation from the crew. Since coming on board, not a single man, with the exception of Captain Lu, had so much as said a peep to me, in any language, or cast more than a furtive glance in my direction. I was, or so it seemed, a one-man social iceberg moving through a frigid, all-Chinese sea.

Kneeling on my bunk, looking through my porthole at the Easter Island men, which daylight had turned back into giant cranes once again, I realized it was do or die. One way or the other, I'd have to break out of my box or this part of the trip would become an even bigger write-off in the reporting department than Vietnam.

3

It was midmorning by the time I climbed the ladder to the wheelhouse and pulled back the hatch. The two young officers standing watch looked up sharply when I walked in.

"Good morning," I said.

The men traded eye-rolling looks and tittered to themselves but said not a word as I approached the large chart table. Pointing to a chart of the South China Sea that was lying there, I asked, "So where are we?" The man with the protruding teeth went goggle-eyed, as if he'd swallowed a frog, but managed to touch a finger to the document and say, "We are here."

Oh, joy and hallelujah! He had spoken only three words of English but in response to a direct question and with surprisingly good diction. Well, things *are* looking up, I thought. Maybe I would find a way to report this story after all.

"So this is where the pirates are," I said, jovially pushing the social envelope. During the night we had cleared the traffic in the Strait and our position, due west of the Anambas Islands, marked on the chart as "P.P. Anambas Is. (Indonesia)," was a well-known pirate's lair. But I'd gone too far, too fast. In the dead silence that followed the men's body language danced a waltz of dissociation. Wherever I moved on the bridge the pair gracefully triangulated away, keeping their distance. My only hope to force a conversation was to cut off the ring, as the old boxing aficionados used to say. When I caught the second guy, the one with the dicky eye, between the hatch to the bridge deck and the chart table I cornered him.

"Where are you from?" I asked. The man stared at me in total silence. Then at length came the reply: "Where is the ship from?"

"No, you. What city are you from? Guangzhou?"

"Shandong."

After a little more teeth pulling, this closet English speaker introduced himself as Mr. Jiang, one of the *Mercury*'s third officers. He then grew cautiously voluble, letting slip that he was twenty-five years old and had attended the merchant naval academy in Jimei. He capped off this startling revelation by saying, semi-emphatically, "Sea life is very difficult."

Okay, it wasn't much of a parley, I'll admit, but if I could trade basic sentences with the men of the *Mercury*, I reasoned, I could do my job, putting names to faces and piecing together the internal life of the ship.

Encouraged by my modest success at breaking the ice, I was back on the bridge two hours later to try again. The watch had changed, and two new men now hovered around the chart table. Word had likely gotten around that the foreigner was haunting the bridge, badgering away in English, and so I decided my best move was to pretend to be totally uninterested in striking up a conversation. Ignoring the men, I strode past, eyes front, and headed straight for the big rectangular windows overlooking the main deck. From the sill, I picked up a pair of binoculars and zeroed in on the flying fish that dove and skipped in the boiling foam around the bow, 176 yards ahead. I was scanning the vast meniscus of indigo sea stretching all the way to the empty horizon, when suddenly one of the men, a short, wiry fellow with a wisenheimer's grin, couldn't stand the suspense. He zoomed up to me with roadrunner energy and demanded, "How tall you?"

Ah ha, I thought, this character is ripe for the plucking. Earlier, I'd seen the man measuring the clearance between my head and the bridge ceiling when he thought I wasn't looking. When I told him I was exactly two meters tall he guffawed and pranced around the bridge, rolling his eyes and flapping his hands. The crew's comedian introduced himself as Second Officer Xu Shujie.

"My uncle was 1.99 meters," Xu said. "Why you not play basketball?"

I did, many years ago, I told him, but no longer—my arthritic knees wouldn't permit the wear and tear.

"My uncle play till he fifty," Xu crowed. He had played for China's national team and afterward in Japan for two years—"Then return to our country!"

Exhausting the sports category, Xu asked, "First time China?" No, I told him, my first visit had been in January of 1978, not that long after China's *annus horribilis* of 1976, when the great Tang Shan earthquake, killing as many as 655,000 people, was said to presage Great Helmsman Mao's death that September.

Xu's eyes widened at a foreigner's knowledge of great events. "That was a black year for China," he said seriously. He'd been a little boy at the time, but he knew his history.

Having covered yesteryear as well as sports, our conversation petered out and Xu drifted back to his duties. But I was tremendously heartened. There was not only better English on the ship than I'd hoped to imagine but also genuine curiosity—about the ungainly foreigner with his amateur's grasp of the Communist past. At that point I was prepared to declare the ice pretty much officially broken.

Curiosity in your sources is a wonderful resource for a long-distance reporter, and when you find it you milk it to the hilt—or let it milk you. That was the case later that afternoon when I encountered the *Mercury*'s chief officer, Wu Ronggui. A soft-spoken man with a cherubic smile, he was standing by the ship's wheel, staring out to sea, when he spoke to me out of the blue.

"I have a sister in New York," he said proudly. "And an uncle and an auntie." I found his use of "auntie" thoroughly charming. "My sister has been there three years. She loves New York."

What about the uncle and auntie? I asked. Maybe not so much, Wu said: "They don't speak English!"

"Maybe you'll go to New York," I said.

Chief Wu shook his head. "No, not me," he laughed. He had no illusions. He circled his hand around his head, as if to say, "This is my world."

But I could tell the chief was a doggedly curious reporter when he asked with the offhandedness of a pro, "Food . . . you like?" I could see Wu had been mulling the riddle of my nonappearance at the ship's morning mess.

"The food's very good," I lied, giving him a thumbs-up sign. Okay, what was I supposed to say? That every morsel was so infernally salty I had been tempted to mug a man I saw carrying a fresh apple?

"Good? You like Chinese food?" Wu asked, skeptically, before adding, "But soap, it is very bad."

The soap? The question caught me off guard. Was Wu suggesting I'd been hiding out in my cabin gnawing on that beautiful bar of Lux bath soap the steward had prepared for me? When in doubt, I have found the wise thing to do is to appear agreeable.

"No, the soap is very good too," I said.

Wu stared at me, puzzled. "No-o-o," he said, shaking his head. "The *soap*!"

"You mean . . ." I said, and I mimed the taking of a shower, rubbing my hands together to lather up and spreading the invisible suds around my chest and arms.

"No, no," said Wu. "I mean the *soap*. S-O-U-P."

"Oh, the soup?!" I said, realizing he was referring to the salty hot-and-sour dishwater that passed for consommé in the mess. "No, the soup is very good, too."

Chief Wu beamed again, but he was still determined to get to the bottom of my unsailorly tardiness. Tilting his head to look me straight in the eye, he asked: "Do you get seasick?"

"Not usually," I said, but I was being modest. The truth is, thanks to inheriting some ancient Nordic seafaring gene, perhaps, the sea has never made me sick.

"No?"

"No. How about you?"

This is where you had to love Chief Wu. "Yes, sometimes," he confessed, his cheeks puckering into a sheepish smile. And with that, I knew I was dealing with an utterly honest man. Only a thoroughly decent person in his position would cast aside macho pride and candidly admit to such a weakness.

I then turned to Third Officer Song, who had been pacing the bridge, eavesdropping on our conversation. Did he ever get seasick? I asked.

"Never," Song said, bristling—and in barely accented English much better than the chief's. But Wu wasn't having it. "You get a little seasick, *sometimes*," he teased.

"No!" said Song, adamantly, before thawing under Wu's level gaze. "Well, maybe a little . . . a very little . . . sometimes."

I was elated. It had turned out that most of the *Mercury*'s officers did speak passable English, thanks to their studies at the merchant marine academy; it just took a little coaxing to get it out of them. Not for the first time was I reminded that the fear of stumbling in a foreign language and losing face was often more of an impediment to communication than the language itself. After the men of the *Mercury* were persuaded I'd lend a sympathetic ear, our conversations ranged from what we shared in common—missing our wives and sweethearts—to thornier topics like China's outsized territorial claims in the South China Sea.

4

In spite of my early reservations, I came to feel very much at home on the *Mercury*. Once or twice I mooched around the main deck but the sun, high and blazing, drove me back indoors after a couple of minutes. Otherwise, I took breakfast in my cabin, munching on my gourmet supplies. After standing the late morning watch with Second Officer Xu, I attacked Mount Ricemore in the mess at exactly eleven forty-five and then returned to the wheelhouse in a food-drugged state where I sat in the captain's swivel chair jotting notes and staring dreamily out the big windows as we rolled on toward the changeless horizon.

One evening after dinnertime I was sitting at my favorite spot on the port bridge deck just outside the wheelhouse, perched on one of those toadstool-shaped steel fittings called a bitt and reading from my copy of Conrad's collected works, when Third Officer Song approached. He had the good looks of a Chinese opera star—a handsome face with arching eyebrows over fierce pupils that changed size as if zeroing in on prey. That last part I found unsettling, but knowing myself to be suspicious as a peasant, I tried to listen to Song's story with an open mind. He had left a young wife behind in Qingdao for nine lonely, miserable months on board the *Mercury*, he said, where, luck of the draw, he was the lowest man on the officer's totem pole.

"My dream is to go to New York, but it is only a dream," he said. Ah, I see, I said to myself, our Mr. Song is a romantic. Then, switching gears, he asked, "How will you write about the sea?"

I told him I didn't know yet; I was still in the middle of my reporting. Did he have any ideas for me?

Song rolled his eyeballs and told me he hated the monotony of life at sea. "Today is the same as yesterday," he sighed. "Tomorrow is the same as today—no change. Sometimes I think I'd like to write something but I don't know . . ."

To cheer him up, I told him about Conrad—how one of the most famous writers of the sea in English didn't start writing in earnest until he was in thirties. "And do you know what was interesting about Conrad?" I said.

Song shook his head. "He was Polish," I said. "He didn't really learn to speak English well until he went to sea."

"Really?" said Song, emitting a surprised laugh.

"So maybe all these things you're experiencing now and think you want to write about . . ." I said, "maybe you *will* write about them some day." Maybe he'd even come to New York.

"Yeah, maybe," he said, with a quick, defeated smile. Song was a charming kid despite his intense, slightly cloying manner. But there was something overly cynical about him, too. Or maybe, I thought, he was just too smart and ambitious for the overly programmed hand life had dealt him.

It was time for Song to plot the ship's hourly position, and so our conversation drifted into the wheelhouse where he made his mark on a chart titled "Southern South China Sea" using a plastic triangle and a lead pencil. But he was still dreaming about New York. All young Chinese wanted to visit the city, he told me, because of a popular TV drama "about a professor who goes to New York and starts a factory."

Song said it was called *The People of Beijing in New York*. He was surprised I hadn't heard of it. He recited the show's catchphrase for me: "If you love her, send her to New York, because it's heaven. If you hate her, send her to New York, because it's a prison."

We laughed at the theatrical way Song rendered the words. I was feeling more at ease with him when he asked, "Do you know the orchestra, 'Take My Breath Away'?"

Yes, I told him, I knew that old Berlin song. "Oh, yes, *song*," he said, correcting his English. "What does it mean, 'take my breath away'?"

My clear memory is that, when I tried to explain, he nodded his understanding, and then simplified the concept into the single word "Fuck," to which I replied, "Yes, well, there's that interpretation too." But my notes only say he nodded his understanding. The long-distance reporter must proceed cautiously where memory is concerned. As Anthony Burgess pointed out in his memoir *Little Wilson and Big God*, "Truth is fabled by the daughters of memory." As for the absolute truth, "God holds possession of that, though God knows what he does with it." Always try to take good notes.

5

When trying to uncover monkey business in the mayor's office or on the local school board, a reporter properly longs to be a thorn in the side of those who would hornswoggle the public or dip into taxpayers' pocketbooks. But it's different with the long-distance reporter. In a foreign culture, the loud and the pushy rarely get beyond creating an impression of wanting to impose their values on others, and that can alter the frame you're trying to observe and offend sensibilities into the bargain. Not always, of course, but much of the time, a lower profile yields the truer picture.

Five days out of Singapore I reached what I considered a milestone on the *Pacific Mercury*, near-invisibility. Well beyond the mere breaking of the ice now, the life of the ship went on unselfconsciously around me—almost—as if I wasn't there. The prime example of this came during Chief Wu's late afternoon bridge watch. Off duty, Second Officer Xu was staring hypnotically out the windows to where sky and sea met like the two halves of a popsicle, lustrous aquamarine on top, dazzling indigo beneath, when suddenly he emitted an earsplitting shriek. "Yeeooow!"

Wiry and quick, he wheeled on a young seaman, who had playfully punched him on the arm, and snapped a gung-fu kick that stopped just shy of the sailor's recoiling nose. "Wah, hah, hah," Xu cackled, staggering around the wheelhouse as if dazed by an invisible right hook to the jaw. A few minutes later he picked up a kitchen knife the officers used for skinning apples and pretended to stick Third Officer Song in the side.

The source of Xu's mood swing wasn't hard to fathom. The following day the ceaseless thrumming of the big ship's engines would carry us into port at Hong Kong, cranes would hoist our cargo of South African steel from the *Mercury*'s big holds, and Xu and his shipmates would go ashore, some for the first time in months.

That the men took me more or less for granted marked a big step forward. Yet it also created a fresh dilemma—how to do justice to the idiosyncrasy of life on board the *Pacific Mercury* in the six thousand words the *Geographic* had allotted for my final story? How to explain, for instance, the way the bridge became crowded with "tourists" after the late afternoon meal, when off-duty crewmen gathered to watch the sun dip seaward, as if observing a primordial ritual? How to deal with the connections between what I was learning of the interior lives of my shipmates and where China might be headed as a country?

I was standing at the chart table one afternoon with Mr. Song, for example, when he blurted out, "If China just had two . . . what do you call admiralty ships with airplanes?"

"Aircraft carriers?"

"Yes. If China had two aircraft carriers . . ." and he didn't have to finish his sentence. If the Chinese had two big warships operating in the South China Sea, they wouldn't have to put up with the pantywaist claims of countries like the Philippines, Vietnam, and Malaysia over all those disputed islands. China would automatically get more respect from the United States. "These islands were always China's," Song said, grandly sweeping his open hand over the entire chart.

"But if China tried to take them back," I said, "wouldn't other countries get angry?"

"Yes," Song said, looking glum. "I'm afraid China lost much of its territory!"

You had to wonder which was the real point, controlling the islands in the sea, and the purported mineral wealth beneath them, or simply establishing a new equity with the affluent West. It was clear that Song and the other young guys on board the *Mercury* were set on a future in which they could afford to buy the Japanese-, Korean-, and Chinese-made electronic goods they saw advertised in the magazines scattered around the bridge. It was clear they wanted a home of their own and a family car. In short, they felt the inherent right to get all the stuff that Americans and Japanese enjoyed in comparative abundance. Lord help us—and the Chinese—I thought, if the day arrived when China's economy could no longer grow fast enough to keep pace with the country's expanding appetites and aspirations.

In the end, however, big pressing issues like nationalism or piracy, or even the immediate danger of typhoons, took a backseat to the biggest enemy on board—the soul-numbing boredom the men felt about their lives at sea. How truly desperate they were became obvious when Chief Wu pleaded with me to stay with the ship after Hong Kong. Apparently, as an antidote to monotony, I compared favorably to the videotaped Chinese bathing beauty contests the men watched as if on an endless loop in the ship's lounge. Wu did his best to make onward travel sound enticing. First we'd steam up to Taiwan and then across the Bashi Straits to Manila, winding up in the magical-sounding Surabaya in Indonesia. We would have a drink in a bar!

I was deeply flattered but I had to turn down the offer. I still had many miles to go before I completed my assignment, and so, when the time came, I went below to settle my chit with Captain Lu. I found him sitting at his desk doing paperwork, levering a toothpick into his gums. "How much do I owe?" I asked.

The captain stared at me for a time as if digesting my words and then sprang to action phoning the bridge to inquire after charges for a shipboard fax I'd sent my wife in New York. That brought Radio Officer Zhou flying into the office with a sheaf of loose papers rattling in his hand, and Lu proceeded to punch numbers into his calculator with such abandon that I grew worried. I was short on hard cash in any currency, a merchant vessel like the *Mercury* didn't take plastic, and I knew my tab was bound to be a steep one. I had spent nearly a week on board, during which time I'd steamed fourteen hundred miles, consumed those huge if blood-pressure-busting meals in the ship's mess, and enjoyed the use of a private cabin with clean towels and all the *s-o-a-p* I could ever want. And despite its delicate beginnings, the trip had turned out to be loads of fun and educational into the bargain.

My palms were sweating when the wire-tough master of the M.V. *Pacific Mercury* finished hammering at the calculator and slid his tally at me across his desk. I couldn't believe my eyes. The chit read: "For entertainments and meals . . . USD 27.00."

He had to be kidding—twenty-seven measly dollars? Mistaking my stunned reaction for a protest, Captain Lu asked anxiously, "Okay?"

"Yes, thank you, captain," I said. "This will be fine."

TO: TOSHIKO DAHLBY
NEW YORK, NEW YORK, USA
FAX: ████████████████

FROM: TRACY DAHLBY
"PACIFIC MERCURY"

AUGUST 4, 1997

DEAR TOSHIKO,

I AM ENJOYING MY VOYAGE ABOARD THE PACIFIC MERCURY. CAPT. LU AND HIS MEN ARE TAKING GOOD CARE OF ME. WE ARE AT 8° 40" N. LAT. IN THE INTERNATIONAL SHIPPING LANE, FAR TO THE EAST OF THE SOUTHERN TIP OF VIETNAM. TROPICAL STORM "TINA" SEEMS TO BE MOVING WELL NORTH + TO THE EAST OF US AND WILL PROBABLY HIT KYUSHU, NOT HONG KONG (OR US!)

I HOPE ALL GOES WELL. IF YOU NEED TO REACH ME IN AN EMERGENCY, CONTACT EITHER ARTHUR BOWRING OR GILBERT FENG OF THE HONG KONG SHIPOWNERS ASSOCIATION IN HK (████████████) OR BERNARD TAN OF MING WAH (SINGAPORE) AGENCY ████████████.

I'LL PHONE WHEN I ARRIVE IN HONG KONG, SCHEDULED NOW FOR THURSDAY.

LOVE,
TRACY

*Faxing homeward from the
Pacific Mercury.*

The *Mercury* had glided into Victoria Harbor at Hong Kong and, once again, I found myself clinging for dear life to that long, snaky ladder as I climbed down toward the deck of a bucking, wave-tossed harbor launch. Whoever was operating the controls added to the excitement when, incompetent or just distracted, he very nearly succeeded in crushing me between the hull-mounted winch motor and the ladder's metal rungs. When I finally reached the safety of the smaller vessel my arms and shirt were pasted with thick black grease.

I was daubing at the mess with a fistful of tissues when I looked up and felt a pang. The men of the *Mercury*, that once but no longer mysterious ship, stood at the rail waving good-bye, so many stick figures receding on the chop. Again, Conrad had anticipated the moment: "A gone shipmate, like any other man," he wrote, "is gone forever: and I never met one of them again."

In Hong Kong, I put aside my newsman's weakness for melodrama and enjoyed a couple of glorious days during which I treated my fragile digestive tract to a series of elegant meals modest in size and low in sodium and, like a crazed fruitarian, ate all the fresh, juicy apples, oranges, and berries I could get my hands on.

6

In *Travels with Charley*, John Steinbeck wrote, "I am happy to report that in the war between reality and romance, reality is not the stronger." Yet the fact of the matter was that tracking down what romance might be left in the life at sea was proving harder than I had counted on.

During my first layover in Singapore I came down with a bad case of the flu. Alternately burning with fever and shivering with cold in my darkened hotel room, I survived on excellent mango smoothies from the hotel kitchen as my ankles swelled to alarming proportions and I grew dreadfully homesick. But marathon reporting requires staying power. And so, shvitzing and coughing, I set out to secure passage on a ship that would get me clear of my personal doldrums.

While still at home in New York I had sent a fax asking for help to the Straits Steamship Company, a proud old name in China navigation, and I now took a taxi to the firm's high-rise offices to follow up. In short order, I found myself honking into a wet handkerchief while a gentlemanly captain named Sairi Bin Ismail, shipshape in a crisp blue oxford shirt and sporting a well-trimmed moustache, lectured me on Singapore's central role in seaborne commerce.

Lest my flu-numbed mind go completely dead, I gasped, "Whad abow da romanz of da sea?"

Immediately, Captain Sairi dropped the data and smiled disarmingly. "If I may be frank," he said, as if confiding a secret, "I miss my time at sea. It's not like an office where you have people hovering over you all the time." We both looked out Sairi's glass fishbowl to a larger office of, well, hovering people.

Now tied to administrative duties ashore, the captain spoke wistfully of the time when as a young man he had served under a flinty British master on one of the last commercial windjammers to ply the South China Sea. There was a faraway look in his eyes. Of course he would find me a ship! "Oh, yes," he said, calling up a shipping schedule on his computer screen. If I got myself along the northern Borneo coast to Muara port in the tiny Islamic sultanate of Brunei by mid-August, I could ship on the M.V. *Straits Star* for a run to Kota Kinabalu with one of the company's most experienced captains, Clifford Royston Rankine.

Nothing beats the promise of a new venture to promote a rapid recovery, and I was quite literally feeling better by the minute. I immediately forgot about my bloated ankles and got on with other reporting chores in Singapore and various points east. In due time, I flew to Kuching, the capital of the East Malaysian state of Sarawak, where I set foot on the world's third-largest island (after Greenland and New Guinea) for the very first time.

On the map, Borneo looks something like a fat-bottomed Chihuahua, the head and sloping shoulders made up of two Malaysian states, Sarawak and Sabah, with tiny independent Brunei wedged in between. The bottom two-thirds belongs to the Indonesians, who call it Kalimantan. Head or haunch, it is madly beautiful in the lush tropical way, with green jungle giving way to blue vistas, and in the foreground all kinds of marvelous curiosities like the occasional vast, radiating spider web inhabited by a ferocious-looking, piston-jointed creature the diameter of a large cereal bowl.

In Kuching, a famous old timber port fifteen miles inland on the Sarawak River, I met Thomas Nalo, whose wife, Kimmy, ran a local tourism business and had been recommended to me by Mike Yamashita. Thomas was a short vigorous man, with a chest that resembled an oil drum and a shy, ironic smile. He was piloting his tiny red car through the clammy gray heat of the afternoon when he asked me what I wanted to do. I told Thomas I wanted to meet some Sea Dayaks. Over the years I'd read about this branch of Borneo's indigenous tribes whose reputation for piratical daring was embroidered onto the standard Dayak traditions of headhunting and black magic. I considered it a great shortcoming that I'd never met a single representative of this fascinating culture or visited one of their customary longhouses.

Thomas stared at me from behind the wheel, dark eyes dancing with mirth. "I am Sea Dayak!" he said, drumming his chest with a meaty fist. Okay, I thought, that takes care of that. I asked Thomas to tell me more.

He said his grandfather had been a warrior, meaning a taker of heads, from the days when shrunken enemy noggins still garlanded longhouse rafters. As a boy Thomas had himself lived a traditional life, from which headhunting had by then been subtracted, and answered to the name Baran. Afterward, he moved to town, went to school with the help of an American scholarship, and then worked in Borneo's timber industry for twenty-eight years.

I must say that Thomas, with his sly jokes and mordant chuckle, was as jovial a companion as you could wish to find, the occasional politically incorrect wisecrack notwithstanding. Yes, he said, with a cryptic smile, "I spent twenty years in Sabah, six years in Indonesia, and two days in Brunei."

"Why only two days in Brunei?" I asked.

"Those Malays"—by whom he meant Malay Muslims—"are fanatical," he said, his eyes flashing comically. Well, the Dayaks did have a long and complicated history with their Malay neighbors just as they did with their former British rulers.

At one point I said, "Thomas, I've read that the Sea Dayaks were famous pirates in the old days. Is that true?"

Thomas emitted what could be described as a soft, piratical chuckle. "No, they weren't really pirates, you know," he said, "but they *were* proud." If you didn't behave in a manly fashion or demonstrate bravery, "the people of the village considered you a coward." In Thomas's book, if I understood him correctly, piracy was more a test of manhood than a desire to accumulate worldly goods, which, I suppose, raises the interesting question of when is a pirate really a pirate or a terrorist a terrorist?

That afternoon Thomas and I scrambled up the ramparts of historic Fort Margherita for a good look at the Sarawak River. From that elevation the river was the color of a rich pea soup from all the foliates and effluvia it contained, and there was a mysterious beauty in the way it folded back on itself, its powerful eddies curdling the otherwise placid surface near the irregular bank. On the opposite side lay Kuching's purposefully charming esplanade.

"This is our famous waterfront," Thomas said impishly. "One kilometer long. Constructed in 1989." Local boosters, like local boosters everywhere in Asia, were hoping to turn their pleasant town into an international tourist mecca and had spruced up the bund with concrete sidewalks, wrought-iron fencing, and stylish gazebos. But for that and its high-rise hotels, the place looked not unlike Lady Margaret Brooke had described it from the 1870s in *My Life in Sarawak*, a book I'd found while rummaging around the stacks of the National Geographic Society's in-house library in Washington, DC:

> The little town looked so neat and fresh. . . . it reminded me of a box of painted toys kept scrupulously clean by a child. The Bazaar runs for some distance along the banks of the river,

and this quarter of the town is inhabited almost entirely by Chinese traders, with the exception of one or two Hindoo shops. . . . Groceries of exotic kinds are laid out on tables near the pavement, from which purchasers make their choice. . . . Awnings from the shops and brick archways protect purchasers from the sun, whilst across the road all kinds of boats are anchored, bringing produce from the interior of Sarawak, from the Dutch Settlement, from Singapore, and from adjacent islands. . . . The Chinese houses of the Bazaar are decorated with coloured porcelains; one sees green dragons, pink lotuses, little gods and goddesses in grotesque attitudes, all along their fronts.

Reading this charming memoir, I couldn't help but admire the intrepid Lady Margaret. Growing up on her widowed mother's comfortable estate in Wiltshire, Margaret had "received the limited education given to girls in that mid-Victorian period," she wrote, and yearned for a life of adventure in the wider world. Opportunity knocked in the eccentric form of Charles Brooke, a cousin twice her age, who happened to rule Sarawak as the hereditary second White Rajah. When Charles proposed marriage, Margaret promptly accepted and headed for the jungles and rivers of Borneo.

If you haven't heard of the Brookes of Borneo, it's quite a story. In 1839, English soldier of fortune James Brooke sailed his schooner, the *Royalist*, up the Sarawak River to discover the Sea Dayaks in revolt against a local governor appointed by the Sultan of Brunei, who theoretically held sway in northern Borneo. In return for Brooke's help in quelling the troubles, the Sultan's chief minister, Pengiran Muda Hassim, promised to appoint him ruler of Sarawak. When Hassim reneged on the deal, Brooke had the *Royalist* train its guns on his palace and the squeamish regent got busy processing the paperwork that established James Brooke as Rajah of Sarawak in 1841. Thus began a line of White Rajahs that held sway, theoretically at least, until 1946, when the last of the Brookes ceded sovereignty to the British Crown.

James Brooke had set about pacifying Sarawak like a town marshal in the Old West. He codified laws and acted as both judge and jury. Exploiting old tribal rivalries, he enlisted indigenous chieftains to help subdue other indigenous chieftains. He worked to stamp out piracy and headhunting, and with some success. But when Brooke tried to extract his full measure of taxes from local Chinese clans, owners of the territory's gold and the antimony mines, the Chinese bankrolled a mutiny that he only narrowly survived. Small wonder the Rajah's coat of arms carried the legend *Dum Spiro Spero*, which translates as "Still Alive, Still Fighting."

Succeeding his uncle James as rajah in 1868, Charles honored his young bride, Margaret, by building the fort that still bears her name. But the ranee's life was no cakewalk. Margaret bore Charles six children, three of whom died of cholera during the same week in 1873. As historian Steven Runciman has observed, the Brooke marriage was a "curious" one from the get-go. On their honeymoon in England, the rajah ordered up a hotel dinner that "consisted of bread and butter" for his bride "while he partook of grilled pheasant legs and two glasses of sherry." In later years, the couple spent most of their time apart, she in England and he at home in the jungles of Sarawak.

Nonetheless, Margaret put a good face on the couple's life together in her Sarawak chronicle, depicting Charles, like James before him, as a kind of benevolent, barbarian-subduing generalissimo and lawgiver. It was the sort of Victorian fairy-tale treatment in which the Brookes frequently sailed valiantly upriver to eradicate piracy and subdue black-hearted rapscallions like the fearsome pirate Rentap when they weren't imparting wisdom and grace on the native tribes.

Thomas Nalo knew the story of the Brookes, of course, and didn't buy it. That much was clear when he and I stood on that catwalk at Fort Margherita, peeping over the crenellated walls, and I shared my enthusiasm for its namesake. Thomas chuckled derisively. "There was only one thing we got from the White Rajah," he said, "and that was the consultative council," a limited form of local government. "They say the White Rajah stopped headhunting but he never did. Education stopped headhunting."

In Thomas's view, even Japanese rule during World War II was preferable to the days of the Rajahs Brook. In contrast to the typically unhappy experience with Imperial Japan in much of Southeast Asia, including atrocities perpetrated on various Dayak tribes, Thomas felt the Japanese had treated people in Borneo comparatively well. It was a bold observation. If Japan's reign had not been cut short, Thomas said—who knew?—"Today we might be on a level with Taiwan."

7

The next morning Kimmy gave me a lift to the Express Boat Wharf, which, in spite of its grand-sounding name, was little more than a long wooden dock on top of which fresh pineapples had been stacked like hand grenades. A catamaran resembling an updated version of the Civil War warship *Merrimac* sat low in the water, its crew preparing for the five-hour run to Sibu. From there, I planned to catch the bus for Miri, a rough-knuckled timber and oil town and a jumping-off place for Brunei.

We bounced downriver and then pelted northeastward following Borneo's upward-tilted spine. I was eager to take in the scenery but the cabin was sealed behind small dirty windows and everything flew by in a green-black smudge. A TV screen embedded in the bulkhead at the front of the cabin produced loud, tinny sounds that made reading or thinking impossible, so I tried to turn necessity into a virtue and learn something about local tastes from the choice of entertainment programming.

"Slamboree" featured professional wrestling from North Carolina and an elaborately staged fight between a wrestler calling himself "Ultimate Dragon," a sinister Fu Manchu character in a Flash Gordon-style helmet, and a wrestler playing the part of a hulking British yobbo in a Union Jack leotard. The fake wrestling was followed by a Hong Kong-produced martial arts movie in which gangsters said memorably sinister things in subtitle:

"You always use violence. I should've order glutinous rice chicken."

"This will be of fine service for you, you bag of the scum. I am sure you will not mind that I remove your manhoods and leave them out on the dessert floor for your aunts to eat."

In Sibu, I missed the bus, which unaccountably left ahead of schedule, and so I took a taxi to the local airport where a ticket agent with a build resembling a Slamboree wrestler and a head shaped like a mallet yelled at me for asking too many questions. Remembering advice Thomas Nalo had given me on the local tradition of amok, the tropical flaring of ferocities that can take you from smiles to mayhem in a few hair-raising seconds, I thanked the agent for his patience and found a plastic chair from which to contemplate the crazy profusion of stars.

The evening was cool and refreshing, and across the tarmac I could see a phalanx of coconut palms silhouetted against the blue-black sky. Suddenly, without thinking about it, I became very happy, and I said to myself, Here I am! The boy who'd escaped his parents' basement in Seattle was now in far Borneo, on the edge of a great canopied forest. Little epiphanies like that have never failed to give me a tremendous boost, even after being yelled at. I waited there for several hours, perfectly content to be suspended for the time being between the last place and the next.

It was late evening when I arrived in Miri and checked into a surprisingly posh little hotel that featured a restaurant with an utterly charming name, the Chatterbox Coffee House. While devouring a late supper of tasty deep-fried prawns, I read in the local paper about a fisherman having been eaten by a crocodile. Riding the elevator with a cheerful red-suited bellman, however, I managed to step on a cultural line I didn't know existed. Short of stature but powerfully built, the bellman stood so close that the top of his pillbox hat hovered like a velveteen saucer on the underside of my chin. After a pregnant pause, he turned, looked up into my face with intense, smiling eyes, and asked: "Professional wrestle . . . is it true?"

The correct answer in such situations is always, "I don't know, my friend, what do you think?" Instead, rummy from a long day of travel, I said, no, it wasn't true. In fact, it was all a big fat fake. That was a foolish mistake.

The bellman's nostrils began to quiver. "Is true! Is true," he yelped, his lower lip trembling petulantly.

Remembering where I was, and what Thomas had counseled, I quickly shifted gears, adopting a conciliatory tone. "Well, maybe it is true," I said, pleading my ignorance. Frankly, I don't know what on earth I'd been thinking.

But the bellman was not assuaged. "Is true!" he muttered, as he jerked my duffel bag from the lift and dumped it grumpily in my room. After showing me how to operate the mini-bar he followed his extended lower lip through the door, letting it bang shut behind him.

8

My next stop was Bandar Seri Begawan, the capital of cloistered, oil-rich Brunei. Many people, if they've heard of it at all, suppose Brunei to be located in the Middle East. It is not. It is, in fact, sandwiched between Sarawak and its sister Malaysian state, Sabah, and it would be hard to imagine a more laid-back Islamic orthodoxy on the face of the earth.

For one thing, all Bruneians (about four hundred thousand today) are exempt from personal income and capital gains taxes and enjoy a highly subsidized lifestyle thanks to the country's sizable if shrinking offshore oil reserves. Personally speaking, the capital reminded me of a devout Orlando, with its high blue skies, spanking-new freeways profuse with greenery, a tasteful downtown mall featuring Pizza Hut and Dunkin' Donuts, and an impressively ornate grand mosque.

My immediate problem was that I had managed to show up at the airport without the required visa. A young woman official in Islamic dress asked me to explain myself, and I said the first thing that popped into my head, which, if memory serves, was that I was writing a story that involved the romance of the sea. The woman's eyes sparkled from behind her designer eyeglasses, as if my answer made perfect sense. Returning my passport, she smiled warmly and wished me a pleasant stay.

My next problem was that I'd never had the pleasure of visiting Brunei before and didn't know a soul in the entire country. So I headed for a hotel with a recognizable name, the Hilton, and there, through a mildly quirky chain of events, made the acquaintance of a young expat entrepreneur named Klaus Lienau. Athletic and handsome, with intense dark eyes and a head of unruly hair that made me think of Beethoven, Klaus ran a local business specializing in diving and jungle tours. And since his business seemed to more or less run itself, he volunteered to show me around.

One night Klaus and a small group of his expat friends took me to Jerudong Park Garden, the amusement center Sultan Hassanal Bolkiah had built at a cost of a billion dollars in honor of his forty-eighth birthday in 1994. What a place! Anybody and everybody could partake of its state-of-the-art roller coasters and rides absolutely free of charge. It was heaven on earth for a fun-ride fanatic like me. No group of mammals in Brunei was better cared for, however, than the sultan's polo ponies, which were housed in air-conditioned stables across the street from the park. As we circumnavigated the royal polo grounds in Klaus's SUV, powerful lights blazed on an immaculate but empty polo pitch. "When you're on the sea at night, you see this big lumen," Klaus said. "You think it's a city."

The following day Klaus picked me up at my hotel in his silver Porsche coupe and we zoomed along the winding coastal road to the Royal Brunei Yacht Club. Klaus and his gracious German wife were throwing a dinner party in my honor that evening and, Brunei being dry, Klaus said we should pop over to the duty-free shop on Labuan Island in neighboring Malaysia to pick up liquor supplies. It would take about an hour each way, and when Klaus said it might be a good way for me to get a sense of the local maritime geography, I was raring to go.

The weather was perfect for a boat trip, gray and hazy and only pleasantly hot. After an excellent cheeseburger lunch on the yacht club terrace, we boarded Klaus's speedboat, a sleek, impressive rig with a sturdy fiberglass hull and a powerful engine. Cruising slowly through the inner harbor, Klaus pointed out the Brunei "navy," a handful of steel-hulled patrol boats that would have had a hard time holding their own against the royal family's corresponding fleet of yachts, also moored nearby. As we passed one of the largest luxury vessels, I couldn't help but make out the letters "TITS" on the prow. They floated above a graphic design that appeared to resemble a pair of female breasts.

Not knowing what to think, I looked to Klaus for instruction and he gave me one of those "don't ask me" shrugs. "It belongs to the Sultan," he said. "Sometimes you really don't know what's going on here."

The outward journey was uneventful and refreshing, and after about thirty minutes, Labuan appeared as a gray-blue hump on the horizon. Thirty minutes later, we rounded the jetty at the island's Victoria Harbor and pulled into the marina. From there it was a short bus ride to the duty-free in a defunct financial center, where a crew of smiling Filipinas did a brisk counter trade in booze and cigarettes and there appeared to be no electricity. Having schlepped our contraband hooch back to the marina, Klaus and I were preparing to shove off when an attendant, gold-filled teeth sparkling under dark glasses, said, "Weather, it don't look so good, Boss." He was referring to the dark, metallic-looking haze that was now suddenly visible in the offing.

The attendant made the situation sound ominous but Klaus ignored him. He'd done this run many times, he told me; there wasn't the slightest thing to worry about. Besides, we had a trusty GPS device on board that would tell us exactly where we were at all times, rain or shine.

That was reassuring, but no sooner had we pulled out beyond the breakwater than the sea grew much rougher than it had been on the trip over. Within minutes, the air temperature had plunged and a chill wind began to howl. The sea grew choppy and the chop turned to whitecaps.

Shouting to be heard over the wind and waves, Klaus observed that he had never seen the visibility so poor. What visibility? I thought, as I watched a clutch of cargo ships on the near horizon disappear into the enveloping gloom. Meanwhile the bouncing outline of Labuan vanished behind us.

Despite the challenging conditions, Klaus remained the epitome of nautical aplomb. If anything, he seemed to relish the challenge. Steering the boat with his right hand, he nonchalantly grabbed the GPS in his left and waited for a reading. When nothing came up, he shook the device and frowned. Forced to shout louder now because of the ambient racket, Klaus explained the GPS was on the blink. Well, that's just dandy, I thought, the adrenaline rushing. So what did we do now?

Klaus instructed me to take the GPS to the back of the boat, out from under the fiberglass sun canopy, and see if I could get a fix on our position. Scuttling, crab-like, to the back of the wildly pitching vessel, I pushed my back up against the stern, steadied my legs against the thwarts, and fiddled with the malfunctioning gizmo. No blasted luck at all. It was dead as a doornail.

My memory is that I bellowed, "Sonofabitch" to the heartless winds and slammed the fickle GPS down hard against the deck but I may have just given the contraption a good chip-rattling shake. In any event, when I looked at the dial again it had flickered back to life and was displaying a set of coordinates!

Ecstatic, I lurched forward and thrust the GPS at Klaus, who seemed pretty happy too—until he got a good look at the read-out. Shaking his head at the numbers on the screen, Klaus said they were all wrong—the instrument hadn't been properly programmed. Yacht club members shared the GPS and apparently the inconsiderate lunkhead that used it last had neglected to either check the batteries or reset the coordinates.

Standing at the wheel, bracing himself like a bronco rider, Klaus turned his head and shouted something I couldn't quite make out. "Do you know how to swim?" Klaus repeated, loudly but coolly.

"Not very well," I yelled back. The truth of it is that not learning how to swim properly had been one of the great lapses of my childhood, which I now deeply regretted.

Looking for something positive to say, I suppose, Klaus shouted for me not to worry—these U.S.-built fiberglass boats were great to hang on to when they flipped over. "Trust your American product!"

Not eager to exercise that option, I wondered if it was really possible to miss the coast of the world's third-largest island entirely? Klaus thought that unlikely. The higher probability was that we'd inadvertently hurtle ashore and find ourselves flying through some unsuspecting farmer's vegetable patch as our good American product came apart around us.

This was serious business now, and Klaus and I hung over opposite sides of the boat, him to starboard and me to port, straining to catch the slightest glimpse of a coastline. Nothing.

Then, incredible, inexplicable relief. Jabbing a finger dead ahead, Klaus shouted, "There it is! I can see it!" Sure enough, the faint gray outlines of Borneo became visible like rising ectoplasm. A couple of minutes later—though it seemed a lot longer—the ghostly vapors revealed a blob off our port bow that slowly metamorphosed into a big, clanging fairway buoy.

Somehow we had bucked and meandered our way back to safe harbor. When I think about it now, I can't help but hear the notes of Beethoven's "Ode to Joy" whiffle through my head for some reason. At the time, I simply felt like dropping to my knees to thank my lucky stars. Klaus, his stony game face once again intact, looked like a bust of the composer trying not to crack a smile. There, he said, I'd had my dangerous adventure: "That'll be good for your story."

Not a single word about our misadventure made it into my final story for the *Geographic*—there simply wasn't room to do it justice. But I like to think we'd have given the croc-eats-man fare in the Borneo press a run for its money if things had turned out differently.

That evening at the party there were beautiful women, both European and Asian, and manly men who bragged about various feats of derring-do of an outdoor nature. As guests were swigging the smuggled beer that had nearly got me drowned, an Australian diving instructor said, "Aw, Klaus has done that trip hundreds of times. He could do it with his eyes closed." It had been a trying day and I must say I resented the stupidly cavalier tone, but I could hardly disagree. He just had.

9

Clifford Royston Rankine, master of the *Straits Star*, poked his head through the doorway of his cabin and extended a large fleshy paw. "Rankine, pleased to meet you," he said, as he shook my hand and invited me to join him inside. The captain was a large, well-constructed man with skin the color of cappuccino and every inch the picture of the stern, capable mariner. He sported gold-rimmed glasses, gold captain's bars on the shoulders of his white uniform shirt, and what appeared to be a yellow curry stain on the breast pocket.

We took our seats as a cargo container, suspended from a port crane, trapezed into view through the porthole over Rankine's shoulder and quickly swung out again. The goods from a Singapore run were still being unloaded, he explained, and in the silence that followed I got the distinct impression that, in spite of his larger-than-life reputation, the good captain was just a wee bit shy. To take off the edge, as one does with sources from time to time, I found something homey and nonthreatening to say. I told him I'd recently rented a house from a landlord with his same last name.

Rankine replied, matter-of-factly, "He must be Canadian and come from the area around Toronto."

I was flabbergasted. I had in fact been living in Toronto, working on that nightmarish documentary film project I mentioned earlier. Yet I hadn't said a word about it to Rankine. Catching me off guard seemed to embolden the captain's inner Sherlock Holmes. "The name is probably spelled R-A-N-K-I-N," he added.

Bingo! "How did you know that?" I asked.

Rankine smiled cryptically at the little demonstration of his deductive powers. "My grandfather was Scottish-Canadian," he said, explaining that the clan patriarch ran a biscuit factory in eastern Canada before, and for reasons unspecified, he had decamped to Sri Lanka to marry a local woman and embrace an early grave.

One of the choicest rewards of the long-distance reporter is the opportunity to meet up with folks whose idiosyncrasies leave indelible impressions on you, and the captain was full of odd surprises. At one point that day—my notes aren't clear on precisely when—he drew my attention to an aquarium tank bolted to a shelf in his office. Inside was a strangely beautiful fish, so long and incredibly thin it looked like an undulating silver ribbon. "You can see numbers on that fish," Rankine declared. "They are printed on the side and they change. The numbers change!"

I'd taken a good look at the fish but didn't see any numbers. Back in Singapore, Captain Sairi had spoken so highly of Rankine that I thought this respected maritime figure had to be pulling my leg. So I joked back, suggesting that such a fish was just the thing for picking winning numbers in the lottery.

Rankine shook his head. Not this fish, he said.

Why not?

"It's not my fish," Rankine snorted. It had belonged to a previous captain.

Thus we arrived at a question worthy of philosophical inquiry. Did the fish have to belong to you before it revealed the winning numbers? Rankine assured me that was the case. I could see I'd be traveling across the roof of Borneo in the company of a man who had invested himself in the art of good storytelling, and I wasn't disappointed.

Meanwhile, though, I had my job to do, and before I completely lost the initiative in our conversation, I asked Rankine to tell me, for the purposes of my assignment, what changes he'd witnessed in his long life at sea:

"Restrictions! Paperwork! You don't have time to train people," Rankine grumbled. "Oh, there is no romance left to this sea life!"

In lilting English he recalled for me the days when the Straits Steamship Company had been the seaborne railroad of empire. Ships with teakwood decks carried live monkeys, orangutans, and snakes in the hold, British grandees in first class, and servants in steerage. "Oh, there were famous storms," Rankine crooned, like the one that chased him from Borneo to Singapore, keeping him 57 hours on the bridge.

In the nail-biting days before commercial vessels routinely carried global positioning systems, Rankine had sailed from Bangkok to Borneo as first officer on a ship blinded by bad weather. "I went below for dinner when we synchronized with a swell," he recalled. "One, two, three—the portholes were in the water! All lifeboats broke loose." Rankine's fleshy hands flew apart, signifying total chaos. What happened? "We altered course and reached Singapore safely," he said nonchalantly, adding that a crewman blamed the captain for almost getting everyone killed and went after him with an ax.

10

At noon, the cutlery was flying in the ship's mess as Rankine, his chief mate, and I tucked into a delicious lunch—eggplant sautéed with small red chilies, a platter of curried beef, a tangy fish soup, and a small sweet apple for dessert, all served by a shy Indonesian cook in blue jeans and a grimy T-shirt. The chief mate, a stolid Filipino with a determined chin, said he was going ashore to rent some movies for the run to Kota. He suggested bringing back *Nixon*, parts one and two.

"Not so good!" Rankine growled. That bluff and hard-shelled man said he preferred something on the order of *Pretty Woman*, the vintage rags-to-riches romance about a Hollywood prostitute starring Julia Roberts and her Prince Charming played by Richard Gere. The chief officer shot back huffily, "That would never happen in real life."

"Of course it can," Rankine thundered. "Anything is possible."

"No," said the chief, shaking his head, "*that* will never happen."

"You *are* wrong," said the captain. "Anything can happen, *anything.*" Rankine glared at the chief while the other man held his tongue and stared stonily ahead, a technique in which he seemed to have some practice.

During that long, slow-moving afternoon Rankine and I passed the time by talking in his office or strolled the decks, pausing to lean against the rails as we idly inspected the mirror-flat harbor waters. We sat drinking coffee in the ship's lounge, where carved into a mahogany bar decorated with Christmas lights was the word "ZANZI-BAR"—a moniker from a time when the *Star*, under a different name, had plied the seas off East Africa. Not nearly as gruff as he first appeared, the captain proved to be a charming host who, among other things, was ensorcelled by his collection of tropical fish. This he kept in two good-sized tanks near the bar—two because it allowed him to separate warring tribes of fishes. A third nursery tank, the size of a large lunchbox, Rankine informed me, served to prevent hungry adults from dining on baby fishes that were no bigger than flicks of sewing thread.

Nodding toward one of the bigger tanks, the captain launched into a blow-by-blow analysis of fish behavior. "There's a big fella back there who comes out slowly, slowly," he said.

"These four small ones," he added, marveling at the ferocity of a gang of flashing silver torpedoes, "they attack any fish put in the tank right away."

And during a later conversation: "Oh, look," Rankine said, smiling in wonder, "today the mama and papa have allowed their little fish to swim. A significant day . . . Yes, yes."

The challenge with Captain Rankine was to keep him focused on topics that might easily fit the confines of my *Geographic* story, and so I asked him at one point if pirates had ever given him any trouble.

"Oh, the pirates were rife," he said, with a desultory sweep of his hand. In the Singapore Strait. At Buffalo Rock. Near the Raffles Lighthouse. Everywhere, they were "roaming, roaming," and you needed to keep your eyeballs peeled. Oh yes. But pirates weren't the only hazard to navigation. Oh no. The pirates you could see.

And it was the unseen, as I discovered, in which the captain considered himself something of an expert. Oh yes, he said, he'd been called in to investigate any number of shipboard hauntings that had ended in grief—an officer killed falling from a ship's riggings, an engineer crushed by a toppling gantry crane, or stevedores fleeing cargo holds in terror. I've always been a sucker for ghost stories, and I could only assume that the mind-reading captain knew a captive audience when he saw one.

In one memorable case, Rankine intoned, the longtime captain of the *Perlis*, a coastal steamer, had been taken ill and was forced to leave the ship in a hurry. His younger replacement had assumed command at Muara, the very port where Rankine and I now sat talking. "The radio officer told the new man, 'There's a ghost on the ship,'" Rankine said, to which the man had replied, "Who's afraid of a ghost?"

Rankine blinked. Of course you always looked for a perfectly rational explanation for shipboard hauntings, he insisted. Yet operating in this part of the world, where the supernatural was part of daily life, only a fool who didn't understand the nature of the peril would make light of the dark forces. And sure enough, when the new man went to occupy the captain's quarters, the hatch refused to open. Thinking one of his unmet crew was playing a joke on him, the new master ordered the prankster to stop fooling around and open up. Suddenly, the door flew back on its hinges and the *Perlis's* new master landed with a thump on the settee. The room was empty.

Now, the man was afraid, said Rankine. That night, "he went down to sleep with the crew—and the ghost attacked him there. They had to carry him off the ship," the poor devil created such a hullabaloo.

When Rankine arrived on the scene he realized he had to make a good show of it for the frightened crew. Before entering the haunted cabin, he spoke directly to the ghost. "You don't disturb me and I won't disturb you," he said, and then walked forward without mishap. Inside, he set up a do-it-yourself altar and made a peace offering of a fresh lime. When word got around that Rankine had appeased the angry spirit, the crew settled down and got back to work.

So it was mainly a public relations stunt?

Oh, no, Rankine said, there *was* a ghost on that ship, and from the way he said it I felt the hair bristle on the back of my neck. "I didn't see the ghost but I could sense it," he continued. "It wanted to get into you and take you over. I fought with this spirit all during the trip."

How did one go about fighting a ghost? I wanted to know. Rankine said he used "prayers, prayers, prayers"—how else would you do it?

So it was that a little window opened through which I could see this private man, the captain of the *Straits Star*, more clearly. In his youth, Rankine hinted, he'd acquired some bad habits—he drank and had experiences he would prefer not to talk about, and I could empathize with him there. When he got his captain's papers, however, he knew it was time to make a change and he converted to Roman Catholicism. In later years, his religion acquired an evangelical spin, and he focused now on the miracles and healing he had witnessed at St. Michael's Church in Singapore. He had traveled to Fatima and Lourdes, and another miracle site in the former Yugoslavia. "Oh, the disbelievers," Rankine said, "they have a difficult time."

In the ghostly battle aboard the *Perlis*, Rankine's psychic defenses were such that the spirit gave up trying to control him and attacked the chief engineer instead. At that point, the captain called in a *bomoh*, or shaman, to conduct an exorcism. The man came aboard, chanted his chants, and made his offerings. When the sun rose the following morning, the demon spirit was gone, and the ship got back to normal.

But why had the ship become haunted in the first place? Being an inquiring man, Rankine asked around the port and discovered the *Perlis*'s original master had been keeping a pocket spirit with him to protect the ship. Nothing unusual there—it was just old-school Malay practice. When the man fell ill and had to disembark, however, there was nobody around to perform the proper rituals and the spirit had gone wild, seeking its revenge. Case closed.

"Oh, you have to have faith," Rankine concluded. "You can make seas calm, storms go, but you have to have faith. Without faith you get nothing."

It was eleven o'clock by the time the stevedores had finished loading the *Star*, and I followed the captain up to the bridge for our departure. We had spent the last twelve hours talking and, in between the ghost stories, he'd given me lots of material in curmudgeonly lament on the lost romance of the sea, which I tried to capture in my *Geographic* story as follows:

> "Oh, there are no real seamen left in this world," Rankine said, waving his hand. "Everything is in the books, not in people's heads!"
>
> Anxious to get out of port, he shouted, "Where's that pilot?" into his walkie-talkie. In a flash a small, petrified man was on the bridge, bowing ferociously and offering excuses in Malay. "He doesn't want to take her out," snorted Rankine. "Pilots today have no experience," he muttered, preparing—not unhappily, it seemed to me—to do the job himself.
>
> "Oh, the last of the Mohicans!" cried the old captain, as the 258th container swung over the side and banged into place and he was finally free to head his ship for the Brunei cut and the darkness of the open sea.

It was after one in the morning when I worked up the guts to say goodnight and head below. Totally brainwashed now, I half expected an unseen hand to be holding the doorknob from the other side when I tried to open my cabin. When nothing happened, I flipped on the fluorescent ceiling lights and was relieved to find everything just as it had been on a first visit earlier in the day. The musty canvas odor, same. The faded lithographs of old-time sailing ships, the *Sophie Gorbitz* and the *Elisabeth*, same. The odd assortment of mirrors that fractured my image in a crazy carnival aspect, same. The single naked razor blade perched on top of the writing desk, same . . .

Single naked razor blade!

Thanks to the novelty of the day, I'd completely forgotten about my discovery of that unsettling artifact. But now, revved up on Rankine's Grand Guignol, I became obsessed. The logical explanation was that one of the crew had used the blade to scrape clean a porthole window or a mirror. But when I looked closely and saw no evidence of window or a mirror having been scraped, my mind raced to more diabolical possibilities. For a frantic moment I thought about snatching up the blade throwing it over the rail into the night sea. Instead, I left it where it was, so I could keep an eye on it from my bunk.

Needless to say, I slept badly and awoke the next morning with a start. Daylight was streaming through the portholes and the book I'd been reading to take my mind off ghosts lay sprawled beside me on the floor. Then suddenly I felt a chill as my eyes involuntarily darted to the desk. *Yes!* The razor blade was still there, exactly where it had been the night before. I was absurdly relieved.

If all this sounds silly to you, it sounds silly to me, too, as I sit in my study at home in Austin, Texas, putting it down in words. I recall I even felt a little foolish at the time—but given where I was and with whom I was keeping company, I didn't have reason to feel all that foolish.

11

My circumnavigation of the South China Sea had entered its last couple of weeks, and my featherheaded fantasies about the romance of place had served me well as a reporting tool. Such images are buried so deeply in the American mind-set that they routinely mess with our perceptions—by glorifying swashbuckling pirates who, in reality, are little more than desperate opportunists; daring and doughty sailors who are generally and absolutely desperate with boredom; and a colonial past that is historically discredited but, as an attitude, is nowhere near put to rest. As I explained it for my *Geographic* readers:

> *Such adventures appeased the eternal adolescent in me but made my inner reporter skeptical. By my third call at Singapore, where I waited for a final run up to Hong Kong on the aircraft carrier U.S.S. Constellation, I had concluded that the glory days of Conrad were pretty much finished. With its mix of Chinese, Malays, and Indians, Singapore was full of "the glitter, the colour of an Eastern crowd" the old master had described—women in saris of red and purple silk or hooded in black Muslim chadors, men wearing turbans or laced prayer caps. But more than anything the city-state resembled a shipshape Los Angeles, with immaculate sidewalks lined with McDonald's, Häagen-Dazs, and Toys "R" Us.*
>
> *I was also having serious doubts about the idea that a rising China might use military force to turn the entire South China Sea into a national lake. For one thing, the U.S., which patrols the sea like a cool-eyed town marshal, takes a dim view of anybody who might obstruct the free flow of maritime traffic through international waters.*
>
> *That was the situation aboard the Constellation when I stood on the bridge with Capt. Rocklun Deal, watching a jet fighter scream off the flight deck every 90 seconds, laying a trail of exhaust fumes over the sundown waters somewhere to the west of the Spratlys.*
>
> *"Technology lets us survey the airspace out to hundreds of miles and tell who's friendly and who's not," explained Deal. That would come in handy if China ever did flex its military muscle. [Meanwhile] diplomatic talk, backed by the admonitory presence of technology-packed mountains of steel like the Connie, might well solve any crisis before it started. Moreover, it wasn't at all clear how eager the American public would be to prosecute a war in a place that few voters—even educated ones—could readily locate on a map.*

Looking back on it now, I believe my strategic thinking, such as it was, holds up well enough. In recent years, China has projected more military hardware into the South China Sea. (In 2012 it commissioned the *Liaoning*, a refitted Soviet-era aircraft carrier purchased from Russia, marking the first step in plans for a Chinese-built fleet to challenge U.S. naval dominance in the China seas.) In spite of Beijing's bluster, though, the balance of firepower has shifted only marginally. I must admit, however, that I was naïve in the extreme, in those halcyon pre-Iraq war days, about the American citizenry's unwillingness to once again countenance war in far places about which most of us don't really have a clue. Well, scratch a baby boomer that, like me, grew up in the quasi-militaristic fifties and, for better or worse, it's not unusual to find a deep-seated faith in America's capacity for wanting to do the right thing in the world.

Riding along as the big gray ships of the Connie's battle group moved deliberately up through the South China Sea, for example, I was totally mesmerized by the show. Here was America at its crackerjack best, I thought, projecting power into the dangerous world, its machines whizzing and whirring and surging and spinning, everything moving forward to signify a determination to keep the waterways free and clear for global commerce. Luckily, I encountered a man on the Connie's busy bridge, a midlevel officer, who got me thinking about the quirky, fallible humanity behind the wielding of all that power. A short, overly precise fellow in a uniform ball cap who reminded me of the actor Danny DeVito, he carried a digital navigation device like a scepter, and with such self-importance that he could have been playing a role in a Hollywood farce in which the missile-launch key goes missing.

Mainly, I think, I liked the Connie because, after weeks in the field, it felt like home. Again, I agree with Anthony Burgess, who once said, paraphrasing Simone Weil, that in the end we are all true to the cuisine of our youth, "and that probably constitutes patriotism." After chopsticking it through Asia I happily walked the chow line heaping my plate with baked chicken, flank steak, mash potatoes and gravy, fruit-flavored gelatin, and other quintessential

American grub. There were lovely breads, cakes, and cinnamon rolls supplied by an unseen force called the Night Baker who I was sorry to leave behind when I eventually blasted off the decks of the Connie and the g-forces sucked the oxygen out of my lungs. I was headed to Hong Kong for the third and final time.

12

Back in what was now, since July 1, the Hong Kong SAR, or Special Administrative Region of the People's Republic, I was flying solo again, and there was no escaping the fact that I was terminally homesick. My hotel, which I'd always considered the height of Eurasian elegance from my days at the *Review*, and where Toshiko and I had spent our honeymoon in 1978, had lost its snap, crackle, and pop. The toilet in the men's sauna was clogged with feces. The chef's salad I ordered from room service came with an athletic cockroach that leapt from the lettuce and sprinted round and round the rim of the bowl. The next morning I was packing for my flight to Taiwan when I flipped on the TV and learned that Princess Di had been killed in an automobile accident in a Paris tunnel. Hong Kong, the recent former colony, was quickly abuzz with melancholy rumors.

By the time I got to Kaohsiung, the big industrial city at the southern end of Taiwan's loaf-shaped island, weeks of fatigue and sensory overload had turned me into the human equivalent of a hermit crab. The smallest inconveniences became infernally irritating to me now. Yet I couldn't very well do a story about China's growing muscle in Asia without reporting from Taiwan, the one-time island province that the mainland wanted back. So I checked into one of the city's better hotels, where the next morning a tall, unfriendly woman intercepted me at the entrance to the dining room. She asked to see my coupon.

"I don't have a coupon," I said. A coupon was mandatory, she insisted, looking me up and down as if I might be hiding cutlery in my pants.

When I casually observed, "This is more like visiting a police station than eating breakfast," the woman stared daggers at me and insisted I print my name above my signature before allowing me to join the buffet line.

Even the best hotels were conspiring against me now. (Did I mention paranoia is part of the long-distance syndrome too?) Anyhow, I clearly needed help. I had put in a call to Taipei to Chih-hong Wang, a globe-hopping photojournalist, to ask if he wouldn't mind serving as my local fixer. Excellent man, he arrived that afternoon. Slim, scholarly, and compassionate, Chih-hong sized up the situation immediately. He said he thought I'd better leave the hotel for a while.

Off we went on a refreshing city tour that included watching the sun drop into Xizi Bay and ended with a taxi driver hijacking us to a distant neighborhood where, in a Japanese restaurant run by his sister-in-law ("clean, no cockroaches," he promised), young waitresses, flirty and pouty-lipped, served passable sashimi and too-sweet tempura so charmingly that the mediocrity of the victuals really didn't matter. Back at the hotel, I bought two cream-filled éclairs with chocolate icing from the fancy patisserie in the lobby—without a coupon—and the next morning Chih-hong and I flew to the tiny outlying island of Quemoy, a trip I realized I'd been anticipating for forty years:

> *Mao Zedong had threatened to invade Taiwan, but when the Eisenhower administration sent in the Seventh Fleet and hinted at the use of the atomic weapon, the Great Helmsman had settled for shelling the bejesus out of tiny Quemoy, a Taiwanese possession hard by the mainland. A third-grader at Brighton Elementary School in Seattle, Washington, I had done my bit by fetching two slightly dented cans of Chef Boyardee spaghetti to a PTA food drive for Quemoy's beleaguered children.*
>
> *As my journey drew to a close, I flew to Quemoy, or Kinmen, as it's now known, where by chance I met one of those children, now a taxi driver named Chen Kuo-chuo. A rugged man of 47, with*

close-cropped black hair and aviator sunglasses, he drove me to the labyrinthine tunnels where he had cowered under that long-ago autumnal fusillade, sustained in part by relief packages from the U.S. ("No spaghetti, thank heavens!" he joked.)

But even as we stared into the bluey haze where, 3,000 yards ahead, rose the green hills of the place we had both feared as Red China, old Cold War currents seemed to be dramatically reversing themselves. Chen, some of whose ancestors left the mainland centuries ago, said that relaxed restrictions on travel from Taiwan to the mainland free him to visit relatives in Xiamen, today a thriving port.

"The communists aren't like before," explained Chen Suei-chai, Kinmen's first popularly elected mayor, when I sat with him at city hall sipping a cup of jasmine tea. A group of high-powered consultants from Taipei lingered at one end of the big room around a wall map of the Taiwan Strait. Heady talk was circulating among Taiwan's savvy capitalists about the emergence of "China, Inc.," a bloc made up of China, Hong Kong, and Taiwan that, old political barriers notwithstanding, might in the new century lead the world and exert a strong pull—political as well as commercial—all along the rim of the South China Sea.

"What people want here and on the mainland is the same thing—economic progress," insisted the mayor, a formal man in a luminous sharkskin suit. "Governments should listen to the voice of the people."

Mayor Chen pumped my hand and thanked me for coming: "We still remember your kindness in sending that canned food!" Frankly, as I stood there, clutching a plastic artillery shell I had bought, a replica commemorating Mao's famous pounding of Quemoy, I was a little sorry I had mentioned that part.

"Yes," teased city official Li Si-heui, "we'll look for the guy who got your spaghetti!"

13

That evening, back in Kaohsiung, I felt relaxed and happy. I was scheduled to fly home to New York the very next day, and I was more or less satisfied with how my reporting had turned out. Chih-hong had arranged dinner with a man expert in Taiwan's relations with China, and I was looking forward to a fine meal in the company of intelligent companions to help me snap what I'd seen and heard into sharper perspective. What I got instead was a character I shall refer to as "The Professor."

Chih-hong and I were waiting in the hotel lobby when a boyish-looking man with a jaunty bounce in his step approached and introduced himself. He wore thick glasses behind which his eyes appeared to trend, astigmatically, in competing directions. I shook his hand and turned on the bonhomie. "Professor, tonight is the last night of my travels," I said. "Let's go out and have a good meal to celebrate." He would be my guest.

The professor smiled or smirked, it was hard to tell which. "Well, we will determine who is whose guest later," he said. As for where to eat, I suggested some brand of Chinese but the Professor shook his head. "The Chinese food in Kaohsiung is not good," he said in brisk, overly precise English. "In Taipei of course it is excellent. Better than in Hong Kong. But in Kaohsiung, not so good . . . but we will try."

We didn't try very hard. After a short cab ride we found ourselves in a Thai restaurant atop a hotel with an impressive night view of the city. Without consulting Chih-hong or me, the Professor took charge, ordering enough dishes for a small symposium. He then began his lecture. The Taiwanese government (that's in Taipei where the Chinese food is good) had dragged its heels on normalizing relations with the mainland and would now face "painful adjustments."

"The Taiwanese have no choice but to go to China," he said. "*No choice.*" The Professor spoke in short, punchy phrases, invariably repeating the point of his last sentence for emphasis. I found this annoying. *Annoying.*

But never fear, he said, "We will find a solution. The Chinese are smart. *Smart.*" After each statement, it seemed, the Professor smirked, cocked his head, and stared in a way that made me feel self-conscious.

China had made big strides economically, I suggested, but didn't the Professor worry that the country's lack of political reform might eventually thwart its economic progress? The Professor looked at me appraisingly and suggested I was probably having trouble following the conversation. How so?

It was constitutionally impossible for Westerners to understand the Oriental Mind, he said. The Asian way of thinking was something that could neither be quantified nor adequately explained. "It's not logical," he said. *"Not logical."*

I groaned inwardly. How many times over the years had some self-appointed guardian of the order fed me a similar line? Such commentators are typically delighted to lecture you about the culture or country or gestalt in question on the implicit assumption that you, being an outsider, are by definition incapable of understanding what they're saying. I have very little patience with the idea that understanding is born in the blood. In fact, it's anathema to me. Followed to its logical conclusion, it's a recipe for shutting down universities, dooming us all to ignorance about "the other," and with the accompanying nasty problems. But of course I was being logical. *Logical.*

I was also attempting to be strenuously civil when our dishes arrived and we began spooning curried fish and eggplant onto our plates. I asked the Professor for his views on America where I knew he'd studied for his doctorate. He looked at me and tilted his head again, asking, "Does America have any core values left?"

I resisted the powerful urge to thwap him between the eyes with a serving spoon. Instead, I suggested that when people talked about core values, it seemed to me, they were usually referring to the received wisdom of earlier generations.

Ignoring my point, the Professor said America's biggest problem was its habitual sloth. Americans were so far gone in fact they could no longer rouse themselves to face the facts or so much as talk about their decline. "It goes like this," the Professor said, his hand tracing large, loopy waves over his plate, as America rose to its apogee after World War II, and then declined into the spicy eggplant. It wasn't personal. "It's history," he said. *It's fate.*

"For the last three centuries, China was down like this," he went on, his hand inscribing a plunging arc. "Now it's China's time. China will be on top and America will be down . . . down. China will be the big power—militarily, economically."

His comments struck me as an impressive demonstration of logic for a man who said logic didn't come naturally. How had he escaped the vagaries of the Oriental Mind?

The Professor said he'd devoted his first three years in the United States to mastering an understanding of the American mind-set. Apparently it hadn't been all that hard. Whereas Americans had once been "arrogant and confident," he said, they now retained the former but had lost the latter, which spelled big trouble for them.

It wasn't until I got back to my bookshelves in New York that I discovered, quite by accident, that British author Somerset Maugham appears to have endured a similar conversation when he met an embittered Confucian scholar he called "The Philosopher" while traveling in China shortly after World War I:

"'I took the Ph.D. in Berlin, you know,' said the man. 'And afterwards I studied for some time in Oxford. But the English, if you will allow me to say so, have no great aptitude for philosophy.' Though he put the remark apologetically," Maugham noted, "it was evident that he was not displeased to say a slightly disagreeable thing." His Philosopher continued:

What is the reason for which you deem yourselves our betters? Have you excelled us in arts or letters? . . . Why, when you lived in caves and clothed yourself with skins we were a cultured people. . . . Then why does the white man despise the yellow? Shall I tell you? Because he has invented the machine gun. That is your superiority. We are a defenceless horde and you can blow us into eternity. . . . Do you not know that we have a genius for mechanics? Do you not know that there are in this country . . . the most practical and industrious people in the world? Do you think it will take us long to learn? And what will become of your superiority when the yellow man can make as good guns as the white and fires them as straight?

My Professor was only a shade more discreet: "We in the East have learned just about everything we can from you in the West," he said. "Now it's time for you to learn from us." Like Maugham's Philosopher, perhaps, he seemed very pleased with himself, as if he had just swallowed a small bird.

Through most of the meal Chih-hong sat quietly by, grimacing and avoiding comment. His English wasn't as fluent as the professor's so I thought perhaps he was reluctant to speak out. Finally, though, he diplomatically pointed out that he'd been all over China, traveling the back roads through some of the country's remotest rural areas. "China has some big problems, too," he said. "It's got a long way to go."

The Professor responded by correcting Chih-hong's English.

14

I don't think the Professor was taunting me. If he did expect me to lash out, however, he had me wrongly pegged. True, I objected to his tone, which was supercilious, condescending, and betrayed the lack of confidence that generally lurks behind nationalistic or cultural arrogance. But here's the thing about long-distance reporting: Ours is not to take offense at even the most unpalatable opinions but to understand the logic that propels them. There was one further complication: Fundamentally speaking, I agreed with the Professor. America *was* going to have a difficult time—harder than most Americans could anticipate—adjusting to a world in which China played a leading role. The reasons related as much to deeply

rooted attitudes about race and political and economic preroga-
tives as they did to fears of economic competition.

So there, at last, was an answer to the first of the two big questions I had set out for my reporting: How well would—could—
America and the non-China world adjust to the realities of a rising China? As for the answer to the second question—What kind
of world citizen would China become?—it all depended. Basically, China wanted what America had, mainly affluence and respect,
and not necessarily in that order, and that hasn't changed. To satisfy
its citizens, then as now, China has been obliged to keep its economy growing at a vigorous clip or risk having to explain to hundreds
of millions of disgruntled Chinese consumers why not. There has
also been a rising, if muted, grassroots demand for democracy. If
the history of nations is any guide, China will do exactly what it has
to do, pragmatically, cooperatively, or bruisingly, to square its political circle and maintain stability.

Working all that out between today's two superpowers means,
in turn, there are many meals at Professor China's table in America's future and we Americans had better get used to dealing with
what's on the menu.

The morning after our dinner with the Professor, I sat at breakfast with Chih-hong before leaving for the airport. That good man,
having unraveled the mystery of the breakfast coupons, smiled
quizzically over his eggs. "I guess he"—the Professor—"must have
had a hard time in the United States," he said.

I told Chih-hong not to worry. Maybe that was precisely the discussion I was meant to have on the last night of my trip, I mused. It
was fate, perhaps. *Fate.*

Leaving Taiwan, I flew eastward across the Pacific on a U.S. air-
liner with faulty air-conditioning, growing increasingly unhappy
with the apparent decline in American efficiency. Channeling Iron
Man Li, I complained bitterly to an uncaring ground agent in San
Francisco. Seven hours later I was turning my key in the lock of our
New York apartment.

Toshiko was still at work and the place was silent but for the rattle of traffic outside on Forty-Ninth Street. And then I heard a familiar thumping sound that filled me with sad homecoming joy—our faithful dog Tammy was beating her tail slowly against the hardwood floor in the shadow of the dining room table. Her illness had progressed rapidly since I left home, and in a few weeks she would be gone.

Tammy rolled her eyes in welcome, and on the spot I had to say a little traveler's prayer. I thanked my lucky stars I'd been able to go where I had gone, see what I had seen, and make it home again in time to say good-bye. My article appeared in the pages of *National Geographic* the following year, in December 1998, under the title "South China Sea: Crossroads of Asia."

PART

TWO

SNAPSHOTS OF THE ISLAND KINGDOM

Kyushu.

HITCHHIKING
IN KYUSHU

1

When people ask me for advice on how to become a globe-trotting journalist, I always say the same thing: Pick a part of the world you can fall in love with and plant yourself there for at least two years. Try your hand at freelancing. Teach English, tend bar, or give body modification classes—whatever it takes to ward off starvation. Meanwhile suck the place into your bones. Absorb its language and politics, its loves, hates, and idiosyncrasies, the alarming as well as the charming.

Here's the thing: The place doesn't have to love you back, at least not right away. But if doing journalism is your goal, make sure it's somewhere the rest of the world wants to know about too.

My first love was China, as I've said. As a college freshman I hungered for the Middle Kingdom's ancient wisdom—anything to make a kid from working-class Seattle more interesting to the world, and the girls, than he really was. Yet even for somebody so feebly grounded in world events, I could see China had its hands full. Wrapped up in the mess and danger of its Cultural Revolution, the Chinese had barred American "imperialists" from entering the country for stays short or long. Not much of a future there, I thought.

Luckily, I had also fallen in love with Japan. Throughout my grade school and junior high school days I'd made friends with Clarke Kido, Steve Matsumoto, and other kids of Japanese heritage who lived in my neighborhood, and I became entranced by the cultural curiosities encountered in their homes. For a kid raised on white bread, canned vegetables, and meat loaf, my friends' daily routines were exotic—from the chopsticks they used at mealtime to menus that included crisp bamboo shoots and crackling green seaweed. The fairy tales their grown-ups told were different, too, pitched in a minor key with captivating little stings in their tails— like the one about the humble fisherman Urashima Taro who returns to his village from miraculous undersea adventures to find that three hundred years have passed and the life he knew, and everybody in it, is long since dead and gone.

Japan had something else going for it, too. Ever since Boeing's B-29 bombers, many of them built on the assembly line in Seattle, had ended World War II by reducing Japanese cities to smoking rubble, our two countries had become the best of friends. That at least was the script as written by Hollywood and other big U.S. media. Postwar movies like *The Teahouse of the August Moon* with Marlon Brando and *The Geisha Boy* starring Jerry Lewis—and the old-fashioned newsreels that movie houses still ran back in the 1950s—added to the idea that the Japanese had seen the light, swallowed their warlike tendencies, and were now devoting every waking hour to becoming more like America. As the Japanese were pictured embracing American jazz, hamburgers, and hula hoops, their factories churned out cheap transistor radios and gewgaws you won knocking down milk bottles at the PTA's carnival night. The message was clear: If Japan continued to work hard at aping America, it might hope to become a third-rate economy one day.

Not everyone fell for Japan's media makeover, of course. Though wartime blood grudges were slowly dissipating, grown-ups in our neighborhood of Scandinavian, Irish, Mediterranean, and Asian descent found it at least mildly freakish that an ostensibly normal, red-blooded American kid, meaning a white one, would nurse a fascination with an outlandish place like Japan. As the father of one of my high school pals put it: "What's a smart young guy like you doing wasting your time on the Japs?"

Such knee-jerk racism made me angry. And though I was far too brainwashed in those socially constipated Cold War days to openly rebel, I harbored a smoldering resentment against a world that would deny me the right to be interested in what I was interested in. To show the naysayers the true depth of their ignorance, I threw myself into my studies at the University of Washington. I read up on Zen Buddhism and haiku poetry, and lorded my counterfeit command of the mysteries of the East over people who didn't seem to notice or care. I spent haunch-numbing hours haunting a cubicle in the language lab, muttering Japanese grammar exercises like a disgruntled drifter. Trapped inside my bubble, I eventually persuaded myself that I spoke flawless Japanese.

It came as shock then, in the summer of 1970, when I got my first big chance to visit Japan on a student tour, that the Japanese refused to acknowledge my mastery of their language. Many appeared not to realize I was speaking Japanese at all. On the streets of Tokyo, Kobe, or Kyoto I'd approached solid-looking citizens to ask directions only to have them brusquely waggle a hand in front of their noses, Japanese sign language for "I don't understand you and I don't want to know you," and walk on. In a restaurant, my request for a glass of water would return a fork; the call for a beer would yield a glass of milk.

The crowning humiliation came during a homestay in Hiroshima. According to Japanese custom, I was removing my shoes to enter the house of my hosts, a young and flinchingly shy married couple, when they began to swoon at the sight of my size 15 oxfords. To put them at their ease, I made the witty, self-deprecating remark, "My shoes are really big, aren't they?" So I was surprised when the attractive lady of the house, who had knelt down before me to tend to her husband's shoes, recoiled, horror-stricken. Belatedly, I realized my mistake: I had confused *kutsu*, the generic word for shoe, with *ketsu*, vulgar slang for the human posterior, and had succeeded in complimenting the woman on the bounty of her hind parts. In Japan for a mere three weeks I realized, as my linguistic calamities escalated, that I'd been infatuated with the wrong country. I vowed I would never, under any circumstances whatsoever, set foot there again.

Never arrived three years later. As I was an uninspired graduate student at Harvard, my professors shrewdly determined I should go away for a while and arranged for me to spend a year in Tokyo ironing out what even I could now see were the serious kinks in my Japanese. Considering the alternatives—unemployment, a return to my parents' basement, or likely both—I jumped at the chance. Meanwhile, in spite of my early misadventures, Japan had turned out to be a wonderful choice of countries to love. Americans were waking up to the disturbing reality that the "third-rate" Japanese were wiping the floor with one U.S. industry after another, from stereos to TV sets and steel to automobiles. Economic jujitsu had grudgingly persuaded a growing number of Americans they needed to know more about the Japanese, if only as a matter of survival. My timing, despite being totally inadvertent, was impeccable.

I had been in Tokyo all of three months, studying Japanese six and seven hours a day, when an unusually outspoken journalist told me from a barstool one night that I spoke Japanese like an effete snob. His name was Tomosuke Noda. To save me from my Japanese teachers, he said I'd better come along with him on a hitchhiking tour of his native Kyushu, Japan's southernmost main island. There he'd introduce me to what he called the "real Japan," a place of salt-of-the-earth farmers and laborers, fishermen and shopkeepers who populated a country most Americans had never seen and didn't know existed.

Without the slightest risk of overstatement, I can say that Tomosuke and that trip changed my life, and we'll get to all that in a minute. (The second bit of advice for living a life abroad, boiled down: Make a good and trustworthy friend and you'll learn more than you ever bargained for.) For now, suffice it to say that two decades later, when, in 1993, Bill Graves asked me to do my first story for the *Geographic*, six thousand words on Kyushu as luck would have it, there was only one logical place to start . . .

It was my first attempt at hitchhiking in 20 years, and we were getting nowhere fast. My partner, Tomosuke Noda, and I had haunted the same remote strip of highway in the mountains of central Kyushu for an hour now. The sun was shining hotly. We had counted dozens of cars zipping past, spraying us with gravel but coolly ignoring our outstretched thumbs.

Tomosuke, an outdoors writer and my oldest Japanese friend, was nibbling a blade of razor grass and smiling with thinly disguised impatience. Then a grinning, wild-haired farmer shot by, waggling his hand at us in rejection, and something snapped.

"You're scaring them," said Tomosuke, referring to my 6-foot-7-inch foreigner's frame, which loomed over the roadway. "For god's sake, go sit down or something."

That hurt. But before I could point out that Tomosuke, with his pencil-thin, gigolo's mustache and rakish peaked cap, hardly presented a beacon of reassurance to the wary motorist, a dusty white hatchback screeched to a stop in front of us. "Notte kudasai!" shouted the young man behind the wheel. "Hop in!"

Yet another crisis in Japanese-American relations averted, we gathered up our gear and crammed our bodies into the tiny car. In a flash, our savior, Gunji Oshikawa, a 21-year-old electronics technician from the nearby city of Nobeoka, was flying down the road as it twisted and dipped high above the churning rapids of the Gokase River.

Watching the scenery whiz by in psychedelic streaks of green and white, I couldn't help but muse at how things had changed since Tomosuke and I had passed this way in 1974 when Tomosuke offered to show me around this southernmost of Japan's four main islands, with its active volcanoes, its long, shimmering coastlines, and a people so passionately hospitable that, on one occasion, we were forced to flee a creaky old farmhouse at daybreak, having been taken into unofficial custody by an eccentric group of young farmers. Now, two decades later, it seemed people couldn't care less.

Wayfarers thumbing a ride, Kagoshima, 1993.
Photo by Michael Yamashita.

"*Everybody's in a big hurry these days,*" *said Gunji, natty in a crisp pin-striped shirt and French necktie. He was himself hurrying back to his head office, 30 miles away. There he would grab a fresh stack of work orders and return to the hills, where, as an expert in outfitting banks with the latest in computerized teller machines, his services were in big demand.*

"*The smallest bank branch in the tiniest town is going on-line,*" *Gunji told us. Just then, we rounded a hairpin curve and swerved to miss a cement truck, and the loose circuit boards beside me on the backseat danced wildly, sending up little clouds of dust.*

Even as we drove, Kyushu was merging with the great data superhighways, endless loops of fiber-optic cable that have now begun to link Japan's major cities and the world beyond.

"*Shinjiraren!*" *marveled Gunji. "It boggles the mind!*"

With the lede, or opening, out of the way, I zeroed *Geographic* readers in on the point of the story, which I wouldn't have known to look for had not Tomosuke introduced me to Kyushu to begin with:

During the four weeks I spent in Kyushu, I was surprised to find people like Gunji all over the island, throwing themselves at the future—determined to make up for lost time. Historically, the rest of the country has tended to view Kyushu, which accounts for a tenth of Japan's land area and population, as a place apart—a sort of squat, volcanic exclamation point on Japan's island tail—and inhabited by a people by nature fiery and rebellious.

That image grew in 1877 when Kyushu's greatest hero, the samurai-statesman Saigo Takamori, led a bloody rebellion against the national government he had helped create only a decade earlier. His goal was to prevent too much of the country's power and wealth from accumulating in its new capital, Tokyo. His flamboyant failure to do so would oblige generations of Kyushuans to leave home to chase their dreams of high-paying jobs and glamorous lifestyles in the centers up north.

Kyushuans today have embarked on yet another ambitious quest: to leapfrog the decades of second-class citizenship. Whether they will ultimately succeed where Saigo failed, nobody yet knows. In the past decade [however], hundreds of corporations, Japanese and foreign, have set up factories here, tapping the island's reservoir of cheap land and well-educated workers and counting on its proximity to the rising economies of Asia to pull them into new global markets.

"Tokyo has always been our magnet," a leading local politician told me, but now the poles are shifting. The Cold War over, pent-up entrepreneurial energies are battering down old ideological barriers throughout the region. Guangdong Province in southern China, for example, boasted a growth rate of nearly 20 percent in 1992, one of the highest in the world. Kyushu's largest city, Fukuoka, a hundred minutes by air from Tokyo, is closer to Pusan (40 minutes), Seoul (65 minutes), and Shanghai (85 minutes).

"Why go through Tokyo any more?" asked the politician.

Besides, the freshest ideas for dealing with the rest of the world in a relaxed, open manner, he insisted, were not coming from reserved, cautious Tokyo but from the south, where, he said, "We've got that frontier spirit!"

2

In understanding a country or a people from top to bottom and inside out, there's simply no substitute for someone like Tomosuke— a guide who can take you deep into not only the practical ins and outs of a place but its emotional core as well. Beginning in 1973, it was Tomosuke's frontier spirit, you might say, that allowed me to see Japan beyond the movie fantasies and media stereotypes. (And since I wasn't yet a journalist in the habit of taking copious field notes, we enter here the realm of studious remembering.)

Tokyo in those days was very much Japan's unavoidable city and nothing in my Seattle upbringing had prepared me for life in its urban beehive. I'd grown up hunting and fishing, and stretching my legs in God's country, as its denizens proudly called the Pacific Northwest, where there was never a shortage of vistas to fill the eye and feed the spirit, with mountains, rivers, and salt water, often all in one picture frame. Tokyo by contrast made me feel like an animal trapped in a zoo. No sooner had I stuck my head outside my microscopic two-room flat up the road from Shibuya train station than my fellow Tokyoites would stop dead in their tracks, dissolve into laughter or just let their jaws drop in disbelief, and announce to the world, as if they'd spotted a visitor from a distant planet, "Hora, mite! Dekai gaijin!"—"Hey, look! A giant foreigner!"

That's not to say I wasn't developing affection for my new home. I was. But the city made me earn it, and Tokyo's famously crowded subways were the worst. Standing head and shoulders, if not half a torso, above my fellow strap-hangers, I was on full-time alert for freelance gigglers, pointers, and hecklers to come forward and remind me of my "otherness." One afternoon I was scanning a swarming car for trouble when I felt a tug, tug, tugging at my long student hair. What nerve! When *would* these people leave me alone, I thought, as I spun around to give my latest tormentor a piece of my mind. But there was only me. I'd been so busy trying to catch someone in the act that I'd let my hair get tangled in one of the car's rotating ceiling fans. The memory of normally poker-faced Japanese doubled over in helpless mirth remains vivid after forty years.

In spite of what I'd seen at the movies back home, I was also discovering the Japanese were not, in the main, a race of obliging American wannabes. If anything, they harbored their own well-worked prejudices. On my way home one evening I was riding a half-empty subway car when a distinguished-looking gentleman plopped down on the bench next to me. Dressed in a pin-neat gray business suit, his silvery hair neatly combed, the man edged up so close that our legs touched. He then cocked his head, smiled a querulous smile, and proceeded to study me from head to toe. Having finished his inspection, he shared his inward feelings: "If I had a sword on me right now," he said with a guttural rumble, "I would run you through! For the honor of Japan!"

Sorting out such daily trials drove me to drink—not that I wouldn't have found my way there anyway. I'd read somewhere that writers were supposed to be big drinkers, and seeing as how I was now twenty-three, I thought I'd better get busy. So I started hanging out in one of Tokyo's bohemian bar areas called *goruden gai*, or Golden Street, near Shinjuku train station, where the raffish back streets were lined with decrepit one- and two-story shanties and churned with prostitutes and poets, transvestites and touts, and everyday working stiffs just trying to iron out their stiffness. Journalists too, of course. And it was there one night toward the end of 1973, at a tiny watering hole called the Art Baroque, that I sat next to Tomosuke for the very first time.

At first blush, he looked like a prizefighter, with a knockabout's nose, a truculent little tilt to his chin, and on this night he was in a defiant mood. Hunched over the counter, sipping a whiskey, he said with a kind of sad-sack brio, *"Toh-ray-shee,* Japan is a nation of sheep," a phrase I would come to learn was one of his favorite mantras. Maybe Americans were under the impression Japan had left its feudal past behind after the Pacific War, but they were wrong. All Japanese were in on the secret, Tomosuke said, whether they liked it or not: Japan was a rigged game in which soul-crushing regimentation was the payoff for the vast majority of its citizens.

After my experiences on the streets and subways, Tomosuke's candor hit me like a get-out-of-jail-free card. The Japanese I'd come to know so far were fine, upstanding people, far more diverse in their tastes and talents than the society of ant-like conformity I'd learned about back in the States. Nonetheless, they did play things close to the vest, particularly around foreigners. But Tomosuke had no such inhibitions. In his middle thirties, he had a chip on his shoulder the size of Mount Fuji and advertised it with a samurai's swaggering pride. In his view, no sooner had two-timing General Tojo and the other militarists who got Japan mixed up in the Pacific War been hanged or jailed as war criminals than the country's corporate elite swooped in to shunt ordinary, good-hearted

Japanese into factories and offices. There, robbed of their identity and independence, they had no choice but to toil in, well, ant-like conformity.

In point of fact, I met a lot of Japanese back then who felt the same way, even if they generally had the good sense to keep their mouths shut in public. The starvation and horror of the war years not that far behind them, people were understandably inclined to trade personal freedom for economic security, and if nothing else Japan, with its paternalistic employment practices, had created a society that offered ordinary folks an impressive degree of diaper-to-shroud security.

How refreshing it was to meet a rebel like Tomosuke! I was even more smitten when he told me he was a *rupo-raita*, or freelance journalist, which of course is exactly what I wanted to be. As far as Tomosuke was concerned, there was only one big hurdle standing between me and making further exciting discoveries about Japan.

"You speak Japanese like a woman," he said bluntly and then went on to mimic the mincing, overly polite speech I was learning to deliver at my Japanese-language school. The point wasn't misogynistic but a political one: The language's demanding, gender-specific grammar rules and withering levels of politesse were tough on everybody, but particularly hard on women—just one more way tradition was used to keep people in line. (I should add here that many women I would come to know, including my wife, Toshiko, didn't like speaking Japanese like women, either, because of how it locked them into unequivocal and unequal social roles.)

Having diagnosed my problem, Tomosuke blamed it on a kind of rampant *gaijin-itis* among the pointy-headed crowd I was hanging out with at the time. University professors, Japanese teachers (though let me stress not *my* sainted Japanese teachers), and other self-appointed interpreters of Japanese culture habitually defended the notion that the same ineffable cultural differences that made Japan unique among nations also made it ultimately impossible for foreigners to understand. The basic problem was that foreigners weren't Japanese enough. Let them learn to speak Japanese well, however, and they became *henna gaijin*, or foreigner weirdos. Such overachievers were viewed as turncoats to their own country and culture, which to most Japanese was the same thing and unimaginable. What self-respecting Japanese would want such an essentially disloyal person for a friend? That, in a nutshell, was Japan's catch-22.

Stick to that prissy path, learn "good-boy" Japanese, Tomosuke warned, and I'd wind up learning nothing about Japan at all. And so it was that in the early spring of 1974, Tomosuke decreed the two of us would embark on a grand hitchhiking tour of his native Kyushu, in search, or so I grandly thought, of the soul of the nation. I had just one reservation. I had yet to see a single Japanese thumb a ride in Japan, where I'd been told the practice carried a stigma of freeloading and rootlessness. Was hitchhiking really okay?

Tomosuke confessed he'd picked up the hitchhiking part from reading Jack Kerouac's *On the Road* and watching James Dean in one of his favorite American movies, *Rebel without a Cause*. In conformist Japan, he reckoned, hitchhiking was a small act of rebellion, and a good way to meet ordinary people and hear their stories.

3

Everybody knows it's an unforgivable cliché to say that travel is broadening. I wouldn't dare. So let me just stipulate that I began absorbing clues about the real Japan as soon as Tomosuke and I hit the Kyushu road in the chilly month of March.

Our first stop was Kitakyushu, where I got an inkling of what it meant to see my "Americanness" through the experiences of others. I was bunked in the guestroom of the big spooky house belonging to Tomosuke's ancient mother when I woke to hear a low moaning sound coming from behind the grandfather clock. It was peculiar and rattled me a bit. When I reported the incident to Tomosuke over breakfast, however, he laughed and said not to worry—it was just the ghost of his dead father groaning in morbid welcome. Then, maybe to make me feel less silly, he suggested that he too knew what it meant to cower under the futon covers.

Tomosuke had been a teenager at the height of the Korean War, when the American military used northern Kyushu as a staging area for the fighting on the nearby Korean Peninsula. By day, big, ferocious-looking GIs tramped the streets in their heavy boots, winning over kids by handing out candy bars and other prizes. By night, liquored up on the local potato vodka, they took to the streets to bellow like wild animals and fire their pistols into the air. Lying in bed, listening to the commotion, Tomosuke was mystified by this strange race of people called *amerika-jin* that acted with such kindness in daylight only to shoot up the joint after hours.

Down the line in Kurume, Tomosuke revealed his gift for inventing boyishly captivating diversions. Staying with his elder sister Hideyo, whose husband, a man named Haraguchi, was a big wheel in the local prefectural assembly, we found ourselves trapped indoors by a thrashing rain. Agitated by the boredom, Tomosuke swung into action. A fan of most things American, including a fascination with firearms that were all but outlawed in Japan, he set up a shooting range on the long second-floor veranda where we passed the time conducting live-fire drills with his pellet gun to the astonished delight of the neighborhood kids.

Local politics made its way onto the agenda, too. One evening Tomosuke and I were haunting the downstairs family room drinking sake and beer, when a curious visitor stepped into the *genkan* or vestibule. A small man with hunch shoulders, a Halloween smile, and prancing feet, he plunked down several big, clanking bags of coins on the entry step—Haraguchi's daily cut from the local pinball racket, Tomosuke said—and then the floor show began. After a deep, solemn bow, the man bent his knees, swung his arms out to the sides, palms facing up, and in voice that started at his belt buckle described his *kuni* or place of origin in Japan, his undying loyalty to his over-boss, and the boss's many virtues. It was the first time I'd witnessed the Japanese hood's ritualized introduction, and it was quite the performance.

"What did I tell you," Tomosuke said, nodding sagely, as if just having proved a complicated theorem. "Japan is still a feudal country."

And so it was my travels with Tomosuke began to radically transform the way I thought and felt about Japan. I could see what the textbooks or magazines said about a place and its people might be important—Japan *was* a conformist, resource-poor island nation, and all of that. But I also realized that book-learning would remain useless for me unless I was able to measure the theory in the light of real circumstances, which I was happily discovering were nearly always unique and often a little crazy.

Inevitably, the question of sex across borders arose in a typically elliptical Japanese way.

Leaving Chez Haraguchi, we hit the road, hitching rides in a rambling, S-shaped pattern all the way down to Kagoshima, the elegant, Mediterranean-style city at Kyushu's southernmost point. From there we traveled another five hours by ferryboat to the small, semi-tropical island of Yakushima, a place remarkable in those days for its giant cedar trees, its dwarfish and sour-tasting pineapples, and one other feature Tomosuke thought might be of special interest to me.

While still back in Kagoshima, bunking in living quarters atop a gynecological hospital that belonged to a Noda family friend, Tomosuke had waggled a tourist brochure under my nose. "Toh-ray-shee," he said, jubilantly, "they have *konyoku onsen* on Yakushima." He was referring to a community bath where both sexes occupied the same soaking pool, a practice outlawed on the main islands since the 1950s. The pamphlet, if memory serves, featured a photo of a rocky grotto with a quaintly thatched roof that was set, alluringly, in a white-sand beach, the whole scene washed by turquoise waters.

The mind boggled. I was just turning twenty-four, and Tomosuke's sales pitch was tailor-made for my desperate hormonal condition. Since arriving in Japan seven months earlier, I'd admired Japanese women from afar for their quiet grace and beauty, but that magical part of the real Japan had yet to become real for me. Suddenly Yakushima offered exciting new possibilities. When you're as young and inexperienced as I was then, you can swallow the bait without ever feeling the slightest evidence of a hook or line.

To hear Tomosuke describe it, the *onsen* was a paradise. Where else could you sit smack in the middle of the southern ocean, drink sake from a pull-tab can, and fish the surf, all at the same time? For an outdoorsman like Tomosuke, it was the perfect alignment of all conditions essential to human happiness. But I didn't really give a damn about the fishing or the sake. In my mind's eye, and thanks to Tomosuke's libidinous hinting, I chose instead to picture myself luxuriating in the bath like a feudal lord while it filled up with the nude and nubile daughters from the local village.

What about, you know . . . I asked Tomosuke.

Oh, yes, yes, he said knowingly, the local villages were famous for bursting at the seams with frustrated beauties that couldn't wait to inflict their pent-up passion on a handsome young foreigner—*everybody knew that.*

Tomosuke and I arrived on Yakushima around noon and hitched a ride into town on a pineapple truck. I wanted to head for Mixed Bathing Central straight away, but Tomosuke reminded me that villagers took their baths after the day's work was done and so, after what seemed like an interminable wait, we borrowed a pair of rusty bicycles from our innkeeper and headed up island in the late afternoon sun. Traversing the endless, spiky green pineapple fields was hot, sweaty work. But Tomosuke promised it would be worth it. Pedaling in the lead, he would turn his head every so often to yell, "Not far now! The girls will be waiting!"

Half an hour before sunset we reached the shoreline, and it really was a dazzling scene. I can still see the blue-green sea crashing against a coronet of big rocks as the yellow sun plunged toward the horizon. High above, wind-sculptured pines clung to a beachside cliff like the subject of a woodblock print. Eager to get the party started, I removed my T-shirt and jeans and followed Tomosuke into the bathing pool.

In short order, Tomosuke produced from his backpack two cans of sake and handed me one; he baited a fishing line and flung it out into the surf, tying the end around his index finger so he could feel for any bites; he then settled back, slumping into the hot bathwater, and smiled blissfully from ear to ear. He looked as regally content as Neptune, god of the seas, on one of his better days.

But I was getting impatient. Where were the girls? "Shimpai suru na," Tomosuke said, "Don't sweat it." The bath would be a steamy jungle of activity any minute now, just wait and see. Then, after what seemed like a further eternity, Tomosuke looked up, and said, "Ah, here they come."

By Jove, he was right. Tilting my head back, I could see a dozen or so villagers assemble at the top of the beachside cliff. All dressed in light, airy summer kimono, they began to slowly file down the steep, serpentine trail. Although they were too far away to make out any distinguishing physical features, my pulse started to race in anticipation of all those pulchritudinous young bodies that would be crowding into the tiny circle of the bath any minute now.

"Yes, yes, here they come," Tomosuke repeated, but this time there was something new in his voice, a teasing undertone, as if he might know something that I didn't. As I watched the pilgrims reach the bottom of the cliff and pick their way toward us across the rocky beach, I gradually became aware of something surprising: the bathers displayed uncommonly poor posture. Backs severely bowed, they walked with a jerky, chicken-winged kind of a gait. When they drew closer, I saw the reason why. Not one of them, female or male, appeared to be less than about seventy-five years old.

Smiling and laughing unselfconsciously, the mummified seniors stopped short of the pool to doff their clothes, exposing sinewy, desiccated bodies twisted from years spent laboring in the pineapple fields. It resembled a congregation of dried-up prunes. Looking at me look at them, Tomosuke snorted with laughter. Any young person with any brains at all left places like Yakushima as soon as they could to find jobs in the big cities up north, he told me with brutal candor. By way of editorial comment, he added that the younger generation had typically lost the stomach for the rigors of farm labor. Just then an old crone, naked as a newborn, slipped into the bath next to me and asked, in the thick local dialect, "So where are you gentlemen from?"

When Tomosuke had explained, the woman turned to me and cackled, "Eigo no shenshay jaroo?!"—"I guess you'd be an English teacher?!" Everybody laughed, including me.

It was like that famous philosopher Mick Jagger once said, "You can't always get what you want. But if you try sometimes you just might find you get what you need." Instead of the lusty experience I'd been dreaming of, our evening in the mixed bath turned out to be a wholly delightful and educational affair. The farmers taught me the words to a couple of odd, haunting lullabies, and together we happily warbled the incredibly sad lyrics, sipping sake till the sun had dropped into the darkening sea, the surf shone as if lighted with fireflies, and our skin had puckered like cheap seersucker.

In sharing the bath with those good-hearted people, I realized that Tomosuke had lied to show me the truth; there was in fact something tangibly real about the real Japan after all.

4

Thus I began to appreciate Tomosuke's instructional methods. He was trying to show me how to look at his country not as an abstraction in a magazine or a film but as the sum total of the people actually living there. The trick was to see them up close and as human beings, as idiosyncratic in their individuality as people anywhere, if expressing their human foibles in ways unique to their own culture.

That grassroots approach would stand me in good stead when a few years later, as a reporter, I was called on to explain Japan to non-Japanese audiences while, back home in America, politicians and ordinary folks, worried about losing jobs to Japanese imports, were itching for a trade war. The Japanese were fierce competitors, it's true. All the same, I couldn't shake the feeling that their biggest sin was to overshoot American expectations. The fact that the Japanese had refused to follow the script Americans had laid down for them during our postwar occupation of Japan came as a shock to those of us who hadn't been paying attention, meaning nearly everybody. And the idea that an economically risen Japan was repaying American largesse with cruel deception produced some nasty consequences.

In 1982, to cite an extreme but telling example, an unemployed autoworker named Ronald Ebens and his stepson, Michael Nitz, made headlines when they encountered Vincent Chin, an American citizen of Chinese descent, in a Detroit area bar and got into a fight. Mistaking Chin for Japanese, and therefore a perpetrator of the American auto industry's decline, the two men pursued him to a local McDonald's where Ebens beat him into a coma with a baseball bat. Chin died four days later. Ebens and Nitz each eventually plea-bargained their second-degree murder charges down to manslaughter and a three-thousand-dollar fine.

America's fear of falling prey to the foreign enemy within is an old, old story of course. Yet it routinely seems to obscure our ability to separate out the actual threats that, in a difficult world, do exist. During World War II, American citizens of Japanese descent living on the West Coast were rounded up and sent to internment camps on unfounded suspicions of spying for Emperor Hirohito; during the Cold War, legions of American moles were said to be working on the Kremlin's behalf to gut the country from the inside; in the 1980s, the Japanese were back, America's sci-fi fears casting them as sore losers bent on conquering by economic means what they had lost militarily in the war.

The U.S.-Japan trade rivalry went on to ignite a furious debate between two main camps in America, each claiming special knowledge of the Japanese and characterizing their opposite numbers as troglodytic "Japan bashers," on the one hand, and members of a spinelessly pro-Japanese "Chrysanthemum Club," on the other. The American news media, caught in the middle and often not knowing what to think, not infrequently defaulted to the bashers' position. Then, in the late 1980s, when the mother of all recessions had clobbered Japan and its economy pancaked, Americans went back to blithely ignoring the Japanese, as if nothing had ever happened. In between, as you can imagine, there was a lot of silliness.

Meanwhile the Japanese pressed on with their magnificent obsession for developing new markets by perfecting products that people wanted and in some notable cases didn't know they needed. Back in Kyushu, reporting for the *Geographic* in 1993, I let the Japanese mania for focusing on seemingly obscure detail lead me to the Kitakyushu plant of Toto Ltd., one of the world's largest producers of toilets, which I captured in my story as follows:

> *I watched in awe as industrial robots spritzed long lines of freshly molded commodes with pastel glazes before they marched stolidly into the glowing red jaws of a giant furnace to be fire-hardened. All this activity, spokeswoman Yoko Okamoto told me, was aimed at a simple goal: to make life more comfortable and environmentally correct.*
>
> *The centerpiece was the company's hot-selling toilet-bidet, the controls of which resemble a small electronic keyboard and, thanks to a microcomputer buried inside, offer an array of jets and sprays—all using no more water than an ordinary toilet.*
>
> *Company researchers had also discovered the alarming fact, said Ms. Okamoto, "that women flush the toilet repeatedly to cover up unladylike noises." She added, quite seriously, that "the excessive use of water has become a big problem." Environmental disaster looming, Toto engineers devised the Sound Princess, a convenience that employs state-of-the-art electronics to simulate a loud flushing sound at the touch of a button—without using a single drop of water.*

5

Build a better toilet and the world may indeed beat a path to your door, but developing an eye for idiosyncrasy also helped me see that the enterprising Japanese were still struggling to feel as if they really belonged to that world. The more economically successful they became, the greater pressure the Japanese felt to fit in with the industrialized economies of the United States and Europe, and that in turn created an agonizing cultural dilemma for many ordinary citizens. One evening I spoke with a newlywed couple at a European-style theme park north of Nagasaki where they had decided to spend their honeymoon. "We thought about going to Europe," Noboru, the husband, told me, "but we wanted to go out at night without becoming crime statistics or having to deal with a foreign language."

That encounter, and the phobias it highlighted, gave me a hook I could use in my story to introduce the larger issue of Japan's ongoing challenges with *kokusaika* or internationalization:

> *That very urge to taste the wider world's glamour without any of its inevitable mess or danger is what worries Nagasaki Mayor Hitoshi Motoshima. In 1945 Nagasaki became the second city in history to be hit by an atomic bomb. Yet today, Motoshima believes, the Japanese have lost sight of the events that led to that tragedy, and such myopia could hinder them as they try to mesh with a rapidly changing world.*

The mayor was a brave, voluble man with an impish smile who had paid a steep price for speaking truth to nationalistic boneheadedness:

> *In 1988 Motoshima broke a long-standing taboo by publicly suggesting that the late Emperor Hirohito bore responsibility for wartime decisions that sent millions of soldiers to conquer Asia in his name. For his daring, Motoshima was shot in the back by a right-wing extremist. "The Japanese," he told me, "have to realize they are not yet truly international people."*

6

Feelings of self-consciousness around foreigners ran deep and could express themselves in unusual ways. During my student days in Tokyo, it wasn't all that uncommon for a Japanese *sarariman*, or white-collar worker, having absorbed a cocktail or two, to sidle up to a foreigner in a bar to inquire, "Okay, how big is it?"

How big is what?

"You know," the man might say, offhandedly, as he cast a furtive glance at the seated part of one's anatomy. It was typically a pretty harmless business and easy to see where it came from. Japanese pop culture did its best to play up the stereotype of the oversexed *gaijin* with improbably oversized parts to match, and exactly how Japan measured up was something of a national preoccupation. Yet I must say the fixation came to an unusual head when Tomosuke and I were on the road back in the glory days of 1974, and this is how the incident has fixed itself in my memory.

We had hitched our way into the sticks of central Kyushu when a local trucker dropped us at a fork in the road where the sun was abandoning a sad-looking country eatery with a jerry-rigged tin roof. When Tomosuke and I entered the establishment to ask after a place to stay the night, however, we found ourselves inside some kind of rural jamboree. A group of young farmers with ruddy cheeks and strenuous dental work were grilling meat byproducts on gas-fired hot plates. Judging from the raucous laughter and empty sake flasks scattered around, they'd been at it for quite some time.

"We're eating grilled pig intestines!" shouted a young man with a face so explosively red it looked like a tomato in extremis. "Please join us!"

Tomosuke and I sat down at the man's table as the farmers gathered around, grinning uncontrollably. Yoked to lives of backbreaking labor, they were enthralled by the idea of hitchhiking and the freedom it represented, and peppered us with questions. Where were we from? Where were we going? How had we managed to avoid working for a living? At length, Tomosuke asked if anybody knew where we could bed down.

Immediately, our self-appointed host spoke up. Why not stay with his family? (I don't remember the man's name but let's call him Ichiro, since he was an eldest son and Ichiro is what farm-belt Japanese traditionally called eldest sons.) It was just over the hill, he said, and his parents would be honored to have such a distinguished pair of guests. So away we went, Tomosuke beaming at the confirmation of his theory that you could live entirely off the kindness of strangers in a real place like Kyushu where people's hearts were smelted from pure gold. I was pretty excited too.

Ichiro's house, with its thick thatched roof and weathered wooden siding, stood on a patch of ground at the head of a long dun-colored valley, and a strange, lovely place it was. As the sun dropped behind the darkening mountains, you could smell the smoke from the village's charcoal fires mingle with the aroma of the terraced, night soil–soaked fields. Here, at last, I thought, was the true eternal countryside of Japan! Ichiro flung back the door to reveal a *genkan* filled with a boisterous welcoming committee made up of his mother and father and assorted neighbors. They all grinned vigorously, showing plenty of gold fillings, and bowed us inside.

The sole exception was an old woman with wispy white hair and a back so doubled up that her shoulder blades were virtually parallel to the floor. "What's that!" she shrieked, her toothless gums working excitedly as she waggled a bony finger at me.

"It's an American," said Ichiro. When the woman let out a keening wail that sounded as if someone had stepped on the cat's tail, he reassured her: "Don't sweat it, Granny, Japan and America aren't enemies any more, you know!" Everybody had a good laugh at that one, except for the woman who continued to stare at me as if Viking invaders had suddenly appeared in her vegetable patch. We went inside.

The house was big and mysterious, its low, dark rooms sealed off from one another by sliding rice-paper doors that were haphazardly patched and yellowed with age. We ate dinner in a cozy family room about eight feet square, and the meal was robust in the country manner with plenty of delicious homegrown vegetables.

A bottle the size and shape of a bowling pin appeared containing *shochu*, the local sweet potato–based white lightning that had driven the G.I.s berserk in Kitakyushu when Tomosuke was a kid.

I hadn't had much experience with *shochu* in those days, except to know that it gave off a powerful odor reminiscent of kerosene and tasted like I supposed kerosene must taste. But the rough edges got quickly smoothed over with repeated toasts: to eternal friendship between Japan and the United States, to our hosts' very good health, to the prosperity of the village now and in generations to come, and so on and so forth.

There were a half-dozen of us in that little room, including three of Ichiro's bachelor farmer pals, who occupied a corner where they sat smiling down at the *tatami* and stealing the occasional peek at the big foreigner. As the party pelted ahead, and one bottle of *shochu* led to the next, the questions came thick and fast . . .

"Can you use chopsticks?"

"Do they grow rice in America?"

"What will you do for sex tonight?"

Ah, I beg your pardon? The question about sex caught me off guard, but Ichiro was only too happy to explain. He and his friends were simple country people, he said, but everybody knew that *gaijin* had famously unquenchable sexual appetites. They'd seen it on TV. So what did I have in mind? The bashful farmers looked up from the *tatami* with clinical interest.

"Well, ah, nothing, I guess. I'm pretty tired you know, and . . ." I said through Tomosuke, who by this time was so thoroughly enjoying my encounter with the real Japan that he was having trouble keeping a straight face.

It was then Ichiro had a brainstorm. There just happened to be a young woman who worked at the village telephone exchange, a real peach, he said, as he sucked his teeth behind a wolfish grin. The bachelor farmers eagerly nodded.

"These poor guys are so desperate," Tomosuke cried, the laughter now swallowing his words. In spite of the large volume of *shochu* that had gone down the pipe, however, I was beginning to feel edgy, as Ichiro continued to press his point, growing tongue-tied as he sang the praises of the telephone lady. Even though neither Ichiro nor his friends had apparently worked up the courage to ask her out on a date, her tastes appeared to be well known.

The telephone lady liked foreigners, Ichiro made a point of saying, as the bachelors grinned wickedly at the *tatami*.

How did he know that? All Japanese women liked foreigners, Ichiro said. In fact, they vastly preferred them to Japanese men. He said this without a hint of the envy or anger you got when the topic arose in Tokyo. Foreigners were big and handsome, something like prized bulls, from the sound of it, and it was natural women like the telephone operator wanted them.

The next thing I knew, somebody had fetched an old-fashioned dial phone on a long twisty cord, and Ichiro was on the line with the telephone lady. Though his face was still beet-red, he suddenly seemed very sober. It's been a long time now, of course, but I remember a conversation that went something like this:

"Hello!" Ichiro said. "We have a big foreigner staying here! An American!" This was followed by an awkward pause, after which Ichiro added, "He is very big and very handsome!"

Having exhausted this tantalizing line of chatter, Ichiro handed me the receiver. The boys looked on expectantly, as if waiting for me to say something absolutely devastating. Instead, I said, "Hello?"

A pleasant, lilting voice at the other end of the line said, in standard Japanese, "Konban wa" ("Good evening").

"How are you?" I replied. In a panic, I'd reverted to speaking Japanese like a woman, meaning overly courteous and dainty for a male speaker.

"I'm very well, thank you. And you?"

"I'm well, thank you," I said, venturing boldly, "You have a nice village."

"Thank you."

"Well, good-night."

I hung up and handed the phone back to Ichiro. He apparently hadn't noticed the preceding half-minute of abject stuttering and stammering because he asked, hopefully, if the telephone lady was coming. I said I didn't think so.

Ichiro and the boys were crestfallen and tried to puzzle out the mystery of the woman's lack of interest. It was pretty clear they felt they'd failed in their duty to satisfy the imagined whims of an honored foreign guest. My guess was then and remains to this day that they honestly thought they were doing all this for me.

At that point the resourceful Ichiro had one more inspired idea. "Listen," he said, as he raised his right hand, closed the fingers into a loose fist, and proceeded to pump it up and down as if milking a cow. "Why don't we all, well, you know . . ."

In spite of my *shochu*-induced stupor, I quickly got his gist. Not knowing whether to be offended or scared witless—I was a little of both—I said, "Oyasumi nasai" ("Good-night"), and did a kind of backstroke across the *tatami* mats and into the room next door where Ichiro's mom had laid out my futon. Pulling the covers over my head, I fell into a sex-free oblivion.

Next morning I was awakened before dawn by a sharp poke in the ribs and found myself staring at a stooped, gargoyle-like figure peering back at me in the crepuscular light. It was the anti-American granny. Working her gums and talking to herself, she circled my futon, probing my body with her cane and mumbling, "I wonder if the big foreigner is still alive."

It was a reasonable question. My head felt large and explosive, and the viscous film that coated the inside of my mouth did indeed taste combustible. In no condition to deal with the gumming granny, I played dead and after a few minutes she went away. To this day, the olfactory memory of *shochu* makes my stomach roll. On the other hand, Tomosuke's campaign to get me hooked on the eccentricities of the real Japan proved as addictive as opium and it became a standard part of my way of looking at the world.

Two decades later, when my story appeared in the pages of the *Geographic* as "Kyushu: Japan's Southern Gateway," a self-appointed cultural watchdog of the type Tomosuke had long-ago sought to rescue me from—this one a foreigner, presumably an American, who had lived in Kyushu but now lived in Colorado—took me to task in a letter to the editor:

> ... The author opens with an admission of hitchhiking in the mountains. Hitchhiking is not looked upon as a proper activity in Japan, where even remote villages are well served by inexpensive transportation. Some of us make diligent efforts to conform to Japan's unique social codes; for example, open urination by a roadway is acceptable in a number of regions, but hitchhiking—never!"

Roadside urination notwithstanding, I must sharply disagree with the letter-writer's point of view. The job of the professional observer is not to mindlessly ape foreign ways but to understand why people occupying foreign parts behave and think the way they do. Limning eccentricity, wherever you find it, however you find it, is a wonderful way to pull a dutiful issue forward without putting your audience dead asleep.

7

In 1993, when I returned to Kyushu for the *Geographic*, the island, with its soundless toilets and immaculate computer chip factories, had changed, but then so had I. For starters, I'd finally learned to listen. Coming to speak passable Japanese had helped; so had marrying into a Japanese family and putting in a decade working as a newsman in Tokyo. My ear was still far from perfect, mind you, but on a good day I could keep my mouth shut long enough to heed what my story was telling me.

Now, in the middle of my reporting month, what my story was saying was this: Unless I found a way to pull it together with a central metaphor, make of it what some long-form writers like to call a journey with a purpose, I'd end up with nothing but a collection of random anecdotes that would read with all the appeal of post-dated sashimi. Luckily I had a plan. I had persuaded Tomosuke, by now a busy, popular outdoor writer and essayist, to join me in Kyushu so we could retrace our long-ago travels. My goal was to compare two sets of reporterly snapshots, then and now, and present the reader with a novel, road-level view of Japan.

We had agreed on a date to meet in Kumamoto in central Kyushu, but when Tomosuke didn't turn up I had no choice, in those pre-cell phone days, but to hole up in a sardine-tin hotel room waiting for the phone to ring. I passed the time by watching TV news coverage of the FBI's fiery siege of the Branch Davidian compound in Waco, Texas. The Japanese media was mesmerized by a shoot-out that jibed with Wild West stereotypes about America, and both the story and its coverage made for a grim, disheartening vigil.

When Tomosuke finally showed up the following afternoon, apologizing for his unexplained tardiness, he suggested we drop in on his elder brother, Yoshihiro, who lived in a village on the outskirts of the city. It was the place the brothers Noda had grown up after World War II, and it had seen big changes in recent years. There were lavish new golf courses. Tax revenues were booming. A big electronics factory had opened providing jobs for young people no longer interested in the hardships of rice farming. What would happen next?

I put that question to Yoshihiro when the three of us, sitting on his porch, watched the sun go down over fields of young rice plants that sloped gently toward the banks of the Kikusui River and the green hills beyond. A retired farmer, Yoshihiro had a turban of wispy white hair, a devilish twinkle in his eyes, and the tooth-sucking grin of the rural card. He prefaced his remarks by apologizing for his nonexistent English: "The war broke out and saved me from learning it," he said. He then suggested that the young folks who hadn't gone off to the big cities for jobs or schooling had lost a sense of direction and acted like zombies. Meanwhile, as I would note in my report, "The old folks, whose stories of village life were once the riveting source of entertainment and wisdom" couldn't compete with the proliferation of electronic games and TV. In the past, the stories that animated life had come not from without but from within:

*When Yoshihiro was a boy, he sat in the charcoal brazier's glow
and listened to tales of Kyushu's mighty warriors. Back then there
were people who remembered actually seeing the squat, bullet-
shaped Saigo Takamori and his rebel army, banners aflutter, when
it gathered on the banks of the Kikuchi River for its last ill-fated
charge on Kumamoto Castle, then a national army stronghold.*

Stirring as the old stories were, however, Yoshihiro was unsenti-
mental about the past. The plot of land where we now sat and
talked was the same place to which his parents had fetched the
family—eight children in all—after the American bombers had set
Kitakyushu on fire. Tomosuke was six; Yoshihiro already a teenager. Back then, Japanese villages could be spooky places, with "one
dark sake shop and a butcher," said Yoshihiro. Days were filled
with brute labor for young and old alike, and because labor was the
dominant measure of life, "Old people used to hang themselves
when they couldn't work any more."

I very much liked Yoshihiro and was sorry we'd somehow
missed meeting one another years before. In contrast to Tomosuke's soulful irony, his brother appeared more comfortable in his
skin, and the contrast made for a lively conversation. As we talked,
however, I thought I detected the contradiction that Yoshihiro was
now negotiating with himself. Still vigorous at sixty-seven, he was
a poster boy for what Kyushuans called *mokkosu*, the stubborn independence to which the locals attributed the fact that people in
Kyushu lived longer on average than almost anywhere else on the
planet. But as I paraphrased Yoshihiro's conundrum in my story:
"What good is a long life . . . if it ends in loneliness and boredom?"

At Yoshihiro's behest, we carried his riddle down the hill and
around the edge of his farm to Kikusui's impressive eldercare facil-
ity, where vacancies were hotly sought after. Yoshihiro had apparently arranged a tour:

*This was despite an unfortunate incident that had marred his
last visit there. An amateur entomologist, Yoshihiro was collecting*

fireflies from bushes near the home's entrance when he was mistaken by a lady resident for a nozoki, or Peeping Tom. The night had erupted in shouts and finger-pointing.

"Are you sure it was a mistake?" asked Tomosuke.

Yoshihiro guffawed. "Who in his right mind would want to peep a rest home?"

In spite of the mix-up, director Kunio Ikeda greeted us warmly, showing us the premises, which resembled a tasteful country inn.

Ikeda introduced us to the oldest resident, a sake-drinking, karaoke-singing 103-year-old woman with a squat, boulder-like build. She was proud of the fact that she had moved in only six months earlier when farm work had finally become too much for her. Shaking my hand in a muscular grip, she laughed and said, "You're an American! I'm a farmer's wife! Let's meet again after we're all dead!"

In an unconscious effort to forestall such an event, perhaps, I had become absorbed in the "Ten Secrets of a Long Life" that were posted on the wall in the big common room:

1. Little meat, many vegetables.
2. Little salt, much vinegar.
3. Little sugar, much fruit.
4. Little food, much chewing.
5. Little worry, much sleeping.
6. Little anger, much laughing.
7. Little clothing, much bathing.
8. Little talking, much doing.
9. Little concern for yourself, much for others.
10. Little riding, much walking.

It was right around then that I noticed that our tour was having a strange effect on Yoshihiro. His jokiness had suddenly disappeared and he grew quietly contemplative. I caught him staring out a window overlooking his acreage next door, smiling wistfully . . .

"If I were to donate that field to you," he said to Mr. Ikeda, "do you suppose I might get accepted here . . . you know, when the time comes?"

The director smiled. Perhaps he was remembering the night of the fireflies. "Thank you for coming," he said.

That evening the brothers Noda and I ate dinner at a frontier-style roadhouse belonging to a member of Tomosuke's extended retinue. A quiet, deputy sheriff–type, the man had created a backpackers' retreat—a series of cabins set in a patch of wild grass and flowering trees that looked more like the Hill Country of Texas than semirural Kyushu. The cabins were built from old electric utility poles and betrayed the faint perfume of creosote.

The proprietor pressed us to sample a glutinous cactus-nectar that he swore had cured him of a deadly intestinal cancer; it tasted appropriately medicinal, like drinking liquid hand soap, and the brothers Noda, I noticed, quickly switched to thimble-sized cups of sake. When the rice wine had sufficiently warmed the cockles, Yoshihiro sat tall on his stool and belted out a song he said he'd been forced to memorize in junior high school during the war against America. The lyrics mostly escape me now but I remember Yoshihiro's ramrod posture and the delightfully bouncy minor-key melody common to old Imperial Army ditties. It ended with the memorable punch line: "And you can tell your Mr. Roosevelt to go straight to hell!"

It was impossible not to be thoroughly charmed.

8

The next morning Tomosuke and I stood in the hotel lobby contemplating forward movement. We had planned to start hitchhiking early but there were new factors to consider. First, it was raining so hard that water pellets were ricocheting off the asphalt of the parking lot with the intensity of falling pachinko balls. Second, Yoshihiro had shown up unannounced with the roadhouse man, who waited out front in his shiny red SUV to give us a ride. In Yo-shihiro's view, two thuggish-looking *chunen*—middle-agers—like Tomosuke and me weren't likely to make it very far thumbing for rides on such a jagged morning.

Frankly, I would have expected Tomosuke to put up more of a fight in defense of rugged individualism. Instead, he looked at the sky, looked at the SUV, and shrugged his shoulders. "Okay," he said, "we'll call it hitchhiking by chauffeur."

We drove through Kumamoto's morning rush hour and, after many gassy starts and stops, began inching up the high Kumamo-to Plain, still in bumper-to-bumper traffic. We were headed for a mountain pass that traversed the great hump of volcanic Mount Aso and connected Kumamoto with Takachiho, a sleepy little tour-ist town that, according to local legend, marked the spot where the grandson of the sun goddess Amaterasu descended to earth from the High Plain of Heaven to lay the foundations for Japan's impe-rial family.

This area, so windswept and rustic when Tomosuke and I had come this way in 1974 that it was derisively referred to as the Tibet of Japan, was now bursting with fast-food restaurants, new tract housing, car dealerships, convenience stores, and tourist traps dis-guised as American-style roadhouses with signage, in English, like "Welcome to Indian Village." It was as if the former farms and paddy fields had been absorbed into some kind of haphazard Old West–style theme park. At that point I had no idea I would be living in Austin, Texas, twelve years hence, but was nonetheless interest-ed to discover that American culture, in its cowboy-western form, had so firmly planted its image deep in the heart of Kyushu.

As we crawled up the mountain, the massive, shadowed-filled caldera loomed off to our right. Observing the scene in brooding silence, Tomosuke appeared to be making a quick trip to the exis-tential crossroads, and the source of the problem wasn't hard to di-agnose. By now he had become something of a cult hero in Japan. Touted as the country's premier kayak adventurer, his stories of far-flung travel, in Japan and around the world, had special appeal for the repressed spirits locked inside frustrated office workers who were, in turn, locked inside routine, dead-end jobs. His books sold like hotcakes and led to his appearance in nationwide TV promotions for ramen noodles.

In sum, he owed his public popularity to the booming demand among ordinary Japanese for leisure activities that the country's prosperity had made possible. And of course it was precisely what that same prosperity had done to change Japan that Tomosuke most hated.

When I helpfully drew the contradiction to his attention, he said he knew he was being paradoxical and selfish but he couldn't help it. "I want the thing that's gone missing," he said in way that was both rueful and rather poetic, I thought. Tomosuke's goal in writing, as he saw it, was to fill a need in his fellow Japanese to know that, somewhere, life pastured in older, simpler, unrushed ways—even if the pasturing for most Japanese was a purely mental exercise. As we drove, he continued to cast a gloomy eye on all he surveyed.

But the good traveler quickly self-corrects, and soon enough Tomosuke shifted his mood so he could focus himself on our mission: finding our way back to the village where the good-hearted Ichiro had once held us hostage to the telephone lady's siren call while pouring firewater down my gullet. When Tomosuke had suggested it over dinner the night before, I was all for returning to the scene of the crime. I had but one demand. Under no circumstances would the setting of the sun find us anywhere near the village of the gumming granny or umbilical Takachiho.

Call me superstitious, but there was something about the general vicinity that creeped me out. True, our experience with Ichiro and the boys hadn't qualified as true rural gothic—no farm animals had been forced on us, for example. Still, the weird night in the hills had been followed by another bad one in Takachiho where we stayed in a depressing hole while I battled the black dog of my *shochu* hangover. When I shared my reservations with Tomosuke, he chuckled at the memory but understood: We would stay well clear of Takachiho, he promised.

On we went, rolling up the mountain and down the other side, when the roadhouse man suddenly turned off the highway, bucketed down a washboard-rough stretch of road, and we found ourselves back in Kugino Village. How Tomosuke had managed to remember the name after all those years was something of a miracle, but the thrill at being back in town was a fleeting one. Absolutely nothing about the place matched up with our memories. The big mysterious farmhouse (on whose low-hanging beams my head had played the xylophone while I searched the night for a toilet—the trauma was still sharp) was nowhere to be found. It had presumably gone the way of the newer prefab jobs that proliferated in the countryside.

The clearest sign of progress was a new culinary institute for the study of buckwheat noodles where a gaggle of day-tripping school kids, girls in pink aprons, the boys in blue, gathered around a big circular counter to try their dough-stuck fingers at the making of soba. Even the art of noodle making had gone from homespun necessity to a gentrified tourist attraction. Somewhere, I thought wistfully, the toothless old granny of yesteryear was rotating in her grave.

Nostalgia duly quenched, Yoshihiro said we had better return to the highway on the Kumamoto side of the mountain so Tomosuke and I could find a decent place to stay the night. Then for no good reason, we reversed course a second and a third time like a bunch of dithering old farts. It was very strange, as if in trying to avoid Takachiho we were being inexorably drawn to it. When we changed course a fourth time, the sun was almost down, our stomachs were growling, and I said to hell with it: Superstition is a luxury and sometimes you can't afford it. So there we were, exactly where I didn't want to be, sitting in a diner in Takachiho eating insipid Mongolian hotpot served up by a sneering waitstaff. The level of hostility was really quite remarkable for Japan. Whatever happened to the old saying "Okyakusama wa kamisama desu"—or the customer is not just king, as we say in the West, but a god? Apparently the restaurant had not received the memo.

Okay, I thought, so Takachiho is having its little cosmic joke. Our pissy reception was one of those tests a place inflicts on travelers, and once we showed we could take it in stride all would be well. After a liberal dose of sake, Tomosuke shared my optimism. He grandly instructed the roadhouse man to deliver us to the best hotel in town where we would rest in lordly comfort. When he rolled us to a stop in front of the hotel, however, I grew concerned: The edifice was oddly backlit, like something from the pages of a Stephen King novel.

Still tipsy from dinner, Tomosuke ordered a modest Japanese-style room for himself but he insisted, absurdly, on a large Western-style one for me. The deskman said they had only one such room, a two-room suite, actually. It wasn't used much but I was welcome to it. Taking a Western-style room in a hotel geared to the Japanese-style is nearly always a mistake. But I didn't want to embarrass Tomosuke in front of the hotel staff, so I followed the bellman up the elevator and down a musty corridor. When he flung back a door on my accommodations, I gasped.

The large dust-laced sitting room was decorated with floral curtains, flying saucer lamps, and a crazy wallpaper pattern straight from the 1950s. The bedroom, dark and narrow, seemed downright demonic. But as I've said before, you make the best of things when you have no choice, and so I was readying myself for bed, vigorously brushing my teeth and trying to take my mind off my surroundings, when I noticed there was no *sekken*, or soap, in the bathroom. I rang the front desk. In spite of still being reasonably fluent in the Japanese basics, however, I couldn't for the life of me make myself understood. It was like being stuck in the subtitles of an old *Twilight Zone* episode—foreign visitor, urgent need to communicate, confronts perverse locals who insist on treating him as if he were speaking gibberish. It's possible that I was getting carried away with myself.

When I finally fell into an exhausted sleep, I had a troubling dream that Toshiko, abandoned in New York, was in physical danger and roaming the streets of a dark, graphic-novel city in need of help. I awoke in a cold sweat and immediately phoned home to confirm that the trouble was all in my head. It was. Toshiko assured me that all was well and instructed me to suck it up and get on with my reporting. She was right, of course—just as I had been right about steering clear of Takachiho, my private Bermuda Triangle. Once again, I'd found myself at Japan's mythological navel, distraught at the dawn, and eager to blow town, this time for good.

Don't get me wrong. What I said earlier still goes: If you want to know what makes a place tick, by all means go there, live in it, and put up with its hijinks. You'll come away with a moveable template you can apply and adapt to the world's other places and, by comparing and contrasting, make better sense out of them. Be forewarned, however, that a few places will have it in for you. I don't pretend to understand it, but for me smiling, sensuous Bangkok, beloved by generations of foreign correspondents, is one such place; harmless, touristy little Takachiho is another; any bed and breakfast in the fifty United States, particularly with easy access to local antique stores, would come in a close third.

<h1 style="text-align:center">9</h1>

Tomosuke and I eventually hitched and rambled our way south to Kagoshima. The city where we'd once holed up in that gynecological clinic en route to our rendezvous with the ancient mixed bathers of Yakushima was now Tomosuke's newly adopted hometown, and his rising fortunes had churned up new wonders. For one thing, there was an elegant apartment overlooking the bay that, as I wrote in my story, "bespoke a lifestyle more commonly associated with California dreaming than the *usagi goya*, or rabbit hutches, that Tomosuke had occupied all the years I had known him." The view really was lovely:

> *Behind us rose conical Shiroyama, the city's hilltop monument to Saigo Takamori, where, in 1877, the old warrior had slit his belly in ritual suicide rather than surrender to Tokyo's hated minions.*

From the balcony I could see the blue sweep of the bay, where a fleet of eight-man shells from Kagoshima University raced over the cresting waves, shouting as they went, while in the background volcanic Sakurajima glowered and belched.

Tomosuke was now free to indulge his weakness for offbeat pets, which explained the presence of Akio, a large white duck that inhabited the *furoba*, the tub room, and so fiercely defended his territory as to make it impossible for humans to bathe or shower. There was also the sudden appearance one night of an attractive young woman easily thirty years Tomosuke's junior. The knock came at the door while we were watching Tomosuke's all-time favorite movie, *Zorba the Greek*, on videocassette. (The film reminded him, he said, of our early friendship—he in the Zorba role, naturally, and me as the callow young foreigner who still had to learn, as Zorba says, "A man needs a little madness, or else . . . he never dares cut the rope and be free"; Tomosuke's interpretation, as far as it went, wasn't wrong.)

The woman was still there in the morning, puttering around the kitchen, fixing bacon and eggs to Tomosuke's exacting standards while glassy-eyed with sleep I studied the bay's smoking volcano. I ate my eggs, asked no questions, and nursed dark thoughts about how to evict that stupid duck from the bathroom so I could wash up. In a spectacular accident with the bidet, which revealed the dark side of Japanese toilet makers' plans for world conquest, I pushed the wrong button and inadvertently redecorated the wallpaper in the stylish WC. In other words, life was unpredictable, but not in a bad way, and almost like old times.

Typically, though, I was nervous about not logging in enough interviews for my story, so one afternoon Tomosuke and I paid a call at the local TV station where the news director, Koji Nakamura, gave me a spirited, Kyushu-direct briefing on what he saw as big changes in the wind for Japan and its historically repressed, renegade island. Japan had indeed been a rigged game centered on Tokyo, but now that was changing and the question seemed to be how fast or slow. As I summed it up in the magazine:

Ordinary citizens were finally demanding a say in the issues that affected their lives: Why they were obliged to pay some of the industrialized world's highest prices for groceries, for example, or to live in some of its tawdriest housing.

Deregulating and decentralizing, Japan might finally succeed in prying open its clam-like economy—to the benefit of both Japanese consumers and chronically irritated trading partners, including the United States. "The makeover might take years," Koji warned. But when it came—if it came—it would move from the outside in— from places like free-and-easy Kagoshima, not bureaucratically infarcted Tokyo.

For an example of the new pluralism, Koji volunteered, "Look at Mr. Noda here."

I looked. Somehow, I had never thought of Tomosuke, who was dressed in an ancient T-shirt bulging with the unmistakable contours of middle age, as a symbolic figure. Still, I had to admit that he did represent a sort of quirky triumph of personal predilection over the forces of organization and control, and I made the mistake of saying so.

Tomosuke smiled smugly. After all, it had only taken me 20 years to figure out what he and every other Kyushuan had always taken as gospel: Given their due, there was no telling where the people of the south, with their fire and fight, might eventually lead themselves and the rest of Japan as well.

So that was my story and everything worked out fine—I had followed my nose to the places where the old Kyushu met the new Kyushu and, with Tomosuke's help, had wrapped it into a journey with a purpose. Mission accomplished, more or less. As time passed, though, I realized I had proved to be as adept at predicting the future as most journalists; I had caught the mood of the place at the time but turned out being largely wrong about the results.

Yes, ordinary Japanese citizens were realizing they had to take more individual responsibility for their communities and their environment, and couldn't rely on a bloated political system that was chronically failing them. In the end, however, the deep bite of

Tomosuke Noda, Lord of the Bath, southern Kyushu, 1993.
Photo by Michael Yamashita.

Japan's recession meant there would be relatively little real change from the outside in, at least in terms of how power was wielded and by whom. Tokyo would remain far and away the country's biggest single concentration of political muscle, wealth, and population. Learning to listen to the story, as it turns out, doesn't protect you from misinterpreting what you hear or letting yourself get ahead of the evidence.

Tomosuke, on the other hand, continued to successfully decentralize his life, ultimately amplifying his cult status by dropping out of sight. He moved from Kagoshima to the hills of Shikoku, the smallest of Japan's four main islands, and by the start of the new millennium I'd lost touch with the man who had taught me to look at the real Japan and try to see what was really there.

REIMAGINING
TOKYO BAY

1

Photographer Mike Yamashita and I got the nod to report a story on greater Tokyo in the spring of 2001 and I should have been over-joyed. I had lived there, man and boy, for nearly thirteen years be-fore moving to New York City in the mid-1980s. Tokyo was the city of my young adulthood, where I'd learned my trade; met, fell in love with, and married my wife, Toshiko; and acquired an extended and generous Japanese family.

So why was I having such a hard time getting stoked? I may have nursed misgivings about overplaying the forces of change in my Kyushu story a few years earlier, but the real answer, I think, is that Tokyo had imposed on me a kind of writer's block—I'd talked and written and talked and written about it from so many different an-gles over the years that I wondered what more I could possibly say.

In other words, I was being lazy. Challenging work is a privilege and, as the saying goes, when there's no wind you grab the oars and row. So I told myself to stop stewing and get busy, and immediately when I dug into the latest news clippings, I realized how dunder-headed I'd been: The Tokyo of the new millennium was quite un-like the Tokyo of the seventies, eighties, or even early nineties I had known so well. I'd forgotten that places and their stories, like the people who tell them, change over time, and thus story and story-teller are almost always meeting on new ground.

Tokyo had always been a formidable shape-shifter. The city had built and rebuilt itself many times over the decades, ever expand-ing its orbit. And thus, it dawned on me, Tokyo's story had to grow

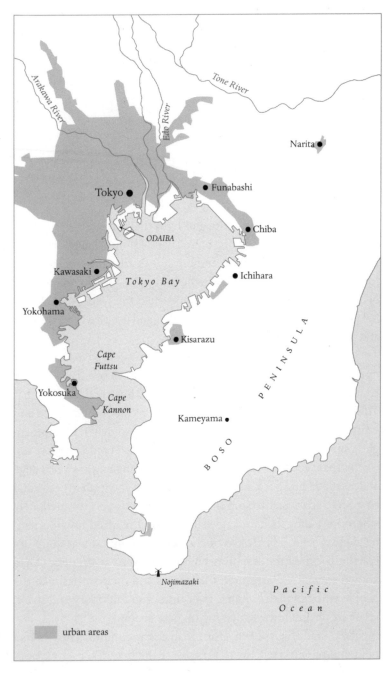

Tokyo Bay.

organically from the city's history of earthquakes, fires, and World War II devastation. That very cycle of destruction and rebirth had shaped an urban psyche that helped make all the transformation possible. Japan's ballyhooed recession notwithstanding, Tokyo seemed to keep on growing and changing, and frustrating those who dreamed of breaking its hold on national life. My problem would not be *what* to write but how to boil it all down into the thirty-five hundred words or so that eventually appeared in the magazine in October of 2002 as "Tokyo Bay."

While still at home in New York, I was wondering how I could bring to life that all-important central theme of impulse and de-struction when serendipity struck. I was reminded, for whatever reason, of my boyhood crush on Tokyo's King of the Monsters, Godzilla. Like many kids growing up in America in the 1950s, I'd been hypnotized by the sci-fi movies that were the rage of the age, shot through as they were with titillating subtextual anxieties about mass annihilation that World War II and the atomic bomb-ings of Hiroshima and Nagasaki had churned up, and my pals and I devoured the flickering black-and-white images and primitive spe-cial effects, agog and agape.

Who knows how a writer's mind works? Not me. (Even that formidable man of letters Saul Bellow said of the act of writing: "I don't know exactly how it's done. I let it alone a good deal.") But I do know that we disregard the pure fascination and curiosity of our early youth at our peril, and, luckily, the image of Godzilla came to me out of the past like a shot of adrenaline. Crazy as it sounds, I could now see the Tokyo Bay story—through the lens of Godzilla. As I wrote in my proposal for the editors:

> Not since Godzilla made his splash in the movies by rampag-ing from the waters of Tokyo Bay 50 years ago has the thumb-shaped body of water and its shoreline loomed so large in the imaginations of so many Japanese. Years of aggressive land reclamation have resulted in a massive man-made urban plat-form that rims the bay with glistening new state-of-the-art

"smart" buildings and enticing high-tech entertainment attractions (including the world's first theme park oriented exclusively toward women and its longest indoor ski slope). Neatly embracing the quiet hubris of modern Japan, Tokyo Bay encapsulates the Japanese belief that planning can make it perfect—that urban sprawl, however vast, can not only be made to work but be profitable, livable and fun into the bargain . . .

One day I was on the phone to Tokyo, talking to my old friend Hideko Takayama, a panoramically accomplished journalist who had agreed to help me set up interviews, when I made a lame joke about how great it would be to talk to Godzilla for the story.

"Do you want to interview him?" Hideko asked.

"Who?" I said.

"Godzilla!" she shot back. It just so happened that among her many contacts was the actor who had played the iconic monster in a number of the films. He taught sword fighting in a Tokyo dojo to make ends meet when he wasn't acting in bit parts in samurai dramas on TV. Mainly, Hideko said, he was a voluble, quirky guy who marched to his own beat—a sort of sword-wielding Tomosuke Noda in samurai get-up.

How could I refuse? One thing led to another, and soon enough I was suspended in a cable car over Tokyo Bay interviewing the monster of my youth. It was a bit of shtick of course, and started as a lark—maybe it would find a place in the final story, I thought, but probably not. It wound up being the lede:

Locked in a tiny Ferris wheel gondola, whirling high above the steely waters of Tokyo Bay, I realized I'd made a mistake asking Godzilla along for the ride. "One swish of my tail," snarled the famous movie monster as he clawed the air, "and that bridge over there is toast!" Seeing as how "Godzilla," an actor named Kenpachiro Satsuma, had earned his living playing the terror of Tokyo Bay, trampling soundstage replicas in a rubber lizard suit, I'd expected an insider's insight into this body of water at the heart of Japan's biggest megalopolis. But instead Kenpachiro grew strangely agitated as we revolved skyward, the bay's overbuilt shoreline fanning out before us like an unruly board game.

"Zzzzsssssttttt!" he hissed, like the afterburner on a jet engine, his eyes eerily agleam. "This is Godzilla's exact line of sight," he declared as we hit the top of the giant Ferris wheel, which at 377 feet was only slightly higher than the mythical monster was tall.

"Hey, I smashed all those buildings down there in my last movie," he huffed, indignantly scanning the horizon. "What're they doing back there?"

Like many residents of the bay area, Kenpachiro was understandably disoriented. In recent years a construction boom has transformed the landscape, and now costly new ornaments—a glitzy hotel or world-class aquarium here, a convention center or two there—mingle with older and more familiar factories, smokestacks, and oil storage tanks. In fact, ever since Kenpachiro's predecessor, Godzilla number one, made his splash on the big screen back in 1954 by rampaging from these waters, the bay area has played the lead role in Japan's rise to stardom. Today its five main cities (Tokyo, Yokohama, Kawasaki, Funabashi, and Chiba) and four encompassing prefectures (Kanagawa, Saitama, Tokyo, and Chiba) anchor the planet's number two economy, after the United States. The center, as the Japanese call Tokyo, and its satellite cities account for nearly a quarter of the country's people and a third of its wealth, dominating its politics, arts, commerce, and communications.

Throughout Japan's steep, brilliant climb from the devastation of World War II, the bay worked like a powerful magnet, pulling in millions of people from around the country, providing them new jobs and new lifestyles. Thirty years ago Kenpachiro came here chasing his dream of becoming an actor but wound up working in one of the area's steel mills, jockeying around molten buckets of iron in front of a blazing blast furnace. His big break came when he got a call to try out for Godzilla.

"The director needed somebody who could work in that hot rubber suit without passing out," Kenpachiro confided.

But as Godzilla and I spun through the silvery air above the waterfront, old dreams were under siege. Japan's deepest postwar economic slump, now a dozen years old, had left the bay area awash in a rising tide of bad debt, busted companies, and lost jobs. Even Godzilla was out of work. Nowadays movie monsters are computer-generated products of special effects studios. "I hate that," Kenpachiro growled.

When it came time to write my story, I tried out various ledes but Godzilla kept harassing me because, in its quirky way, Kenpachiro's tongue-in-cheek ill temper captured the story's dominant mood: anger. Indeed, popular ire over the country's systemic failures in coming to grips with its political and economic challenges was as much a part of the new Tokyo as its frenetic overbuilding. The formula that had once seemed to make Japan invincible and fueled its dramatic rise in postwar living standards was in trouble, and the citizens of greater Tokyo felt confused and betrayed. As I put it in my story . . .

Despite all the flashy new construction the bay had become a breeding ground of disillusionment. "Look at Tokyo Bay, especially at night, and it looks exactly like New York City," said novelist Koji Suzuki, whose macabre bestseller, The Ring, *is set against the backdrop of the bay. "After the war, becoming like New York was our vision of the future. But now that we've reached the future, are we satisfied? It doesn't feel like it."*

2

Koji Suzuki was talking specifically about Odaiba, a reclaimed piece of land in Tokyo Bay that I found particularly impressive if only because it turned my sense of the city inside out:

In the dozen years I'd lived in the bay area this 1,110-acre island had been an empire of weeds and warehouses known as Landfill Number 13. But Japan's boom times of the late 1980s—the infamous "bubble economy"—set the stage for the transformation of Odaiba into an outpost of ultramodern office buildings, lofty condos, and sleek techno-pop amusement centers. There was even a waterfront replica of the Statue of Liberty.

Indeed, visiting Odaiba reminded me of standing on the promenade in Brooklyn Heights and looking back on a newer, sleeker version of Manhattan—the glass-and-steel spires of the world's richest metropolis, Tokyo, booming into the ozone of a brilliant day. The perspective was so dramatically different from what I remembered, in fact, that I could hardly believe this was the same city where I'd once struggled against that chronic case of urban claustrophobia.

Tomosuke did not share my enthusiasm. "Fake, all fake," he muttered as he looked up from his work—he was methodically assembling a big two-man sea kayak to take us on a waterline tour. But from the way he hummed along under his breath with a xylophone rendition of "Zippity Do-Dah" or whatever it was tinkling from speakers posted at precise intervals up and down the picture-perfect boardwalk, I could tell he was getting into it. And sure enough, when he looked up again, swiveling his head to take in the pleasant bight of beach with its jetty-sheltered cove, pellucid water, and an unblemished and uniformly white sandy bottom, he had to grudgingly concede: "Okay, unnatural nature. Not bad."

Japan might have become overly concentrated in Tokyo, but Tomosuke, now living the decentralized life in Shikoku, had more or less stopped answering his phone or responding to e-mail. Old friends had started referring to him as "the Hermit." Run to ground by the intrepid Hideko, however, Tomosuke agreed to come all the way up to Tokyo, determined to show me, among other things, how he'd brought the recreational sport of kayaking out of the hinterlands and into the hip heart of the big city.

I was helping Tomosuke stretch the heavy canvas skin over the kayak's aluminum skeleton, when a young man on a bicycle rolled to a stop in front of us. His jaunty polo shirt and preppy slacks belied a badge that identified him as a minor city official. Boating wasn't permitted here, he said, smiling blandly and without introduction.

Why not?

"It's dangerous," said the official.

I know a professional journalist should avoid getting too involved in a story lest he or she lose perspective. And, yes, I did say earlier that the long-distance reporter should strive to be a fly on the wall, not a thorn in the side. Sometimes, though, there's just no getting around it. So for the official's benefit, I pointed out a group of kids horsing around at the water's edge.

"That kid just threw a rock into the water," I said. "Isn't that dangerous too?"

"Well, he didn't throw it *at* anybody," the man said, lamely, as he looked down at his shoes and smiled. When Tomosuke, still bent over his work, ignored him, the official restated his message that boating was not permitted, under the impression perhaps that the raffish-looking older gentleman fitting out his kayak might be hard of hearing.

Suddenly Tomosuke reared up, as if from a great depth, a vein bulging in the center of his forehead. "What about the windsurfers?" he asked in a tone that was dangerously even. He was referring to three men in wet suits who were slicing merrily through the waveless waters of the cove not a hundred yards away.

"Windsurfing *is* permitted," said the official. "It is boating that is not permitted." He spoke politely but slowly, as if explaining the rules to a moron.

Tomosuke stared at the man. "You've got to be fair," he said sharply, but of course Tomosuke was wrong. All the official had to do, in the time-honored way of the Japanese official, was to explain what wasn't permitted—in this case, no swimming, no fishing, and *no kayaking*. Nothing except the mysterious windsurfing.

Tomosuke suspected a political payoff on behalf of what he imagined to be a windsurfing lobby, and said so. He then lectured the official on old-fashioned feudal arrogance, a protest for democratic transparency that was taking on the trappings of a samurai drama. Behind us, our loyal retainers, the guys from a local sporting goods store, stood by, snorting derisively and kicking at the sand. But the bureaucrat didn't budge.

"I'm sorry," the man said, mustering a mirthless smile that was old when the mighty shogun of Tokyo set up an artillery battery here on Odaiba to ward off interlopers 150 years before. "It's a matter that has been decided."

Tomosuke chuckled sardonically. Did he give a hoot about what had been decided? Not a bit. Vexed by years of bureaucratic fiat that had favored the bay's powerful industries and moneyed interests over the interests of its ordinary citizens, he turned on the callow, just-following-orders official and yelled, "You're like a pig! You're not a human being!"

The official blanched but stood his ground, and from the way that vein on Tomosuke's forehead was visibly throbbing now, I thought a little comic relief might be in order. So I jumped into our kayak, grabbed an oar, and began stroking furiously while being careful not to disturb the sand, which I reasonably assumed would be included on the list of banned activities.

Tomosuke and the official stopped and stared at me. I asked the official if there was any regulation against dry-land kayaking? Temporarily out of rules, he wracked his brain and then fired off his coup de grace: He couldn't think of any, but if we wanted to take a photo of dry-land kayaking, he said, there would be a fee for that.

Tomosuke tilted his head back and laughed at the absurdity of the thing. But of course nobody got to go kayaking, not then and not later.

3

Tokyo's churlish new mood extended to urban planners, environmentalists, and politicians who were engaged in a running argument about the physical contours of the bay's future. Perhaps the most startling—some would say outrageous—new ideas were contained in a plan conceived by prominent architect Kisho Kurokawa:

> *It calls for scooping up the polluted muck that lines the seabed and using it to create a huge central island covering as much as a third of the bay's surface area. Theoretically the massive structure would also ease Tokyo's population jam by providing living space for up to a third of the city's 12 million people. "The average citizen," Kurokawa says as a part of his promotional pitch, could have "a house—with a yacht harbor attached."*
>
> *Staring at me confidently through tortoiseshell glasses, Kurokawa declared, "I will save the environment."*
>
> *Leading environmentalists hotly disagree, arguing that such massively engineered solutions smack of the same postwar hubris that brought on the bay's ecological woes. When I raised Kurokawa's plan with Toshio Furota, a marine biologist, the genial professor raised his fists and said, "I'm ready to fight."*

It was a good thing somebody was ready to put up their dukes because so many other Tokyoites seemed to have lost interest. On our day of Godzilla, Hideko and I spent the afternoon with Kenpachiro parading around futuristic Odaiba. When the actor wasn't wearing his rubber lizard suit for a photo session with Mike, he was dressed in a samurai's black kimono with a cell phone dangling from a cord around his neck in lieu of the traditional long and short swords at the waist. The funny thing was that none of the hundreds of young people walking the shopping arcades or hotel lobbies gave him a second look, which appeared to irk him no end. He was a Tokyo samurai dropped into an Odaiba food court and nobody seemed the slightest bit interested.

Over lunch Godzilla bit back. Japan's affluence had created a postmodern kind of monster (his word), Kenpachiro said, in which kids "want to become famous but they don't do the preparation. Instead of educating them, everything is put into what they desire." As a result, he went on, "Japan is losing its important sense of values now. Look at the young Japanese family. Kids don't take their fathers seriously. No respect. The entire nation is in a vicious cycle of pampering its children."

That evening Kenpachiro invited us to join him for a drink in an outdoor eatery on the edge of the city's fashionable Ginza district and we got a look at the flip side of the Japanese dream. The yakitori stall, located under a train trestle up the street from the stately Imperial Hotel, gave an impression of viewing the high life from inside a cave. Sitting around us at the cheap plastic tables was a cohort of Japan's ubiquitous "salarymen," or white-collar workers. Alone or in pairs, their collars undone and neckties askew, it was hard not to feel for them. The country's brisk march to postwar prominence, from dead in the water in 1945 to the world's juggernaut economy of the 1970s and 1980s, had come to such an abrupt halt that its long-suffering foot soldiers seemed to be in a state of complete befuddlement. Collectively estranged from their wives and kids as they often were by a pattern of long hours of dutiful work at the office, their by no means inconsequential sacrifices now seemed brutally devalued.

No stranger to my own middle-age grumbling, I was nonetheless suspicious of Kenpachiro's carping about Japan's broken social formula, and so I invited the daughter of an old friend to tea. A bright, stylish young woman in her mid-twenties, she surprised me by agreeing with Kenpachiro about the widening generation gap. She loved and respected her father and so it hurt that her friends were openly contemptuous of theirs. They complained their dads were, in essence, unclean—smelling of tobacco and dirty socks. It was the ultimate put-down in a culture where age-old Shinto traditions of ritual purification still put a high premium on personal hygiene and cleanliness.

Thus had the recession, by pulling at the seams of the old order, brought about a society split in a way I'd never seen before. On the bright side, you had perhaps the world's most fashion-conscious, fastidious country, in which people lunched and shopped, and kids texted and grooved to music on their mp3 players. On the other hand, you had members of one of the most successful economic armies in the history of the world being openly disparaged by those enjoying the lifestyles their work had made possible. My young friend agreed it was an odd and painful situation; her friends said their fathers stank and they didn't want to even look at them.

After that, my reporting refined itself into following a fairly straightforward course. I would search out people who could tell me about how they'd been affected by the big changes buffeting life in greater Tokyo and to what extent these changes were affecting the strict social pecking order on which Japan's successes had been built. One bright Sunday morning that pursuit led me to the people living in a neighborhood of cardboard boxes down by the Sumida River, Tokyo's storied old waterway . . .

Near the coffee-colored river's confluence with the bay, I spied dozens of men and women scuttling in and out of neat, boxlike structures. Squatter's camps were all but invisible when I lived in Tokyo, so I stopped and asked a muscular, well-spoken man what had landed him here.

"I lost my job in a metal pressing plant," said Sadao Yamashita, 38, offering me his only chair. When rent money ran out, he'd built his box—roughly eight feet long and five feet high—from scraps scavenged at building sites. Inside there was an alarm clock, a cassette tape player, and neat piles of clothing.

"My father worked for the same company for 35 years," said Yamashita, but Japan's vaunted 'permanent employment' system had failed people like him. Still, Yamashita felt lucky. Though homeless for now, he had just landed work at an express delivery company for 175,000 yen (about $1,400) a month, not plush in high-priced Japan but enough to get by on.

Prosperous bay residents had complained to me how their luxury condos had cratered in value since the slump began, but Yamashita wasn't bitter. "Passersby give us dirty looks," he said, but homelessness had taught him to live without fear of not fitting into Japan's conformist society.

"In Japan," he said, "it's always been one rule after another. But here I can be my own man."

4

Japan's well-deserved reputation as a stronghold of male privilege notwithstanding, the pace of change now so obvious in Tokyo seemed to be breaking in some positive ways for the city's females. Although absolute numbers were still comparatively low, more women were running for elective office. Equally important, it seemed to me, women were taking a lead in voicing public concerns about "soft" issues like education and the environment that had typically been sidelined by more "manly" policies favoring economic competitiveness.

Akiko Domoto, a women's rights advocate, former parliamentarian, and then-governor of Chiba Prefecture, told me that women and young people were aching for change and there were fewer impediments now that the old-boy network had begun fraying at the edges. The paradigm shift wasn't complete, of course; there was still plenty of discrimination against women. On the other hand, she said, "Young people are looking at their mothers and seeing how hard a life they're spending. They don't want the same thing."

I talked to many women—including OLs, or "office ladies," the female counterpart of the salaryman; business managers; high school students; and a popular poet—all of whom shared to a significant degree Domoto's rejection of the old-boy formula and the straitjacket of traditional gender roles. To try to convey that sea change in the limited space available in my article, I focused in part on Venus Fort, an upscale, gender-specific shopping mall on the

Tokyo waterfront that was then in the public eye and seemed to mingle a number of relevant themes . . .

Billed as a "theme park for ladies," its main concourse resembled an antiseptic Italy, whose upscale shops attract a new species of bay dweller—the parasaito shinguru, or parasite single. Mostly young women in their twenties and thirties, they generally live with their parents and seem intent on liberating themselves through conspicuous consumption.

"Is it getting dark in here?" I asked my appointed guide, Tamami Yamanaka, a young single with chic auburn hair. "Yes," she replied. "People buy more in the late afternoon," so a computer-driven "sky" in the high vaulted ceiling produces a new sunset every two hours. I was intrigued. Had sales data confirmed the sundown buying theory? "No," said Yamanaka, smiling. "I think the owner"—a man—"just heard it someplace."

Personally, Yamanaka thought Venus Fort's popularity stemmed from a potent shift in gender roles. For centuries survival in Japan's male bastion forced most women to focus on attracting a mate, but bad economic times cut deeply into the perks and power of the country's corporate samurai. As young women take up the slack, getting more and better paying jobs (though at salaries comparably lower than males), they are postponing marriage and rethinking their options.

"We women don't expect much from men today," Yamanaka said matter-of-factly. "But we do want to better ourselves." We had paused near a boutique called Accessory Creation Mix. Inside, customers pressed the counter, ordering cosmetics tailored to their skin's precise complexion. Did today's freer spirit connect with bigger ideas of feminism and equality? I asked. That might come later, said Yamanaka, but for now women were enjoying the gender jujitsu. "Men are good for taking you out to dinner," she said, "but in the future women will make the decisions."

5

Long ago brainwashed by Tomosuke's vision of the "real" Japan, I would never rely on the views of city folk alone, and so I had to see how far the urban malaise extended into the countryside. That meant hitchhiking into Chiba Prefecture, which occupies the Boso Peninsula, a swollen knuckle of land separating Tokyo Bay from the Pacific Ocean. Historically, the Japanese viewed Chiba in the way that Americans sometimes see New Jersey—an area maligned for its polluting industries, corrupting politics, and a challenging relationship with high culture. As one popular guidebook put it: "There are few compelling reasons to visit the area." But for a reporter there are always good reasons to do the exact opposite of what the guidebooks say . . .

> *Thus one brisk May morning I stood on the shoulder of Highway 16 on the eastern shore, marveling at the area's transformation. Twenty years ago this part of the prefecture had been as developmentally remote from Tokyo as rural Iowa is from New York City. Now it was peppered with video stores, pizza restaurants, tire dealerships, and places with fancy names like Pâtisserie à Chiba. Having spent the night in a dusty, mite-ridden inn, I was having mixed feelings about the progress of civilization here.*

I was also having mixed emotions about my traveling companion. I was grateful that Tomosuke had ventured north to join me in Chiba for what would be our third major hitchhiking ramble in thirty years. It became quickly apparent, however, that our dynamic Japanese-gaijin duo, which had worked together so well for so long, was now undergoing some midlife strain. In short, Tomosuke and I were bickering like an old married couple.

The previous evening he had sharply rebuked me for talking on my cell phone. "Your voice is too loud," he groused, mimicking something that sounded like a horse speaking English. "When you speak it just goes bah-bah-bah and breaks up."

Now, as we stood on that dewy patch of highway, it was payback time. When I noticed Tomosuke was only sticking out his thumb for the biggest, nicest cars, I chided him for being overly selective. I may have also mentioned my annoyance with his near-total lack of enthusiasm.

Tomosuke tilted back his head and appeared to look down his nose at me, despite the foot or so difference in our heights. "I want a big car, not a small one," he said, regally, by which he meant a late-model Mercedes Benz sedan—"air-conditioned."

The squabbling helped explain why my old traveling companion didn't play a more prominent role in my story this time—there was simply no space to illuminate the complications.

Language was one problem. Tomosuke spoke English painfully now and often had a hard time explaining anything more complicated than the time of day. When I helpfully pointed this out, he grew testy, countering that I had become, as he was fond of saying, "one point two five lingual," meaning that my Japanese was kaput as well. The sad truth was that we were both losing one another's language rapidly now. In due time, we'd be drooling into our soup bowls, our adventures together at best a series of ghosts flitting through our respective heads.

We were observing a period of sullen silence when a white minivan that said on its side, "Flower Arrangement—Petit Fleur," rolled to a stop.

"Need a lift?" said the driver, Yoko Maru, an effervescent woman in her forties. Squeezing into the car, I complimented her on how lively Chiba had become. "Are you kidding me?" said Maru, who grew up on the citified Chiba-Tokyo border. "Before we married, my husband said this was such a great place, but he lied," she said with a chuckle. "Everything moves so slowly."

As we talked, Maru-san piloted her van at high speeds, leaving the highway to make a series of breathtaking turns through backstreets lined with weathered storefronts and sad-sack mom-and-pop eateries. She said she was looking for a shortcut. Trying to appear nonchalant as he surreptitiously fastened his seatbelt, Tomosuke asked Maru what her husband did for a living.

"He's a middle school teacher," she said.

"That's great," said Tomosuke, who had once been a teacher himself, in Kyushu, and considered it a high calling.

"Is it?" Maru said, defiantly. "The salary is pretty thin!"

Down the shoreline you could see the metallic spires of a big electric power plant, their spectral lights arcing in hazy sunshine. Maru blamed the local electric utility, which she referred to as Enemy No. 1 in those parts, for polluting the local waters. She was precisely the kind of live wire who wanted Chiba to change and fast.

"I got tired of being a housewife, so I opened my own flower shop," she said, adding in complaint that business was too slow. "People around here have land and grow flowers of their own. Except for carnations and chrysanthemums. So I sell carnations for Mother's Day and chrysanthemums for funerals. That's my market!"

Okay, maybe Chiba's hinterland wasn't that exciting, I conceded, but what about all those new conveniences lining the highway?

Maru admitted the area's burgeoning consumer culture makes life brighter and more convenient. But people here worry about waves of drug abuse, school bullying, teenage prostitution and suicide now sloshing into Chiba from Tokyo. Yet despite the arrival of these and other modern ills, Maru felt most residents are still behind the times.

"This place is in a time warp," she said. "I want to go to New York!"

6

Later that afternoon I spied a roadside billboard announcing an outstanding reporting opportunity, the NEKO DA! PARK—or IT'S A CAT! PARK. When I broke the news to Tomosuke that we would be paying a visit, he stared at me as if I'd lost my marbles. I was compelled to remind him that our hitchhiking tours had always aimed at tapping the essence of the real Japan, and to take what came our way. Well, *NEKO DA! PARK* had come our way and we *were* going to tap.

The "park" was situated just off the main highway in a squat, dusty prefab building that reminded me of a plumbing supply outlet. When our taxi pulled up, Tomosuke had to be coaxed from the car, not unlike a cat staging a sit-down strike. "This is close to Tokyo so there are plenty of suckers who'll spend their money on anything," he groused, as I shelled out the equivalent of sixteen dollars for our entry fees. A human cat facilitator in a brightly colored uniform sprayed our hands with a perfumed antiseptic—to protect the cats from infection, I was told—and we went in through a kind of amateurish airlock. After all that, the "park" was a letdown—just one large, open room where, under florescent lights, dozens and dozens of domestic felines lounged and groomed themselves in the manner of a George Booth cartoon while wall speakers blared out a pulsating, synthesized chorus of cats meowing "Born to be Wild."

"I don't like this place," Tomosuke said, eyeballing a big gray Persian that was reclining on a carpeted pedestal and regarding him with an air of lazy superiority. I had to admit that it was odd in the extreme to have all those cats sizing you up all at once like that; it revolutionized my perspective on the cat-human relationship, but not in a good way, and I felt pretty silly.

Yet the long-distance reporter, having invested time and effort, is obliged to make the most of even a harebrained idea. So I suggested to Tomosuke that we chat up the only other humans in the room, a pair of forlorn-looking young women in raincoats. They were sitting on a bench, knees held tightly together, while they jointly cuddled a large, disinterested-looking tabby. In a whispered aside, Tomosuke said they appeared to have been lobotomized. As we approached, however, he turned on his antique charm to ask where they were from. "We're from Nagoya," one of the women said without making eye contact. "We love cats," said the other. Though riveting, it was a short conversation.

"The cats here appear to be smarter than the people," Tomosuke sniffed, and the argument wasn't without merit. The cats did look as if they might be covertly planning a jailbreak, and there was clear evidence of submerged ferocities. A dozen or so animals, staking out the mockup of a Japanese-style family room, licked themselves with vigorous, flicking tongues as they stretched out on *tatami* mats absolutely torn to shreds from mighty and sustained clawing. It struck me that working as a cat warder might be a harder job than I would have thought.

Indeed, Hisao Sano, the friendly park manager, said it wasn't a love of animals but the lousy local economy that had brought him to *NEKO DA! PARK*. Sure, you could still sign on at the big petrochemical plants that had been Chiba's hallmark industry. Or, like many of his high school classmates, you could head to Tokyo for a white-collar job for more money and where you didn't have to dirty your hands. But Sano was now thirty-four, and he said he wanted to stay put while staying out of the factories.

What was the hardest part of his job? I asked. Training the cats "not to attack the customers," Sano said. Apparently your committed cat lover not infrequently lost control in close proximity to a beguiling feline and squeezed too hard, provoking in return bared teeth and scratching claws. Sano-san and his colleagues had erected a big poster on the premises with helpful illustrations to show people the proper way to pick up a cat, but he said it hadn't helped. What could you do? Cat people were just inveterate squeezers.

Outside on the driveway I struck up a conversation with one of Sano's young assistants. She had a country girl's round smiling face, bright orange hair, and angry red scratches up and down her forearms. Grimly cheerful, she confided to me that the park had been forced to intermit its foster care program "because some bad guys adopted cats and then sold them for experiments."

Alas, the cat park saga didn't make the story's final cut and for good reason. In long-form journalism, the offbeat and the truly odd can keep the reader engaged, and the story's lifeblood flowing. Too much in too short a story, however, pulls readers away from the through-line and leaves them bewildered. The best you can do while in the field is to hoover in all the details you possibly can and sort them out later. But here's the reporter's psychic reward for doing all that work: The cat-park anecdotes are the ones that will stay in memory long after the dutiful parts of a story have been reported and forgotten.

7

In getting to know a country or a city well, it stands to reason you need to get to know the people who live there. I've said that before, but here's a corollary: Since you can't very well develop personal relationships with everybody on your beat, which could run into the millions of people, you become, in effect, captive to those you do get to know well.

A correspondent colleague in Tokyo in the late 1970s, for example, had some years earlier made friends with a charismatic man of letters, who had slit his belly in ritual suicide to make his point that Japan was forsaking its samurai soul in heedless pursuit of material gain. Not unreasonably, my colleague concluded there were some dark stirrings at the bottom of the Japanese psyche and foreigners who hoped to deal successfully with Japan had best take note.

His was an intriguing cultural snapshot, but thanks to my friendship with Tomosuke I had formed a markedly different picture of Japan. To my eyes, the country was by and large a place of middle-class strivers, lately risen from the farm or the working class, and not very different at root from the folks I grew up among in Seattle—honorable, hardworking people, conflicted with guilt over money and sex, and cursed with bad marriages and dysfunctional families or blessed with good ones in roughly similar proportions. That's not to say the Japanese were immune from bamboozlement by their elected leaders or the odd revanchist demagogue. Having been hoodwinked and materially shattered by nationalistic ayatollahs in World War II, however, the Japanese were, if anything, it seemed to me, somewhat less delusional in their politics than, say, we Americans.

As far as Tomosuke was concerned, his existential conflict made sense when you knew a little of his personal history. To put it simply, as a young man Tomosuke felt he had been "centralized" against his will. An athletic college kid with a talent for writing and a good brain, he saw little choice but to head for Tokyo after high school to seek his fortune. A student at Waseda University from the late 1950s, he inhaled books, rowed on the crew team, and chafed at Tokyo's big city ways. Above all, Tomosuke was intensely loyal to his friends, especially those he thought were being treated unfairly.

Ko Shioya, one of Tomosuke's *kohai* or protégés, remembers getting into hot water with his mates on the rowing team, then in contention for a berth in the 1960 Summer Olympics in Rome. Ko, who went on to become a prominent journalist, was from Hokkaido, Japan's northern outback and, like Tomosuke, faced the challenges of fitting in.

"I was constantly bullied by my seniors for my big mouth," Ko told me, and "Tomosuke always rushed to my aid whenever I was in trouble. He fended for the underdog with all his might," and not infrequently with his fists. "I assumed he was willing to help me because he had always been an odd man out himself." And after Ko had made the point, I could see how Tomosuke must have sized me up when he and I first met: one outlandishly large, foreign oddball who would never fit into Japan's cloistered society no matter how hard he tried.

After college Tomosuke returned to his beloved Kyushu, but there was little work for a budding wordsmith and soon he found himself back in Tokyo, the proverbial fish out of water. It was a conflict I recognized in the stories of my own westward-tramping forebears in America—the tension between the untrammeled out-back and the complicated urban core, each with its own unique deviltries—the city's corrupting pleasures, the loneliness and ele-mental fear of the countryside. In the first instance, however, it wasn't philosophy but an addiction to fish or fishing (it was never entirely clear to me which one he liked best—the pursuit or the conquest) that drove Tomosuke toward the wilds.

Tomosuke and I spent many a weekend on Japan's wild rivers chasing darting specimens we'd either net or Tomosuke, braving swift currents in a ratty wet suit, would catch, I kid you not, with his quick, bare hands. (As far as I could ever tell, and I was never far enough underwater to see it actually happen, he would sneak up behind his quarry while they idled in the current and grab them by the gills before they knew what had hit them.) In the evening, when the shadows deepened along the riverbank, we'd build a roar-ing fire, cook and eat our fish, and then drink sake and sing songs, Japanese ballads and American folk songs, into the night.

It must be said that when Tomosuke came across a fish of truly irresistible charms (determined by guidelines I never fully under-stood), he adopted a different modus operandi. These squamous beauties he would lovingly wrap in wet newspaper and fetch all the way home to Tokyo. There he added them to the wild fish col-lection he kept in the Japanese-style bathtub in his small city apart-ment. Looking back, I can see how that did a lot to keep his boyish spirits alive in the urban setting, but it also led to problems with his wife, Akiko.

Originally drawn to his devil-may-care, fish-out-of-water wild streak, she grew to lament Tomosuke's inability to behave like a normal Japanese person. It didn't help that Akiko, a refined, porcelain-skinned beauty from a well-to-do Tokyo family, was also required to leave home to bathe in the neighborhood *sento*, or pub-lic bath, where she shared the cloudy pool with hunchbacked gran-nies and street urchins.

After the couple divorced in the early 1980s, Tomosuke was more of an odd man out than ever. He moved to Kameyama, a hamlet in the hills of the southern Boso Peninsula, where he rented a room above a combination bait shop and filling station so he could lick his wounds. When I visited him there a time or two we got out the kayaks, as usual, and horsed around on the big dammed-up lake, but I could tell Tomosuke's heart wasn't in it. He'd be sipping whiskey from a pocket-sized flask at eight in the morning and by ten had lost his focus. Tomosuke credited the good-hearted people in that little town—the couple that ran the microscopic Chinese takeout restaurant, for example, and the guy who owned the tackle shop across the big bridge over the gorge—with such kindness and generosity of spirit that he eventually regained his equilibrium.

And so it was that on the day following our cat park misadventure in 2001, Tomosuke insisted on paying a visit to Kameyama. I guess he was feeling nostalgic for his bittersweet days there, especially now that he was back on top of his game. I suspected he also wanted to show off just a little, as the famous writer now starring in those famous noodle commercials on TV. In any event, after the cat park fiasco, I owed him one, and so we hopped a train, switchbacking up into the hills under mackerel-colored skies, for the grand homecoming.

By way of prologue, you should know that ordinary Japanese not infrequently found Tomosuke's anti-establishment views hard to swallow. Some people just wrote him off as a Communist, a Japanese libertarian or some kind of a nut. His rambunctious ways could occasionally rub even his most ardent supporters the wrong way, and Tomosuke—who among us is immune?—wasn't always adept at picking up on such vibes. Which may help explain our reception in Kameyama.

Our first stop was the Chinese restaurant where the man and wife were still slinging fried dumplings and steaming bowls of noodles. The place smelled pleasantly of soy sauce and vinegar when we walked in and sat down at one of its two or three tiny tables. The cooks, busy filling lunchtime orders, bowed and smiled but weakly as Tomosuke wedged himself into a corner and proceeded to dredge up fond memories that no one but him seemed able to remember. The monosyllabic character at the tackle shop appeared so disinterested in rekindling his acquaintanceship with Tomosuke that I thought he might be mentally impaired.

As we walked out the last door and over the bridge above the gorge, I could see Tomosuke was deeply wounded, and it hurt me. "Tell you what," I said. "Let's get the hell out of here and to hell with these people."

"Yeah, okay, you're right, Toh-ray-shee," Tomosuke said, as if the world couldn't end soon enough. We climbed the hill to the train station, but when we reached the ticket window the stationmaster told us, as luck would have it, we'd managed to just miss the last train that day by a matter of minutes.

"Hey, I've got an idea," I said as we shuffled aimlessly along the station access road wondering what to do next. "I hear there's this thing called hitchhiking . . . you stick out your thumb and . . ."

Tomosuke guffawed in spite of himself and took a playful swing at me with his walking stick. We hadn't gone more than a few dozen paces when a late-model delivery van barreled down the station road and suddenly slammed on its brakes, skidding to a stop in front of us. The driver was in such a state of excitement that he momentarily lost control of the clutch and his van hiccupped forward in a couple of yard-long leaps down the hill. When he got things reined in, he rolled down his window and shouted, "Aren't you Noda-san?!"

Tomosuke grunted his samurai grunt in the affirmative. "I knew it!" said the man with an awed smile. "I read about you hitchhiking around Kyushu with some big American a couple of years ago!" And no sooner had the word *amerika-jin* passed his lips than he stopped and stared at me, mouth agape.

"That would be us," I said.

The driver shifted his gaze from Tomosuke to me and back again as if in the presence of rock music royalty, and then invited us to climb on board. Resembling a fireplug dressed in khaki pants and a navy blue polo shirt, he said his name was Nobutaka. He was on his way back to Tokyo, and he'd consider it an honor to take us wherever we wanted to go. No sooner had we started rolling than the story of his dreams and anxieties came spilling out.

"I wanted to join the national police force and passed the first test," he said, his dimples puckering into a rueful smile. "Then they checked my background and found out I had a record—stealing bicycles and getting into fights when I was a kid." His police career had ended before it could begin. Nowadays, he was the district sales rep for a big supplier of Chinese restaurants. He kept a far-flung network of eateries in abalone, bear paw, and shark fin for soup, but such pricey delicacies were hard to move in any volume during the country's endless recession.

Nobutaka said he hated living in Tokyo and that the great Noda-san's tales of outdoor adventure had helped make life bearable. In the big city, he said, "I try and act friendly but my neighbors won't even say hello. They won't look you in the eye," and then there were all those kids who sported the dyed orange hair. He found them surly and aggressive, and they scared him a little too. One day he said, dimpling again, that he hoped to move to Hokkaido or one of the remote places Tomosuke had written about in his books.

Well, the world is full of woes and wonders, and for the traveling man there is no substitute for motion—streaking down the highway like a trout in a stream. The adulation of adoring fans doesn't hurt either. And so it was that Tomosuke and I rolled along, high above the vibrantly green, neatly geometric paddy fields, while we listened to Nobutaka's troubles in a story that was old but new again in the retelling. Best of all, I knew Tomosuke was feeling his old self. Out of the corner of my eye I could see him smiling a smile of amused contentment. And he kept smiling it all the way down the mountain and into the next city.

8

Persuading Tomosuke to stick with our hitchhiking plan was growing increasingly tedious. Now in his early sixties, the famous traveler liked nothing better than to hoist on board a big, satisfying lunch of fish and rice, wash it down with a couple of big bottles of beer, and then find a place to snooze away the afternoon. The upshot was that we'd spent only a handful of hours on the road, all told, when a rainstorm beat down, interrupting our forward motion once again.

We were standing inside the train station in a town called Kisarazu, looking out on the pleasant little artificial town square, where a sign read, in English, "Humming City," when Tomosuke revived the concept of self-programmed hitchhiking. "We need a chauffeur," he declared, and not particularly interested in hearing my opinion, punched a number into his cell phone. The following day a young assistant named Munetaka Yaginuma materialized to rent a van and drive us around the rim of the bay and back home to central Tokyo.

How the mighty have fallen, I thought. Once Tomosuke and I had prided ourselves on traveling the countryside like a pair of *furaibo*, a great old Japanese word for vagabond, meaning a leaf that comes floating in on the wind. Now, more often than not, we seemed to be made up mostly of wind and ill tempers.

When Yaginuma had picked out a vehicle with seats that reclined at an angle acceptable to Tomosuke, he climbed in the back and stretched out so he could get on with his harmonica practice. He was scheduled to take part in a "save the rivers" benefit concert in the band shell at Tokyo's Ueno Park in a couple of days, and he sat back there playing the sad old country ballads, stepping on notes with abandon, as we drove past sprawling factories—steel, chemicals, and nitrous fertilizers—where orange flames leapt from intricate ductwork. When we stopped to stretch our legs, the bulkhead at a desolate seaside park at Ichihara was covered with graffiti, including, in English, "FUCK DA POLICE."

I asked Yaginuma, then in his late twenties, to interpret the antiestablishment tone for *Geographic* readers:

"Young people are spoiled," said Yaginuma. But in his view the root of the problem goes deeper than that. When his father grew up in

the 1950s, the drive to rebuild their devastated country had infused people with a keen sense of national purpose. You went to work for a big company, adopted its values, and in return you were guaranteed a job, often for life. But hard economic times have changed the social contract, leaving many Japanese to fend for themselves.

You can see the result in the growing number of young people around the bay who take part-time jobs—some out of economic necessity but others as an act of personal liberation from Japan's rigid pecking order. They call themselves freeters, slang for freelancers, and Yaginuma is a prime example. He wants to be a professional sportfisherman or writer, he isn't sure which. To make ends meet he delivers mannequins to bay area department stores for $150 a day—a radical departure from the traditional career track taken by his father.

"He gave me hell for wasting my life," said Yaginuma, a prep school and college graduate, as he ran his hand through his dyed blond hair. "Then Dad's company went bust." The elder Yaginuma was forced to take a job driving a Tokyo taxicab. "Now he says he knows exactly how I feel."

In the back seat, Tomosuke, still sucking on his harmonica, and being irritating in the traditional manner, launched into an old lullaby. It was one he and I had sung with the elderly farmers that long-ago night in the mixed bath at the edge of the pineapple fields on Yakushima and, in spite of some wild notes, the sad, minor chords seemed like a message from a muffled past. We all sang along, Yaginuma needing a little help with the prehistoric lyrics, while, up ahead, the big Ferris wheel on Odaiba grew closer and closer.

Much had changed in the three decades since Tomosuke took me under his wing and together we hit the Kyushu road in 1974. In between times, Japan's economic successes had so rattled America that the Japan bashers, with the help of the U.S. media, made the Japanese seem ten feet tall and, like the Soviets before them but with much less reason, invincible. In the end, however, Japan turned out to be a disappointment in the bogeyman department.

At the turn of the new century, with the Japanese economy chronically depressed, Japan and the United States enjoyed what the foreign policy types called a mature relationship. Islamic terrorism had yet to hit the U.S. homeland (though 9/11 was then only weeks away), and China had emerged to promise a bigger long-term threat to America's interests in the world than recession-clobbered, zero-growth Japan ever had. America likes an enemy with staying power.

As for Tomosuke and me, to say our friendship taught me a lot would be a wild understatement. Like any good teacher, he steered me to the right places and then stood back so I could see for myself that the Japanese weren't as standoffish or changeless, dunderheaded or ineffably artistic or wise as people in America sometimes liked to think. You just have to lean in closer and a little longer before you see the dynamism and peculiarities of a people or place, that's all—just like others do when they considered that most confounding place of all, the United States.

In short, my travels with Tomosuke affected all that I have done or will ever do as a reporter or a person. He was the perfect guide to Japan for me, and I thank my lucky stars that I ran into him. May travelers, everywhere, be as lucky in their choice of friends.

JAPAN'S MAGIC
MOUNTAIN

1

A reporter should always keep an open mind, but sometimes we jump to conclusions. In the spring of 2001 I was at home in New York preparing for my Tokyo Bay assignment when Bob Poole phoned me to ask if I wouldn't mind doing a second story while I was at it, this one on Japan's signature peak, Mount Fuji.

My antennae shot up immediately. "This won't involve climbing the mountain in any way, will it?" I asked, to which Bob replied drily, "Yes, but send me your notes for safekeeping before you go up."

Bob was joking, but I wasn't. I had climbed Fuji once, in 1976, and hadn't been impressed. I remembered it being less of a climb than an excruciatingly hard uphill walk along barren, trash-strewn slopes studded with unscrupulous vendors charging outrageous prices for a bowl of watery miso soup or a can of soda. To put it bluntly, I was appalled by how the Japanese, reputed to be some of the greatest nature worshippers in the history of the planet, had let their iconic mountain go to hell. That and memories of a hellacious altitude headache and the knee-rattling upward tilt of the trails had confirmed for me a life of seeking my adventures at or near sea level.

Unexamined prejudices are fatal for a journalist, and talking to Bob made me realize my error in thinking. In keeping with his advice to me over the years, he said I should look at Mount Fuji as a metaphor. What did Japan's national symbol have to tell us about the heart and soul of the nation and its people? Any contradictions

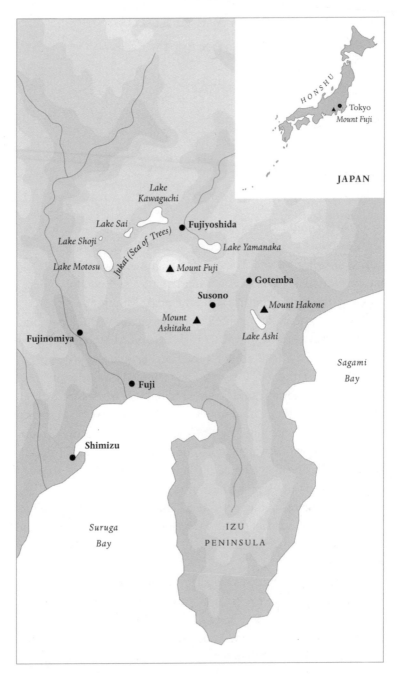

Mount Fuji and vicinity.

between the popular imagination and starker realities would be pure gravy for an alert reporter. Bob was right: It is precisely by exploring the crevasses between image and reality that journalists often turn up the most illuminating stuff.

In any event, I accepted Bob's offer of a double assignment. It had also occurred to me that my qualms about Fuji weren't based exclusively on a high-minded concern about the nature of the story. Beset with an aging boomer's anxiety, I was secretly afraid my arthritic basketball-damaged knees were no longer capable of carrying me to the top of the world. Now, however, I had no choice but to swing into action to prepare for a story that eventually appeared in the magazine as "Mount Fuji: Japan's Sacred Summit."

I spent the next few weeks hiking four to five miles every day, up New York's East River from our apartment on East Forty-Ninth Street and back again. Deteriorating cartilage notwithstanding, I paused at the Seventy-First Street pedestrian overpass and ran up and down its concrete steps half a dozen times or more while the cars on fuming FDR drive played bumper-to-bumper chicken at high speeds. It was like preparing for death, but not in a lugubrious way. Given my arthritic joints, I knew my second assault on Fuji would surely be my last, and, despite straining and kvetching, I secretly started to look forward to the challenge.

Once I arrived in Tokyo, of course, I put off the climbing part as long as possible. Instead, I consulted as many "experts" as I could find—Japanese journalists who had written about the climbing of Fuji and mountaineers who had climbed it. I talked to scientists and historians who filled me in on volcanic Fuji's time-honored habit of intermittently blowing its top, spewing the surrounding territory with fire and ash and injecting fear of the mountain's darker side into the Japanese psyche. I spent a pleasant day observing ruddy-cheeked farmers conduct a disaster preparedness drill like it was a community festival. In other words, I was thoroughly enjoying myself. Ultimately, though, there was no avoiding the climbing part, which I used to open my story:

*It was 25 years since I climbed Mount Fuji the first time, and my
51-year-old knees reminded me, painfully, of the old saying: Only
a fool climbs Fuji twice. But there I was, at 2:35 in the morning,
clinging to the inky slopes with my old friend, Gerry Curtis. Only
the lights strung around the ubiquitous climbing huts were visible,
running in a crazy line to the top, as we hunkered down in a cold,
gritty wind.*

*Gerry, an esteemed professor of Japanese politics at Columbia
University and a streetwise New Yorker, was making his first
ascent. And now, exhausted, walking stick in hand, he looked
dangerously cranky.*

"We're lucky," I said, trying to avert a mutiny.

*"Yeah, how's that?" muttered Gerry, as Japanese climbers
stepped around us shouting brisk words of encouragement.*

*"For one thing," I said, "we don't have altitude headaches"—
the clanging pain that comes when reduced oxygen forces a climber's brain to expand against the immovable skull. "Turns out, as
we get older, our brains shrink—so fewer headaches."*

*"Is that so?" said Gerry. He took a hit from an oxygen canister
and stared at me. "My brain must have really shrunk to let you talk
me into this."*

*I couldn't blame him. Climbing Fuji isn't the snap many people
think. Yet every year, during the July-August climbing season, some
400,000 mostly enthusiastic tenderfoots (20,000 on a good day)
scramble for the summit of Japan's mighty beacon. For the Japanese,
Fuji (early Chinese characters for which mean "without equal") is
unrivaled in its capacity to stir a sense of national identity even
in a society that is more individualistic than in the past.*

*"People my age can't even name Japan's second highest peak,"
said Atsushi Yamada, a sturdy 22-year-old climbing instructor
with a bushy head of dyed orange hair. (It's Kita-dake in the Japan
Alps). "But everybody wants to climb to the top of Fuji." And at
12,388 feet you need neither rope nor crampon to get there. Just energy, particularly if you do it a popular way—a lemminglike dash
to glimpse goraiko, or sunrise, from the highest point in the Land
of the Rising Sun.*

Our foursome, including my guide, Munetaka Yaginuma, and godson, Arthur Mitchell, a student of Japanese literature, fit right in. We started up with gusto at 11:30 p.m., but as dawn lightened the sky, the thin air and lack of sleep slowed us to a head-bowed crawl. Then, nearing the summit, a sudden miracle—a luminous egg yolk peeped through ruffled clouds, spreading golden fluid through the heavens. Climbers halted to savor the moment. Some applauded. Others whipped out cell phones, describing the scene for loved ones back home. Elated, possibly from oxygen deprivation, I called my brother Dave in Seattle.

Gerry, rejuvenated, looked like a man who had planted a flag on a distant planet—"Spectacular," he beamed.

2

That's an accurate description of our assault, as far as it goes. But the problem with a crisp and classy professional editing job of the type you expect at the *Geographic* is that it can make something really arduous sound easier than it was.

That was the case with Fuji. After an endless night of climbing, somewhere above the last commercial hut, I stood in the flat light of dawn, head tilted skyward, to see how far we had yet to scramble before overtaking the *torii*, the traditional gate, marking the entrance to the summit. Still in miniature, the marker hovered at the top of a twisting, vertiginous path that reminded me of a Bruegel painting, in this version, littered with the bodies of pooped-out climbers who gasped like so many rock cod on a slab.

Pop-eyed with oxygen debt myself, I scribbled a few notes that looked like cardiographic squiggles and then stopped writing altogether. I severely regretted stocking up on the grape-flavored energy jelly that Yaginuma and I had purchased at a sporting goods outlet in Tokyo the day before; losing steam during the wee hours, I sucked down a tube of the glutinous stuff in two seconds flat and the ensuing sugar rush left me feeling queasy as a puppy on a merry-go-round. The canisters of sandalwood-scented oxygen we'd counted on to stave off altitude sickness did absolutely no good at all. My body ached, my lungs were on fire, and now, more than anything, I simply wanted to sit down and catch my breath.

Which is exactly what one of the Fuji experts I'd talked to in Tokyo had warned me *not* to do. Having accurately pegged me as a fair-weather climber and total rookie, this lord of the peaks had advised me that, in the final approach to the top, I should keep on moving at all costs or risk deflating, as I interpreted it, like a spent, middle-aged gasbag. When he warned that once down you weren't likely to get up again, I thought he was being melodramatic.

He wasn't.

Now within sight of the top, my legs moved jerkily, like animated pieces of concrete, as I acquired a kind of hallucinatory affinity for my surroundings. Everywhere I looked, I could see rock formations, big ones and little ones, that seemed to suggest anthropomorphic characters I remembered from the animated movies I'd seen as a kid. Some looked friendly and camel-like, others bellicose and ceratopsian. Meanwhile, the bed of frilly white clouds spread out below me looked so soft and inviting I thought of one of those TV commercials for bathroom tissue that feature the prancing bears. When I spied a rock in the shape of a comfy cartoon ottoman, I plunked myself down. When nothing bad happened—what did the god of climbing know?—I went from rock to rock, until I went one rock too far.

Instantly, I found myself inside a kind of phantasmagoria with violent purples, yellows, and reds flashing impressively before my eyes. Luckily, I had planned for just such a moment. A traveler must try to prepare for all eventualities, and given my age and bad knees I'd brought along Yaginuma and my godson, Arthur, and not only because they were good and sturdy companions but mainly on the theory that when I started to lose gas the two younger men could, in effect, put me in harness and drag me up to the summit. That, it turned out, was a very good idea.

Hunkered down on my rock, I was watching the light show inside my skull with a kind of detached fascination when I heard the voice of God. He commanded me to rise up, as if to receive some kind of important message. Struggling to obey, I discovered my legs had completely stopped working. "Stand up," God repeated, and suddenly another miracle occurred: I felt my body slowly, effortlessly begin to levitate off the face of the mountain.

In groggy ascent, I managed to put two and two together and realized that God's voice was, in fact, coming from none other than my godson Arthur, as he and Yaginuma, grabbing me by my elbows, lifted me to my feet.

My master plan for conquering Fuji worked brilliantly but for one final complication. Punchy but mobile, I was trudging up the last few hundred yards toward the summit when Gerry suddenly zipped past me—though "zipped" may be an exaggeration, since to any casual observer it would have appeared that both of us were lurching forward in extreme slow motion like astronauts released from a moon capsule. But speed is relative and so is human nature, and the lack of velocity didn't reduce by one iota Gerry's glee at pulling ahead. Pumping his elbows as he stepped around me, he wheezed, "I'm going to beat you!"

I must say I found that very unsporting. I had invited Gerry along to maintain generational balance on our four-man team and because, altruistically, I thought any prominent Japan scholar really ought to have at least one Fuji climb to his credit. And this was the thanks I got? Gerry, by the way, was the same man on whose behalf, earlier in the climb, I'd retraced my hard-won steps, going back down the trail at least twice, to check on him and, out of Mother Teresa–like compassion, encourage him to keep on climbing, however slowly.

"Ha, ha, I beat you," Gerry taunted, as he passed under the *torii* ahead of me, slick as a very slow-moving whistle. I had learned a lot about Japan from Gerry over the years but made a mental note to reevaluate the nature of our relationship.

That evening, our quartet was resting up at a comfortable country inn famed for its volcanic hot springs, when my post-climb arthritis kicked in big time. After an excellent dinner of sashimi, deep-friend prawns, colt's foot, and other wild mountain vegetables,

Arthur and Yaginuma were obliged to extract me from under the low table. Pulling on my arms, they slid me backward across the tatami mats and hauled me to my feet while Gerry, annoyingly ambulatory, made uncharitable quips amusing only to himself.

Life is wildly unfair, of course, but let me say it again: Karma is often repaid quickly and in kind. In this case it took twelve hours. Early the next morning I was painfully lurching down the hotel corridor, making my way to the men's bath, when I saw Gerry ahead of me. Bleary-eyed with sleep, he appeared to be wandering into the ladies dressing room by mistake. Perhaps I should have said something. As it was, Gerry removed his cotton kimono, slid back the door, and entered the steaming grotto, much to the delight of a group of voluble, soaking matrons who erupted in a chorus of shrieks and bawdy laughter.

I smiled to myself as I heard a sliding door slam shut followed by the august professor proclaiming, "Oh, shit," as he fled back into the corridor, trussing up his cotton kimono as he came. It's hard to describe how really very good I felt just then.

3

The Fuji story taught me just how big a deal the mountain was in the minds of ordinary Japanese. I wondered how, after all my years living in Japan, I could have overlooked this crucial fact about the national gestalt. So in writing up the story, I tried my best to supply the reader with a decent nut graph that pulled the key themes together, with some efficiency, and then allowed me to drive on to my first character to rivet the point about Fuji's "psychic hold." Here's what I came up with:

> It's hard to overstate Fuji's magnetic pull. Its solitary cone rises from the Fossa Magna, a tectonic hinge that bisects Japan's boomerang-shaped main island, Honshu. With its flattened top, Fuji-san, as the Japanese call it, resembles a giant mound of powder (flour in winter,

graphite in summer) sifted onto a cookie sheet, and on a clear day can be seen from Tokyo, 70 miles away.

For centuries Japan's holiest of natural sanctuaries, Fuji shows up today in more worldly ways—as a popular brand of mineral water and a lucky logo for hundreds of businesses, including multinational giants Fuji Photo Film and Fuji Xerox. "Japan without Fuji," one veteran climber told me, "would be like America without the Statue of Liberty."

Fuji's psychic hold was evident the day I visited Hikotaro Omata at his home on the shores of Lake Kawaguchi, one of five lakes bunched along its northern slopes. "I was a climbing guide for 60 years!" cried the squat 80-year-old, whose barrel chest and earthy manner suggested he might have grown directly out of the side of Fuji itself. "I went to the top more than 800 times!"

I was feeling less the fool for climbing Fuji only twice, when Omata-san fixed me with a steely gaze and declared, "Fuji-san saved my life!" In World War II, he said, Japan was still the "land of the gods," but he was in the jungles of New Guinea, a soldier in the emperor's army, when Fuji appeared to him in a vision. "I was nearly dead from starvation," the old man said. "And she was snowcapped and beautiful!"

So when Fuji thundered, "Return and climb me!" Omata-san had to obey. But the old magic faded fast during Japan's postwar "economic miracle." In the 1960s a famous pop crooner hired Omata to help carry up a grand piano for a concert. "We got all the way to the top," he said, "when word came this singer fellow wasn't feeling up to the climb."

There was that look again. "It'd taken us three days!" barked Omata-san. "They could've flown the damn thing up in a helicopter for less money!"

Omata boasted about his role in guiding former president Jimmy Carter up the mountain and how he had once bawled out two clueless young women (a woman's presence on the mountain being considered bad luck among the shellbacked climbing guides) who had had the temerity to show up on the climbing trail wearing high heels and carrying parasols. "Why do you come up to the mountain dressed like that?" he had demanded, adding as an aside: "That's why it's raining!"

The old man of the mountain then went on to complain about Japanese news outfits not paying him enough money for interviews, which, since I never pay for interviews and would pay him nothing at all, I took as one of those three-cushion complaints not uncommon in subtle cultures. Though I realized I would have to climb Fuji a few hundred more times before I could properly judge him, interviewing Omata became tiresome and I confess I was happy to wind it up.

4

That all-knowing editor who warned me against sitting down on the slopes of Fuji had one other piece of advice. If I really wanted to understand the mountain's power to turn a man inside out, I'd better talk to a fellow named Masuko.

What was so special about him? I wanted to know.

For starters, the man said, Masuko-san had climbed to the top of Fuji ninety-seven months in a row, in a bid to break one hundred; when after eight years he fell short of the mark, he immediately started over from zero until he had reached his goal. The numbers were impressive, but they didn't begin to tell the story. Unlike most climbers, who tramped around Fuji only in summer, Masuko also climbed during the icy winters when the mountain was a wind-ravaged sentinel in some ways more treacherous than Mount Everest. From the way the editor sniggered a little in recounting Masuko's derring-do, however, I sensed there was more to it than he was letting on. I wasn't wrong.

I was still limping from my own assault on Fuji a few days earlier when I met Mr. Masuko at the bottom of the staircase in the busy lobby of the Imperial Hotel in Tokyo. You could have spotted him a mile away. Somewhere on the uphill side of sixty, he glowed like a beacon of outlandishly good health. His wiry torso wrapped in a crisply laundered safari jacket, his hair shaved down to a sun-cured scalp, Masuko didn't appear to have enough fat on him to grease a sukiyaki skillet.

Over the clatter of cups and saucers in the lobby tea lounge, Masuko-san confirmed that, yes, he had long intended to climb Fuji one hundred months in a row, not merely to get himself into the record books, which he eventually did, but because he was also a rapt connoisseur of Fuji's many moods. Every time he climbed the mountain, he said, it seemed to present a different face—green and peaceful, serene and lovely, stark and forbidding, all depending on the season and conditions.

Masuko had been ridiculously close to his goal that first time around when, in 1987, disaster struck. A computer scientist by trade, he was taking the train home from work one evening when his blood sugar plummeted from overtraining and lack of sleep. He tumbled down a flight of stairs at Tokyo's Ueno Station, fractured his skull, and woke up in the hospital.

It was early January then, and though the room flew round and round for a time, he wasn't about to let a bump on the head get between a man and his mountain. He calculated he still had sufficient time get out of the hospital, resume his training, and get himself up snowy Fuji before the calendar flipped to February. Just as he was plotting his next ascent, however, the doctors got wind of his plans and ordered him held over for an extended period of observation. The calendar flipped.

Masuko didn't let on what he thought of his doctors but said, simply—and not unhappily, it seemed to me—that he had had no choice but to start over. Old-school Japanese love an impossible task, especially when it requires *gaman*, or perseverance, a word that not infrequently implies some kind of incredible act of self-denial and sucking it up in the face of adversity. For Masuko, I thought, the setback, and the seemingly insurmountable obstacle it presented, may have only added to the nobility of his quest.

In any event, it was on March 28 of his year of concussion that Masuko reset the climbing clock with ascent number one, and eight years, four months later he finally summited Fuji for the hundredth time. Then, pretty much for the hell of it, as far as I could tell, and almost certainly to make the very clear point that he was undisputed champion of consecutive Fuji climbs, he summited thirty-one more times in thirty-one months. And that wasn't all. While he was at it, he had also set another record—conquering Fuji ten years in a row on January 1, Japan's pinnacle New Year holiday.

Having just gasped and stumbled through my own Fuji ascent, I really couldn't think of anything more extraordinary. What on earth would possess somebody to do what Masuko-san had done?

Smiling from under cheekbones that resembled sturdy promontories, Masuko told me the plain truth was "my love for the mountain is beyond imagination." He was seven or eight years old, he said, when he scrambled up a hill behind his village home and laid eyes on Fuji for the first time, and after six decades the original image was still indelibly lodged in his brain. Thrusting up through clouds that looked like frozen waves on the sea, the mountain was wreathed in a magical golden light, and he was a goner. It sounded to me as if Fuji had imprinted itself on him like a gosling gets stamped with a migratory route, but whatever it was, it had gotten to him in a profound way.

A love like that is risky business, of course, and Masuko said he knew only too well that once he started pressing his daring ascents, his cherished mountain could turn on him at any moment and kill him. He described that part with a kind of morbid joviality, and I was reminded, oddly, of the female preying mantis's habit of biting off the head of her inamorato after copulation. Frankly speaking, that part of the story struck me as a bit unusual.

Masuko pressed on. In winter, he explained, it took him nineteen hours to conquer Fuji. Starting from the very bottom, he would have had to first tromp up through the cathedrals of pine trees that cover Fuji's skirts and then onto the blue, ice-glazed slopes, where subzero winds routinely blister escarpments at speeds of seventy miles an hour. "You start at 2 a.m. at the foot and you're down about 9 p.m.," Masuko said. "It's nineteen hours of fighting yourself, the lack of sleep, the severe weather conditions, the loneliness."

Masuko made me feel better about my own hallucinatory experiences on Fuji when he talked about his. High-altitude cerebral edema results when blood coagulates in brain tissue due to the lack of oxygen, and because it can make you do some very foolish things, it's nothing to fool with at all. On one ascent, for example, Masuko was traversing Fuji's rocky shoulders, when a building-size boulder he was using to orient himself suddenly metamorphosed into a coffee shop. It looked so homey and inviting, Masuko said, he thought, "I'll just drop in and have a cup of coffee before continuing up the mountain." When he was about to reach the charming little oasis, a gust of wind slapped him in the face and, in a flash, the coffee shop turned back into a big rock. Masuko realized he had come very close to stepping off the side of the mountain.

I wondered if Masuko didn't consider himself just a bit obsessive. The short answer was no. First of all, he said, his adventures gave him an "overwhelming feeling of accomplishment. . . . I'll be on the train and I'll see Fuji-san in the distance and I'll say to myself, 'I was at the top of that mountain, I was up there yesterday.'" And then there were the aesthetics. Some aspects of Fuji he said he'd seen only once in twenty-four years of climbing and they were experiences to be savored.

What did Masuko-san's wife of many years think of his exploits? By this point I was dying to know. Wasn't she just a bit jealous of his love affair with Fuji? I said it in a half-joking way, but Masuko-san got the point and smiled confidently. Basically, he said, his wife was ignorant of the dangers, so he was free to act as he pleased. "She's given up on me," he said, in the way men say when they don't really answer the question. Learning to read something as fickle as Fuji's shifting moods, I gathered, didn't necessarily lend itself to mastering connubial sensitivities.

My big dilemma came later, when I was back in New York trying to piece together my story and I confronted a common tragedy of long-form storytelling. My Japanese editor friend had been right: Masuko the Climber was unrivaled in his obsession with Japan's unrivaled peak. Try as I might, though, I couldn't squeeze him into the paragraph or two I could spare in a story my editors had decreed would be no longer than three thousand words, period.

Unhappily, I had to substitute the shorter, less interesting anecdote about Omata-san, the snappish climbing guide. Though I'd found him to be a testy old codger, I really had nothing against Omata—except to say that in the end he edged out a vastly more complex character with the heart to risk all for love, however unwise. Writing, as they say, is a brutal business.

5

It was late July, and the rigors of scaling Fuji were behind us, when I rehired Yaginuma, Tomosuke's twentysomething protégé, and together we drove around middle Japan, conducting a thorough study of Fuji's sprawling foothills. We rambled through a giant amusement park where the fun-ride fanatic in me was excited about riding the Fujiyama, a state-of-the-art roller coaster with a heart-stopping 230-foot drop. Alas, the monster coaster was closed for repairs, and I was disqualified from other adrenaline-pumping rides because none of the demure safety harnesses could be made to snap shut over my giant *gaijin*'s torso.

On Fuji's wooded flank, I interviewed the daughter of a dead mystic who told me her mother had awakened from a trance one day to inform her father, "I am the goddess of Jimba and I have decided to take this woman's body. Please allow me to use it as a place of religion," to which her father had replied, "Please, be my guest!" The woman went on to found a cult that continued to flourish in a bosky hollow where the upswept roofs, covered in pricey titanium tiles, bounced back the long rays of the afternoon sun. At a coffee shop on the backside of Fuji, I questioned a ufologist with the face of a surprised cat. He reported having seen a flying saucer emerge from Fuji and produced a helpful diagram that resembled a pair of giant flashlight batteries.

It was exceedingly pleasant duty. We tramped around Fuji's foothills in the sunshine, ate buttery Fuji ice cream, slurped fat, delicious Fuji udon noodles, and found big parking lots in which to play Frisbee. Each night Yaginuma and I picked out an elegant *ryokan*, or Japanese-style inn, with a soothing hot-spring bath to soak away our cares, of which there were few. In the mornings, we climbed into our dented white rental van (Yaginuma had insisted on the dents to ward off insurance defrauders who were then in the news for targeting fancy cars to slam into) and listened to old rock-and-roll tunes, as the elevated countryside, with its twisty roads and broad vistas, stretched out before us. Yaginuma, his hair dyed orange one day and flecked with yellow or red the next, asked me to teach him what I knew about America's golden age of rock and roll. As a basis for our study he compiled a mix tape including Wanda Jackson's 1957 chart-topper, "Fujiyama Mama," which I was startled to discover goes like this:

> I've been to Nagasaki, Hiroshima too.
> The same I did to them baby I can do to you.
> 'Cause I'm a Fujiyama mama and I'm just about to blow my
>   top.
> Fujiyama-yama Fujiyama.
> And when I start erupting ain't nobody gonna make me stop.

Luckily, Yaginuma, who was not alive in either 1945 or 1957, didn't appear to understand the historical import of the English lyrics, and educating him about that part now proved too complicated for my disintegrated Japanese. Not even my remorse at losing my language skills could break the happy spell we were traveling under, however. We threaded our way in and out of Fuji's five finger lakes, communicating well enough, Yaginuma drumming the steering wheel to the sounds of Elvis, Jackie Wilson, and the Supremes, while I let the story seep through my brain like groundwater finding the surface.

But the long-distance reporter must be ever mindful of those who help him on his way, and so I felt a serious sense of mission in finding a suitable reward for the lady concierges at the Imperial Hotel back in Tokyo, my home base of nearly two months. Going above and beyond the call of duty, these thoughtful young women had upgraded me to a series of better and better rooms they deemed conducive to my work. (Gerry Curtis was impressed when, ringing me at the hotel one day, the operator asked, "Which of Mr. Dahlby's rooms would you like?" At that point I had two. That was a nice day.) And so, I instructed Yaginuma to drive miles off our circuit to a farming area northwest of Fuji famed for its softball-sized peaches, which the Japanese consider a great delicacy and rightly so. Royally pampered, each and every peach, and there are several dozen such beauties on the average smallish tree, suns itself wearing a rice-paper hat the farmer has dressed it in to ensure the ripening process will be slow and even. The fruit is incredibly delicious.

Just to make sure we had the pick of the crop, Yaginuma and I sat in the grower's yard, sampling peaches until the juice ran in rivulets down our forearms. We ate them both hard and soft, the natives preferring to take them hard and crisp like an apple. The natives had it right. I bought a large gift box of these perfect specimens for the hotel ladies, and when I eventually delivered it in the Imperial's cavernous lobby they laughed and clapped. They then upgraded me to the ultimate "sunny room" in a quiet corner of the hotel where they felt the light-filled alcove would be ideal for writing. Life was perfect.

And yet there was something indefinably strange in the air that summer too. During all that time I was enjoying myself, like a man traveling in a light-filled dream, the end of summer was approaching and, I kid you not, I began to detect—how should I say?—the hint of a whisper of something coming in on the autumn breeze. I came to think of it as a voice, though it may have been no more than a recurring thought. In any event, I couldn't explain it then and don't understand it now. What it said was, "This is the last good time."

That's what it said—the last good time—but not in a menacing way. The emotion behind the words, as far as I could tell, was simply that this was a moment to be savored, the last rose of summer and all that business. And so Yaginuma and I drove on, the words cycling through my head from time to time, reminding me about the last good time. I got used to it. In a summer of pleasant distractions it was just another precinct heard from.

6

It stands to reason that any national symbol worth its salt should reflect the dark side of the psyche as well as the light, and during the course of my reporting I dutifully looked into such hypothetical horribles as the more or less constant swarming of low-frequency earthquakes around and under Fuji. Scientists were carefully monitoring this activity for signs of mischief at the level of deep magma flows that could signal Fuji, the biggest of Japan's eighty-six active volcanoes, was preparing to blow its top. As I eventually wrote:

> *Only fear of Fuji's fury may run deeper than devotion in Japan's collective consciousness. Records show that since A.D. 781 the mountain has erupted at least ten times, with flaming skies and molten rivers. Its last blowout, in 1707, followed a colossal earthquake estimated today at magnitude 8.4. (The 1995 Kobe quake, which killed 6,400 and caused massive structural damage, registered 7.2.) It cratered Fuji's southeast face, raining ash so thick, one diarist noted, "We lighted candles even in the daytime."*

At the same time, there was a more directly disturbing aspect of the mountain's morbidity that I explained in the following way:

> *Fuji's jukai, or sea of trees, is its garden of dark visions. This swath of old growth forest northwest of the summit, deep and tangled as a fairy tale, is infused with caves formed by lava flow cold now for*

a thousand years. From a cloistered compound on its verge Aum Shinrikyo, a fanatical religious cult, staged a poison gas attack on Tokyo subways in 1995, killing 12 and sickening thousands. But today the jukai's beauty belies its image as the suicide capital of Japan.

"This is where people go in and don't come out," said my guide one sunny Saturday morning when I joined a group of cave explorers at the entrance gate where Fuji's lower flank gently tilts upward. It was barely 11 a.m., but the forest was already in twilight. Tree roots roiled the hard lava crust like moss-covered snakes. "That's the tree," said our leader, pointing, "where, two years ago, we found a human head in the branches"—the remnants of a self-inflicted hanging.

Too many such grisly discoveries had led local firemen to stop yearly cleanups for fear that media coverage of the bodies only added to a national suicide rate that was soaring in the midst of Japan's deepest postwar recession.

I was shining my flashlight inside a low vine-covered cave, watching a caver wriggle forward on his belly, when one member of our group, a brusque man with penetrating eyes, said, "I found some bones over there."

He led me toward the ruins of a campsite that rose from the underbrush as we approached. There was a soggy green tarp tied between two saplings, a muddy sleeping bag, an empty gas can—and a nondescript pelvic bone. Stuck to the side of a collapsed tent were clumps of thick black hair.

"Thirteenth body I've found," the man said matter-of-factly. But there was in fact no body or ID, just the possible traces of a tragedy. A woman put her palms together in prayer, and then the jaunty spelunkers were off galumphing through the dense pulpy forest, laughing and joking.

That struck me as callous. Somewhere, surely, old parents pined for word of missing children. A homemade poster tacked to a trail gate said as much. It asked for help in locating a 36-year-old salaryman and displayed a weathered snapshot. Through the cracked

emulsion you could make out high, round cheekbones, a haunting,
almost girlish smile, and the pomaded hair of a vanished man.

Let me say a further word about that pelvic bone. I don't know why
I was being so cagey about its provenance in the story except to say
the research department at the *Geographic* was always topnotch and
eagle-eyed, which meant exceedingly picky, and required incontro-
vertible proof of all statements of fact. Yet while there was no scien-
tific evidence the bone was actually human, there wasn't a shred of
doubt in the minds of the cavers or me, even though it looked only
a little larger than if it had once anchored a good-sized pork chop.
The main point is this: Those cavers and I were equally unhappy
about the discovery but in very different ways.

A half-dozen of us stood in a circle staring at the bones, there
being a few smaller ones too. They lay in a muddy trench dug when
the purple sleeping bag had been dragged, by whatever means,
from the red-and-white tent, the sleeping bag pulling the tent behind it like a stillborn pupa emerging from a cocoon. The bones, a
dirty liver color, had been picked absolutely clean.

"Bear," the head caver speculated. He sported a brushy, well-
trimmed goatee under those severe eyes of his, and had an authoritative way of speaking that discouraged dissent. According to my
notes, he was an ex-military man—Japanese air force, if I remember correctly.

"Ah, it was a young guy," he said, clucking his tongue, as he
squatted down to pick a Swiss Army knife holder out of the muck.
His hand hovered over the bones as if warming itself by a fire. He
speculated a bit more and then expanded on his theory that the
hapless camper, whom everybody assumed was male, had been
killed by a black bear.

I thought that was silly. Having spent my youth hiking the for-
ests of western Washington, where black bears were common, I
had come to think of them as grumpy, overgrown dogs. I also knew
they resorted to violence against man only in the most desperate
of circumstances. It seemed vastly more likely to me that a bear or

maybe a wildcat had caught the scent of a freshly decaying body and, coming to inspect, had pulled the corpse from the tent for a closer look.

But the cavers didn't want to hear what I thought. Their leader groused that after reporting that head hanging in the tree branches two years earlier, the cops had made everybody wait around all afternoon answering routine questions and spoiling their fun. No, his mind seemed made up: "The bear probably smelled food and did him in."

It was then the penny dropped and I thought I realized the nature of the game: Death by wild animal was an act of nature, not a crime, and that got the cavers off both legal and existential hooks.

"No," the goateed man went on, "this doesn't look like a suicide." He was pointing to a nifty little scoop or trowel, or whatever it was, lying there in the mud. This camper had a purpose for being inside the suicide forest that didn't include suicide, the man insisted—maybe he was an amateur botanist collecting plants. There was some further desultory discussion and then—as they say in the Mafia—that was *that*. Old-school rules. The group consensus was to not notify the authorities.

The verdict troubled me. I grew angry that the cavers might have made me party to a cover-up. But what was the crime? Failure to report a *possible* crime? Obstruction of justice? Whatever it was, it didn't seem right to ignore such mysterious circumstances, particularly when you thought about what could lead a person to make the choice to die up there in the lonely mountains, his world shrinking to a small, dismal clearing in the thick underbrush before he crawled into his tent for the last time. Was that where he thought his last obsessive thoughts, as he smelled that resiny waterproofing the canvas gives off? Had he used pills or a razor? Given Japan's stringent firearm laws, it wasn't likely to have been a gun. Was that how it ended? How many variables could there be?

That evening we all put up at a local Japanese inn where my room featured a mounted deer's head with staring glass eyeballs. At dinner we sat at long tables in a common room on the ground floor. I didn't feel like eating, but I was famished nonetheless. One caver had failed to show and somebody set the missing man's dinner tray in front of me, smiling and inviting me to dig in. I ate the extra helping with gusto, as the cavers drank beer and sake, and sang and laughed the night away. They were good and friendly folks, by all accounts, and by this time I disliked them quite a lot.

7

Looking back on it, my reasons for accepting the Fuji assignment were pretty straightforward. First, while only a fool climbs Fuji twice, only a complete idiot turns down a chance to report a story for the *National Geographic*. But I also reminded myself how good it was to be alive, traveling around the country, seeing the sights and all. Lord knows I wound up having some of the best adventures of my life after my cancer diagnosis in 1996. The magazine had sponsored most of the big ones, and I felt a duty, exactly to whom or what wasn't clear, to prove I could climb the mountain, ford the river, or go to hard places to get the job done.

Thus, at the end of the Fuji trail, I found my way to a group of kindred spirits who, though they had faced far greater challenges than I, also relished the opportunity to walk the world and have their adventures. Here's how I used them to bring the story to its summit:

Tramp around Fuji long enough and you'll very likely trip over some obsession of your own. I proved that when, at journey's end, I found myself trudging up the mountain's gravelly trails once again, my knees still hurting from my earlier ascent. I'd heard that one of Japan's big daily newspapers was sponsoring a climbing expedition for young cancer survivors. As a fellow survivor for whom Fuji's rigors had a special meaning, I was curious to see what the mountain would mean to them.

It was late summer, and the road up was a green tree-lined chute with Fuji at the end—a vibrant red immensity. But by the

Fifth Station, where the highway ends and the main climbing trail begins, the peak had transformed itself from red to a dusky emerald green. The Fuji-obsessed had told me the peak shifted moods like a quick-change artist, and I was getting the point—underscored two days earlier by a freak lightning storm that had killed a 61-year-old climber near the summit.

On this day hundreds of happy greenhorns panted in the hot sun, crowding trail turns as if waiting for an escalator. Panting a little myself, I encountered Tomoko Omata resting over a cup of green tea inside one of the many ramshackle huts where climbers can buy sodas or candy bars or rent a few square feet to catnap at ridiculously inflated prices.

"I had a tough time getting this far," said Omata-san, 32, who had leukemia at age 13.

"Really tough," chimed in Yoko Nomo, 27, who survived a brain tumor, "but Fuji-san is the number one mountain in Japan!"

When I told Omata how event sponsors had tried to keep me, a reporter, from joining her, she smiled wearily. "We need the media," she said. "When young people get cancer in Japan, everybody thinks they're going to die." Families are overprotective. Companies won't hire. Potential mates pass them by. "Many survive," said Omata, "and people need to know that."

"You should have seen us on the bus ride up," Nomo broke in, her face glowing in the hut's dim light. When they slipped above the clouds and Fuji revealed itself, it was such a thrill she said, "Everybody started clapping!"

"Till then nobody knew what climbing a mountain meant," said Fumiko Ikeda, a social worker and chaperone. I understood. But gazing at the canny faces around the table, I also knew that each of these women was a seasoned veteran in treading the uphill path. Today Fuji-san, the culture's malleable old symbol, had simply confirmed that fact for them.

And that got me thinking. Maybe it was time to retool that old proverb about Fuji and fools, the first part of which says the man who climbs but once is wise indeed. Lucky enough to get a second

*go, I realized how many people grew just a little taller in spirit
from any opportunity to measure themselves against Japan's inevitable mountain.*

8

So that was the end of the story, but not really. Reporting necessarily gives way to the prison-like conditions of writing and a powerful nostalgia for the freedom of the field. As a charmingly wayward
Newsweek colleague once said, "I love everything about being a correspondent there is—it's just the writing part I don't like." And so
back in Manhattan now, the streets sun-fried and hazy gray in the
heat, my good feeling about my summer in Japan refused to go
away, as did that voice whispering about the last good time.

Basking in the afterglow, I spent the dog days of August holed
up in our apartment, sifting through my notes by day as I wran-
gled my writing outline. In the evenings I watched the old Japanese movies I love, particularly the early postwar classics directed
by Yasujiro Ozu like *Tokyo Monogatari* (Tokyo Story) and *Banshun*
(Late Spring), with their focus on change, loss and dislocation, and
a sweet, wistful mourning for a prewar lifestyle that was forever
dead and gone.

I even thought about making a film of my own, a documentary
on postindustrial Japan and its noisy evolution or quiet revolution,
I was still trying to decide which. Ko Shioya even suggested a primo
title: *Kizashi*, which means the shape of things to come but also carries with it a delicate sense of foreboding about the future. By that
time, though, China's rise had pegged it as America's new bogeyman supreme, and nobody wanted to fund a film about a wistful
anachronism like Japan.

So there I was, sitting at my writing desk one morning, working on my story and unusually happy at my task, as I glanced out
the window and down Forty-Ninth Street to where the East River
shone like a highway paved with freshly minted nickels. I could see
the geyser at the tip of Roosevelt Island spraying plumes of toxic

water into the channel and, on the far Queens shore, the landmark red-neon Pepsi-Cola sign. Encompassing all, high and low, was a sky of deep, flawless blue. It really was a gorgeous morning.

The telephone rang. It was my upstairs neighbor, Robert Schonfeld. "Turn on the TV," he said. "A plane's hit the World Trade Center."

What followed was a short but profoundly disorienting time. It was either the same day or maybe the next or the following one, I can't remember which, when the phone rang again and one of the very helpful hotel ladies from Tokyo, a recipient of the giant peaches, was on the line. As luck would have it, she was making her very first trip to New York City. In a voice that was brave and afraid, she apologized for her bad timing. It was a quintessential Japanese exchange. The destruction of the World Trade Center Towers never came up directly, that I recall, but loomed large in the background.

The woman apologized for not being able to keep her promise to meet me. She said she was staying with a friend in Brooklyn and would not be coming into Manhattan, after all. I felt badly, too, as if I'd somehow failed her for having to welcome her to a city of smoking ruins. After that, the voice talking about the last good time fell silent and I never heard it again. A year later, in keeping with the glacial pace of *Geographic* time, the Fuji story appeared in the magazine with haiku-like brevity at, by my count, 2,754 words.

PART
THREE

ACROSS THE
FLOORBOARDS OF ASIA

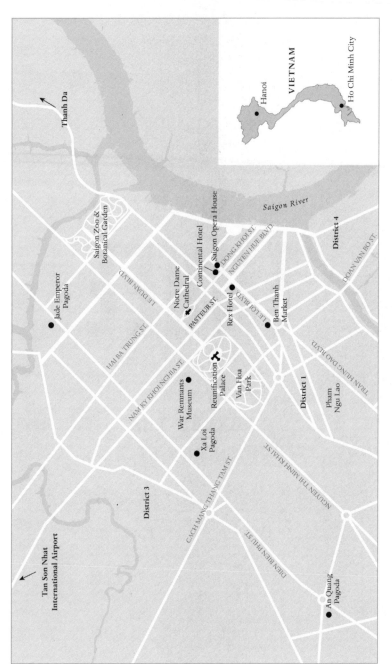

Ho Chi Minh City (Saigon).

VIETNAM
RECONSTRUCTS

1

For the long-distance reporter, each assignment is a quest, particularly the really complicated ones, and here the ancient Chinese book of wisdom, the *I Ching*, gives us some advice: "At times one has to deal with hidden enemies, intangible influences that slink into dark corners and from this hiding affect people by suggestion." To tease out the subtleties and bring that which is hidden to light, that sage tome prescribes, "Priests and magicians are used in great number."

Which brings us to Vietnam.

I had rarely felt in such need of some kind of divine intervention when Bill Graves assigned me to do a story on Saigon, a.k.a. Ho Chi Minh City, to coincide with the twentieth anniversary of the end of the Vietnam War in 1975. There were truckloads of fine journalists who knew something or a lot about Vietnam, including men and women who had covered the war at personal risk and sacrifice. I was not one of them. Still a student at the time, I'd missed reporting the conflict and was spared from serving in it by drawing a high number in President Nixon's draft lottery. As such, my thinking on Vietnam, a country I'd never visited, was conditioned by a set of dark, fluctuating, and vaguely guilt-ridden images about what had happened there and who or what was to blame.

In short, I didn't have a clue.

So I needed to find a guru to home me in on Vietnamese realities, and fast. From my reporting experiences in China, I knew that in a sequestered, Communist society you either got to sources on the inside or risked being left with whatever misinformation a government handler threw your way. But in Vietnam I didn't know a soul. While still at home in New York, I turned to my friend David Halberstam. David, who had won a Pulitzer Prize for his Vietnam War reporting and also had written the best-selling book *The Best and the Brightest*, qualified as a sort of high priest of war reporters, though he and I had only occasionally talked about that in a relationship that included going to Madison Square Garden to watch the New York Knicks lose and a collaboration on a film project about America in the 1950s. When I asked him for help, however, he was typically generous and incisive.

"Go see my old friend Pham Xuan An," he said, reminding me that An had a reputation for being the most gifted Vietnamese reporter to cover the war for the American press, so good he eventually became a full-fledged correspondent for *Time* magazine. An had continued to file dispatches after Saigon fell to Communist forces in April 1975, and for months after other Western journalists had left the country. But commitment to deadlines wasn't An's main claim to fame. Unbeknownst to his press colleagues at the time, he had also been a top spy for the Viet Cong and, in that role, helped pave the way for the American defeat he had so diligently reported on.

My priest, it seemed, was introducing me to some kind of shape-shifting magician, and being desperate for inside contacts, I couldn't wait to meet An. How could you not be curious? While many American colleagues ultimately accepted An's double life, others had felt betrayed. That David spoke so fondly of him discombobulated me. How could a journalist of Halberstam's stature, a stickler for the old-school values of transparency and truth, consider such a duplicitous character a friend? How could anybody trust a man who had been so patently two-faced in a time of war reporting when truth was an easy casualty and lives were on the line?

The case for An was this: He was, first and foremost, a patriot fighting for his country's independence, but in so doing he had never betrayed his press colleagues or fed them false information. In fact, he had gone out of his way, risking his cover at times, which meant risking his life, to keep American friends out of trouble. In a time of extremes, An was a man saddled with the impossible mission of reconciling ultimately irreconcilable loyalties. That was the argument anyhow.

When I persisted in my questions, David said, "Ask An. He'll lay it all out for you." Then as an afterthought, he said that I should be sure to take him a book. An avid reader, An apparently had a hard time getting his hands on the latest American titles in Saigon. So I tucked into my duffel bag a copy of *The Fifties*, David's history of America's signature decade, the basis for our TV miniseries, and off I went to sum up the Vietnamese gestalt in five thousand words for an article that would eventually be called "The New Saigon."

In July 1994 I arrived at Tan Son Nhat airport in Saigon. It was a sweltering afternoon, and after engaging in a brief shouting match with a bullying security official, who insisted on putting my laptop through one of those ancient death-ray X-ray machines, I checked into the Rex Hotel in District 1, the city center. Feeling the mixture of excitement and dread that comes when you arrive alone in a strange country, I was famished for context and could think of little else but contacting my Mr. Inside, Pham Xuan An. In the event my room was bugged, I dialed An from a pay phone in the lobby. (An may have been a top agent, but after the war his superiors had never permitted him to leave Vietnam for even short trips and kept tabs on his visitors.) An was polite but also to the point. In a raspy voice that reminded me of leaves skittering across a courtyard, he said, yes, he'd meet me—but not now. Wait until I got myself oriented, had seen more of the city and talked to more people—maybe then he could help me establish perspective.

It sounded like a classy snub and I felt disheartened. On the other hand, I'd given myself only a month in Vietnam and had no choice but to get busy, spy or no spy. So I reached out to others, including an American businessman I would describe in my story as "an affable old hand of the new Saigon," and who provided me my story lede when I found myself on the back of his scooter, hanging on for dear life, as we pulled away from the Rex . . .

"You don't mind the motorbike, do you?" asked Gerry Herman, pretty much as an after-thought, before inching us into the swirling, darting chaos at the intersection of Le Loi and Nguyen Hue Boulevards, where, in the tropical night, motorbikes flew in all directions.

"Not at all," I lied, knuckles clasped to jellied knees. In a flash we had whipped around the redbrick edifice of Notre Dame Cathedral, as if fired from a slingshot, and were speeding under a canopy of towering tamarind trees. Farther on, families hunkered down in community video parlors that glowed like snug electronic caves, young lovers hugged the shadows, and peddlers hawked tourist T-shirts proclaiming, with presumed irony, "Apocalypse Now."

"This is the ultimate video game!" yelled Gerry, as he expertly navigated a sea of taillights and headlamps. I was just working up the courage to share his enthusiasm when we fishtailed slightly and—thwack!—I felt a hand slap my shoulder. Turning, I found myself staring into the ambiguous grin of a scooter-borne teenager.

For a fleeting moment I felt uneasy. Like many Americans making their first trip to a city that had once served as the capital of our country's failed efforts to bring American-style democracy to Vietnam, I had harbored qualms about just how I might be received.

I needn't have worried. The youngster flashed me a luminous smile and the thumbs-up sign.

"There is great affection for America here," Gerry told me later over a mercifully stationary dinner, "in spite of, or maybe because of, the wartime trauma we shared." Indeed, as my own travels would confirm, foreigners, and particularly Americans, were symbols of the resurgence of light and color in a city that had a decade earlier hovered on the edge of darkness. President Bill Clinton had lifted America's 19-year-old economic embargo of Vietnam six months before. All Saigon, it seemed, was speeding toward the light.

"I came here for a week as a tourist and was amazed at the energy and drive," said Gerry. Flying to nearby Singapore, where he was working at the time, Gerry sank his life savings into computer equipment and returned to help a Saigon company set up Vietnam's first state-of-the-art graphic-design studio. Three months later the firm won the advertising account for Vietnam Airlines, the national flag carrier.

That kind of promise had begun to lure back growing numbers of exiled Vietnamese too. "Money, brains, hard work," said Gerry. "That's the fuel that's going to help this place catch fire."

Gerry turned out to be right, of course, but as I traveled around the city and talked to dozens of people, it also became clear that outdistancing the past would be an enormous challenge of the type often underestimated by the U.S. media. In setting up my story, I tried to spell out the main reasons:

Twenty years after its "liberation," Ho Chi Minh City remains the captive of a struggling economy. The country's communist rulers in Hanoi are embarked on a tricky bid to steer toward the open market under cumbersome communist discipline. Daily life, meanwhile, is shaded by resentments between victor and vanquished, north and south. City dwellers speak, with a wink or a frown, of the reemergence of the "Old Saigon"—shorthand for a troubling surge in drug trafficking and prostitution.

2

My early misgivings about writing on Vietnam had been exactly right: I sorely needed help in seeing beyond and below all that frantic, contradictory dynamism. And so, while waiting a decent interval to try phoning An again, I embarked on a modest double life of my own. For a few hours each day, I took whatever Mr. Duan, my government-supplied fixer, had arranged for me. A smart, organized, and charmingly cynical young man, Duan introduced me to farmers, intellectuals, and entrepreneurs, some of whom were even mildly critical of government policy and seemed pleased with their daring. It pays to be leery of any session that sounds neatly scripted, of course, and my anti-propaganda filters strained to keep up with the incoming data. It helped a bit when Duan told me, persuasively, that he wanted a career not in government but the private sector, and I came to trust him to a degree.

Nothing could change the fact, however, that he worked for a government that ultimately brooked little genuine dissent. If push came to shove, as I've said before, it's the rare and insanely brave person anywhere in the world who is going to go out on a truly long limb for a foreign reporter. As the old Korean saying goes, "When the whales fight, shrimp get crushed."

In my second life, therefore, I used the remains of each day to develop my own contacts. I tramped the rambunctious, sun-bleached city streets making cold calls on a sampling of diplomats, ex-pat businesspeople and journalists, Vietnamese émigrés from the United States, and foreigners who worked for nongovernmental organizations and charities. Like the generous Gerry Herman, these folks generally saw Vietnam caught in a yin-yang cycle of light and dark, past and future, but were nonetheless bullish about the country's trajectory. So were the Vietnamese college students I talked to. The American War was ancient history to them, something their parents and grandparents prattled on about; they expressed great enthusiasm for all things American, particularly the good-paying jobs American businesses were now bringing to Vietnam. Listening to this upbeat chorus, it was possible to believe the war had been little more than an unfortunate blip in a long-running American-Vietnamese romance.

It would have been possible to believe, that is, if the past didn't weigh so heavily on so many others. Like the émigré, now an American citizen, who had been obliged to abandon an infant son in Saigon when he and his wife fled the country during those last chaotic hours before the fall in April 1975. After arriving in the States, he fought a guilty conscience, working so devilishly hard at multiple jobs, he told me, "so my brain wouldn't kill me." One of the most memorable characters of all was the man story photographer Karen Kasmauski and I affectionately referred to as the Scissors Man. Him I met one day when I visited the Nguyen Dinh scissor works on Thanh Da, an island in the Saigon River:

Owner Nguyen Manh Tuan steered me through a jungle of stamping machines and drill presses to a mound of old military-truck suspensions. "Top-quality steel," he said triumphantly, kicking one of the slats. "Left behind by your army!"

A former lieutenant colonel in the South Vietnamese Army, Tuan was captured in combat in March 1975 and spent 18 months in a communist reeducation camp. After his release, he said, he was "homeless, penniless, jobless." Then lightning struck: Why not turn the wastage of war into something useful, like quality, hand-ground scissors?

Today, Tuan, a genial man with a level gaze and a salt-and-pepper mustache, has sold his scissors, with their snappy orange-plastic handles, in 14 countries around the world and also provided hundreds of jobs for Army of the Republic of Vietnam (ARVN) veterans and their family members, who still had trouble finding steady work.

"But I am not a real capitalist yet," insisted Tuan, elevating his eyebrows toward seven tumbledown wooden sheds that were as much artifact as factory. Steel fence posts that had once helped ring villages in barbed wire in the U.S.-backed "strategic hamlet" program now supported a thatched roof over the workers' canteen. Homemade grinding machines were pieced together from old howitzer shells. "I can make one for $50," he said proudly.

I couldn't help but like this inventive man with the tungsten constitution. But how was he able to put his painful past behind him?

"I knew I must forget the past if I wanted to survive," he said. "Any military man knows the best way to win a victory is to persuade the people who are against you to think like you and respect you."

3

How do you get people to like and respect you when you lie to them? That question overshadowed my brief relationship with Pham Xuan An, a series of three long conversations over the course of as many years that began on August 1, 1994, when my pedicab driver dropped me in front of An's walled villa in Saigon's District 3.

In spite of my worries of a brush-off, An had been true to his word. When I phoned him a second time, after I'd chased around town for a few days, he invited me over for a chat. I pulled the cord at the left-hand side of the gate, as An had instructed, and the tinkling bell brought the master spy scuffing forward in his sandals. What an interesting-looking man he was! His head was large for his emaciated body, his bright eyes sharply contrasting with a face so gaunt and sallow I thought he might be a cancer patient. (He was, in fact, a heavy smoker suffering from emphysema.) His most striking feature, and the one that sticks with me still, was the way his mouth smiled while his eyes studied.

An guided me into a big and airy room on the main floor and we sat down in an alcove where he did his work amid an empire of old-fashioned gray filing cabinets and a collection of books betraying the faint pong of mildew. A ceiling fan stirred the torpid air and, occasionally, a tropical bird broke the silence by burbling a melodious, intricate chord from a bamboo cage nearby.

I handed An the book I'd brought for him from the States and told him I was acting under orders from David Halberstam. He smiled wanly, remembering David with obvious fondness, but he didn't linger with the nostalgia. Instead, An poured us each a cup of jasmine tea, lighted a cigarette, crossed legs skinny as chopsticks, and got down to business. In that conversation and a longer one on August 18, he gave me a brisk, sharp-witted tour of the horizon and the challenges facing Vietnam.

An would stipulate that he didn't mind being quoted by name about his wartime experiences or Vietnamese history but he preferred not to be directly quoted on his analysis of current events

Pham Xuan An, Saigon, 2000.
AP Photo/Charles Dharapak, File.

while they remained current. Suffice it to say, now two decades later, he generally talked about the same contradictions roiling Vietnamese life and politics as other sources— the rigors involved in a closed political system trying to open its economy to the world, and the internal rivalries, urban vs. rural, Buddhists vs. Catholics, northerners vs. southerners and victor vs. vanquished, that complicated the process. His biggest favor was in getting me to think about the overall framework for my story, the many moving parts it must necessarily take into account, and how to assign values to them. That, in turn, helped me ask better questions of other sources and figure out where their answers fit.

I don't know what I'd expected exactly, but I found An's forthrightness both surprising and refreshing. There wasn't the slightest hint of subterfuge, which meant he was being honest or was simply exceedingly good at the spinner's art, or both at the same or different times. In any event, talking to An, along with others, led me to believe that Vietnam would continue to open and close like a bivalve, absorbing nutrients from the outside world and shutting down again any time the elite felt threatened. In short, I was able to see how I might turn a puzzle into an acceptable story.

Every country is a puzzle in its own inimitable way, of course, as are the individuals who populate it, and An was a gifted, if at times mesmerizingly opaque, briefer. (What he told you was fascinating, but he told you in a way that made you wonder what the submerged part of the iceberg looked like.) In any event, after our talks, each of which lasted several hours, I came away feeling better able to identify the puzzle pieces in play. I was also beginning to understand why Halberstam and others admired An so ardently. He was wonderfully seductive. His intellect was elegant and well exercised, his sense of humor wickedly ironic, and his mastery of conversation A-No. 1 prime. When I later read about him in the old days, I could easily picture An, as legend had it, holding court in the Givral coffee shop near the Continental Hotel, briefing friends in the foreign press—"General Givral," they called him, so impressive was his command of information that nobody else could get.

In those first two sessions we tiptoed around the edges of his spying career; it wasn't until I returned for a visit in 1997 and An greeted me like an old friend that I zeroed in on the nagging question: How could he have worked as a journalist for the Americans, snooped on them at the same time, and kept his double identity a secret?

For An, it was an old question by now, and he didn't miss a beat. When he was a boy attending the French *ecole*, he said, "we learned about *Liberté, Fraternité, Egalité* . . . very captivating for young Vietnamese," and all three of which had been denied the Vietnamese during a century of French domination that ended in 1954. Later, when he encountered Marxist ideology, An said he found the lodestar of the modern European revolutionary "very appealing to bring social justice . . . to bring happiness to my people."

At the same time, An had learned to make an important distinction—to separate ideology from humanity. In other words, you could hate French policy, but only an imbecile would hate all things French. Later, after he had studied journalism at Orange Coast College in Costa Mesa, California, in the 1950s, he said, "I had respect for those who did good things for me. The American people, my [press] colleagues, too, taught me a lot and opened my mind. I could tell the difference between friction between cultures and what people did for me. The American people . . . taught me the right thing and the wrong."

So there was the fulcrum of An's narrative, the answer to everybody who had been pestered by the thought I'd had about the enigma of divided loyalties. Loving your country, wanting to see it liberated (*Liberte!*) from foreign meddling, and alleviating social injustice (*Egalite!*), didn't mean you couldn't love Americans for their bedrock ideas and culture (*Fraternité!*).

An elaborated: In the 1960s, when he worked for Reuters news service, the *New York Herald Tribune*, the *Christian Science Monitor*, and eventually *Time*, he developed a sense of loyalty to his foreign colleagues. He shared stories with Halberstam and the others, and competed against them too. "To have a free press, you have to compete, not to lose a scoop, if you had it. But there was sportsmanship. We competed but on fair ground," An said.

How remarkable, I thought: He's talking about a free press when he fought for a Communist movement that lived and died by its own strident propaganda!

An had professional and personal boundaries he wouldn't cross, and for good reason. Former colleagues have pointed out, for example, that he was careful never to pass on disinformation to his friends in the Western press. Behind the argument is the suggestion that An would have considered that disloyal, and there's evidence to support that. Planting lies would also, as a practical matter, have destroyed An's credibility as a reporter and blown his cover. Well, life is complicated and, as every reporter needs to remember, there is almost always more than one answer to any question that's really worth asking.

Puffing the ever-present cigarette, An acknowledged his reporting complemented his spying but insisted the two things were different. Intelligence work required greater depth. If he got inside information from the ARVN central staff or American officials, he said, "I could use part of it for the press." But there you only needed "a kind of snapshot." In strategic intelligence you needed "the big picture." For example, "If there's a coup, the press only reports why it happened. For strategic intelligence, you . . . have to analyze the doctrine of war and how that will affect the outcome."

Sitting across from this skeletal chain-smoker, so alert and astute, I recalled another of my favorite passages from the *I Ching*: "The caution of a fox walking over ice is proverbial. . . . His ears are constantly alert to the cracking of the ice, as he carefully and circumspectly searches out the safest spots."

Indeed, An had spent his entire life picking his way carefully along treacherous paths. In the 1950s, he had been a de facto double agent, working for ARVN military intelligence while reporting to the Viet Cong. Later, as a reporter, he had been "double" in an unofficial but highly effective capacity, serving both the American press and the Vietnamese communists.

One way or another, it was a life that had required An to master tradecraft. He wrote his reports in invisible ink, for example, what he called "Chinese medicine." "You dissolve it in water and you write," he said. When you wanted to decode the message, "you have another medicine you put on and you can read what's written." Thicker, more detailed reports he microfilmed. His dispatches went by courier "into the jungle," at the network of secret Viet Cong tunnels at Cu Chi on the Saigon outskirts. Occasionally An would go into the weeds himself to be briefed on strategy, he said. It was a dangerous business but also a small world. The secret agent had many old friends in the South Vietnamese secret police, who, lucky for him, didn't know his secret. "I'd show up at a checkpoint and they'd let me go through," he said—no questions asked.

In contrast to the way many Americans have come to see the war, An insisted the outcome was far from inevitable. "America came close many times to winning," he said. From 1957 to the end of 1958, for example, "eighty percent of our Communist cadre was either killed or captured," and again in 1970 following the success of America's Operation Phoenix in capturing or killing suspected Viet Cong. But An and his colleagues were always sure they would win the "software" war, what the Americans used to call the war for "hearts and minds."

Eventually they did win, of course, but not until the fighting had dragged on for another bloody decade and a half. Throughout it all, An's superiors deemed his work so risky, his role so vital, they left him alone for fear of outing him. When it was all over, An was declared a hero of the revolution and heaped with war medals. Eventually he was promoted to the rank of general in the Vietnamese People's Army. Because of his ties with the Americans, however, his superiors worried he might have been conducting a triple life and sent him north for "political reorientation."

What was that like? I asked him. "Very difficult," he said, after all those years of operating independently. "I was not used to this kind of indoctrination."

The question of An's role in the war and what he did afterward remain subjects of controversy to this day. There was the argument, adopted by Halberstam and others, that An was a man split more or less in two—loyal to his foreign friends, if ultimately loyal to the cause of liberating his country from foreigners, which he had first taken up in 1944, after the Japanese invaded Indochina and temporarily displaced the French. That was An's basic story line and one that historian Larry Berman adopts in *Perfect Spy: The Incredible Double Life of Pham Xuan An*, whose cover proclaims Berman the man "An considered his official American biographer."

Not everybody has agreed. In his biography, *The Spy Who Loved Us: The Vietnam War and Pham Xuan An's Dangerous Game*, author Thomas A. Bass argues that An was a master of deceit to the very end. Simultaneously "presenting himself as a strategic analyst, someone who merely observed the war from the sidelines," Bass writes, An "was actually a master tactician involved in many of the war's major battles" and by extension responsible for the deaths of many Americans, a people he professed to love. The spy's "brilliant sleight of hand" blinded those who loved him to the true nature of his intelligence work, which Bass contends continued until his death in 2006. (Berman writes that he, too, discovered "An had never really retired from the spy business; he remained a 'consultant' for Hanoi's General Department of Intelligence"—but he puts less weight to it.) So there you have it: Two well-written, well-researched books on the Vietnam War's famous spy reach different conclusions.

A certain mystery is likely to always hover over An's legacy, but my encounters with the man left me with the distinct impression that, whatever else could be said of him, he was, epistemologically speaking, an old-school stickler too. By his lights, honest observers might differ on the interpretation of events, but a fact was a fact was a fact. Communist officials were capable of doing good research, but because they were always trying to satisfy their superiors, uncomfortable facts had often been ignored. "You can't have good analysis without good debate," An told me, "and their data was sometimes falsified."

That viewpoint inevitably created a divide between the veteran reporter in An and others in military intelligence. It was, he said, "a conflict of cultures, of . . . ways of research. . . . I did research based on fact, not ideology," just the way his American press colleagues and editors had taught him. What had chronically escaped some of his Vietnamese colleagues, he said, was the basic truth that "perception is different" from action. Sometimes they talked like the facts had changed their minds and they were willing to act, but then did nothing.

We paused our last conversation at one point so An could show me his collection of tropical fish, quicksilver bullets in a big aquarium tank outside his first-floor window. He talked about his German shepherds with a light in his eyes but looked sad when he said his dreams of breeding the dogs had stalled because one of them had died for lack of proper medicine. As for Vietnam, he was sure the healing would come, but, speaking personally, he was disappointed: Freeing the Vietnamese to chase money without a deep sense of social commitment wasn't what he'd had in mind when he went to war against foreign tyranny in the name of social justice.

I watched the old spy open the bamboo cage and feed his bird a few rice worms. It was a little green and yellow thing and, as the creature flitted around excitedly at the approach of his hand, An looked at me, his penetrating eyes smiling. "He sings beautifully," he said.

As our talk drew to a close, An waved a hand, as if the words were birds on the wing. "I'm too old to solve the problem," he said. "Young people have to do it. In history, everything changes. You fight for social justice and when you cannot achieve it in your lifetime, you feel a little upset about it. . . . Older people are stuck looking through the lens of war."

I pursued a similar point in my *Geographic* story:

Cutting through the debris of history has been critical to improving Vietnam's relations with the United States. I discovered this one morning at the War Crimes Exhibition [today, the War Remnants Museum] when I found myself in a deserted courtyard with the rusting relics of war: an M48 tank and a large yellow bulldozer allegedly used by the Seabees to raze a village. A guillotine purportedly belonging to the U.S.-sponsored regime of former President Ngo Dinh Diem bore the cheery legend, "The blade weighs only fifty kilos!" But why were there so few Vietnamese visitors, I wondered?

One reason, as an amiable government guide later explained, was that half the city's residents had been born after 1975 and, for them subsequent clashes with China and Cambodia had made sharper impressions. A thousand years of fending off overzealous neighbors and colonialists had taught the Vietnamese to be realistic, he said.

Equally important is the city's frenzied dash for dong (Vietnam's official currency) and dollars (its preferred one), which leaves little time for dwelling on the past. . . . Americans I met found a few of Saigon's cash-based values less than appetizing. Everywhere you went, they said, somebody expected "rich" foreigners to redistribute their wealth in the form of tips, inflated prices, even bribes. "Cowboy capitalists," as the more freebooting Vietnamese-American entrepreneurs are called, get the blame for promoting this "fast buckism." Many older Vietnamese complain that it tempts the twentysomething generation into a moral vacuum of motorbikes, Hong Kong movies, American fashions, and rock-and-roll.

This made me wonder: If the city that fell to communism 20 years ago was becoming a Madison Avenue-style beachhead, what had the "war of liberation" been all about?

Tran Van Giau tried to set me straight. "Bienvenue, monsieur!" said the 83-year-old former revolutionary when I visited him behind the gates of his villa. Giau had served many years as a top agent and propagandist and told me bluntly that Karl Marx never said people had to be poor.

I'd give him that, but what would Ho or Marx make of cowboy capitalism or the rise in drug abuse and prostitution? "When economic development is so quick, there are bound to be side effects," Giau acknowledged. Then he added, "But poverty is always more threatening to society than wealth.

"When the Americans left, the economy was booming," he said. "Then our mistakes nearly killed it." Thanks to doi moi, the government's reform policy, the economy is now back on its feet.

Still, wasn't he bothered by the billboards for credit cards, hair tonic, and video recorders that wallpapered the streets? Or the city's proliferating discos?

The old revolutionary stared at me. He didn't know about me, but, he said, "even I used to go dancing when I was 18!"

4

Good reporters can get a bad rap for seeking out conflict, points of tension, and contradictions. Yet would we really want it otherwise? Like a doctor trying to make sense out of a battery of conflicting test results, it's precisely by looking at the anomalies and trying to rectify them that we're likely to come closer to the reality of a situation. Conflict necessarily drives the reporting puzzle. And so, it stands to reason the more opportunity you have to observe your subject over time, the better shot you have at resolving the irregularities that obscure the truer picture or simply confirming trends that were less evident but hinted at before.

The latter was the case when I returned to Ho Chi Minh City in 1997, three years after reporting "The New Saigon," and found the city had become more paranoid. I checked into the Continental Hotel and after inhaling an excellent *croque monsieur* in the lobby bar, I tried phoning Tuan, the Scissors Man, but I couldn't get through. Later, when I had a Vietnamese speaker try, a man got on the line to say, cryptically, that Tuan was now in the Mekong Delta and couldn't be reached. A reliable friend told me word had come to him that another entrepreneur of my acquaintance, flying high three years earlier, was now in jail. The Saigon rumor mill was flourishing but the larger idea seemed to carry weight: Officials might resent commercial success for doctrinal reasons, but certain parties got especially nasty when you failed to cut them in on the action.

Saigon was more contradictory than ever. Walking the streets, you could see the city was brighter than before, with more fancy new hotels, more stylish shop fronts, and newer, trendier restaurants. In spite or maybe because of the new brightness, though, the darkness at the edges of the picture had only seemed to deepen. Expat oilmen I spoke to farther south in Vung Tau told me how lower-level Vietnamese involved in their business had been executed for corruption; it wasn't clear whether officials had targeted them in order to clean up the system or for failing to include them in their side deals, or both. In sum, there was a feeling that people who stepped out of line could be eliminated at any time, and it wasn't always clear where the line was.

Even the ebullient Gerry Herman seemed a little spooked. I was sitting with him in a coffee shop on Dong Khoi Street one afternoon eating ice cream when he told me that an Australian friend had been put under house arrest for espionage. His crime? All he appeared to be guilty of was sending monthly business reports to Singapore in line with his job as a corporate securities analyst.

"I felt sorry for this poor guy," Gerry said, so he'd treated him to dinner at a neighborhood restaurant, which was permitted under the terms of his friend's confinement. The pair sat and talked while two plainclothes policemen occupied a nearby table. A short time later, Gerry was leaving for Singapore on business when the authorities stopped him at the airport. "They'd found their courier pigeon," he said with an ironic smile. The police photocopied Gerry's papers and business cards, and then allowed him to board his flight. When he got back to Saigon, they hauled him in for questioning.

That's where the story took a peculiar twist. Out of the blue, Gerry's interrogator asked him about his father. What on earth did his father have to do with anything? Gerry wondered. Hadn't his father served in the OSS, the precursor to the CIA, during World War II in Europe? the policeman asked.

Gerry was dumbfounded. Okay, so what? To him, it was an ancient war story. But in a traditionally nonlinear, dynastic way of Vietnamese thinking, he knew what the cop was thinking—*Like father, like son.* Gerry was let go but had wondered ever since about the security cops' source for his father's antediluvian activities. He concluded the information must have spilled out of Russia after the fall of the Soviet Union in 1991 when KGB archives had become accessible. It wasn't a bad guess. And up to the time we met, Gerry had had no further encounters with the Security Police. "Perhaps I earned a star," he suggested. "After all, Ho Chi Minh worked with OSS during World War II as well!"

In the space of three years, a growing debate inside the Communist party and the government, and growing paranoia over how to maintain control in a country opening to the outside world, had become an important measure of the extent to which Vietnam might overcome its deep divisions. While reporting my Saigon story in 1994, the key elements had all been there. What would continue to remain unclear after 1997 was whether the grinding of society's various tectonic plates would eventually produce a political or social earthquake, workable reforms, or something in between. In the meantime you couldn't help but be impressed by the vigor with which Vietnamese and foreigners alike were engaged in a high-stakes gamble, not really knowing how smoothly or disastrously things would go.

5

I had been reporting my initial Saigon story for two weeks and was beginning to worry about the quality of the material I had in my notebooks. A half-dozen or more separate interview appointments isn't too many for me to squeeze into a single day if travel between and among them doesn't eat up too much time. On this assignment, though, try as I might, I wasn't filling my quota. More to the point, I had a sinking feeling I wasn't burrowing far enough into the woodwork of the city or seeing far enough into people's lives.

As I've said, one of the big causes of social disharmony was the unenviable position of the millions of Vietnamese who had found themselves on the losing side when the Communist forces overran Saigon in 1975 and the last American helicopter had lifted off the roof of the American embassy. Overnight, the Scissors Man, and others like him, became pariahs in a war-shattered country where the victors had little sympathy for making meager resources stretch to aid yesterday's foes.

By 1994, resentments between victor and vanquished had reached a boiling point, and the country's leaders faced a dilemma. If they lifted the lid on the ARVN veterans, no one could predict the outcome but the consequences might be bloody and disruptive; if they didn't heal the breech, how would the country move forward? Fixer Duan dutifully laid on an interview with the head of a government-sponsored veterans' organization and, predictably, the man didn't give a damn about the ARVN vets. The question for me was this: How did I get a good look inside this important angle of the story?

As I pondered that challenge, I was also beginning to go a little stir crazy. Life at the Rex Hotel was comfortable but stifling, like staying in a homey, threadbare museum. The hotel had housed U.S. Army personnel once upon a time, which may have explained the presence of macaroni and cheese on the room service menu and the old-fashioned wooden rocking chair in my room that could have graced the front porch of a leafy Iowa town circa 1960. By contrast, the damp, fragrant bathroom maintained a local sense of humor: The "Toilet Paper of Tourism" promised "the softest bathroom tissue" while delivering sandpaper; the garbage pail spoke philosophically with the motto: "for those who wish to enjoy simple and rational lives." I really needed to be getting out more.

I did so by getting introduced to the habit of hiring a pedicab, or cyclo, driver and touring the city at street level, delving into a different nook or cranny every day. It wasn't hard to arrange. A ragtag contingent of Cyclo Irregulars, as I thought of them, routinely camped out on the little traffic island across the street from the Rex, waiting in the muggy heat for foreign tourists to materialize. They would then swing into action, fighting for fares and using their cabs, bumper-car-style, to push one another out of the way. The drivers, mainly ARVN vets, had few other job opportunities, and the competition was dog-eat-dog.

After my self-imposed isolation, I looked forward to these excursions when one or another of the Irregulars would pedal me around the elegant, seedy, up-rushing city center with its tree-lined boulevards, démodé French architecture, and new construction sites, the driver shouting into my ear what English he knew in short, sharp bursts: "New hotel! Six hundred fifty rooms! Many Chinese! Many foreign people!" In Pham Ngu Lao, Saigon's backpacker district, I saw a troop of European tourists, awkward as baby fawns, recoiling on the sidewalk from an onslaught of street kids hawking postcards, maps, and ancient coins of dubious origin. I loved the way these ubiquitous, pint-sized hustlers typically greeted their marks: "Hello, Money!"

It was by venturing into District 4 that I learned something fundamental, however. An island bordered by the Saigon River, the area was heavily populated with people who had worked for the government of South Vietnam, or the Americans, or belonged to the defeated ARVN forces. Being an island, it was a convenient piece of geography for the authorities, since it could be sealed off from the rest of the city in the event of an uprising by the disenfranchised. In other words, it was the place you wanted to see if you wanted to understand the price of defeat . . .

The sun was burning down as my driver pedaled across a bridge, where emerald green palm fronds drooped over a fetid canal, and plunged down a trail of broken pavement. Suddenly a wild-eyed young man in a soiled green shirt rushed our cyclo, arms flailing in anger. "He wanted to know what country you from," said my driver, unconvincingly, after fending him off with a few brisk shouts. No wonder few outsiders ever ventured here.

As we burrowed deeper into the heart of the district, with its collapsing wooden shanties and septic ditches, the streets closed to little more than a cyclo's width, bringing us within a fingertip of the daily round. A toothless old man leaned from his window to say "Harro," with a friendly flap of his hand. A sad-faced young mother in flower-print pajamas cradled her baby under bunched mosquito netting in the cool darkness of a metal-roofed shack, as an unseen boom box crooned a tinny rendition of an old Everly Brothers song:

When I feel blue in the night
And I need you to hold me tight
Whenever I want you
All I have to do is dream, dream,
dream, dream . . .

It was a depressing scene. Had I to do my job over again, I might have tried to augment the Everly Brothers with a passage from Vietnam's epic poem, *The Tale of Kieu*, which I was then just discovering. It spoke about the burden of Vietnamese history in a different, more organic tongue:

A hundred years—in this span of life on earth
talent and destiny are apt to feud.
You must go through a play of ebb and flow
and watch such things as make you sick at heart.
Is it so strange that losses balance gains?
Blue Heaven's wont to strike a rose from spite.

(One more belated tip for the long-distance reporter: Find a country's Homeric poem and you've found an invaluable window on a people's collective consciousness.)

My trip to District 4 continued as . . .

Nearby I stopped to talk to a middle-aged resident with rheumy eyes and a thin mustache, who proffered a snapshot, grainy with age, showing a rakish young soldier in combat fatigues. "Airborne," he said proudly, his backbone stiffening at the memory of his role in a long-gone army.

The man holding the photo was an older brother of Tuan, one of the Irregulars, and he and I were shaking hands inside a small, strange room—a restaurant, I thought, but with only one small table and no customers. The brother gripped my hand in both of his and shook firmly. As we sipped hot tea from crusty shot glasses, Tuan interpreted for his brother. "Government has done nothing," the brother said emphatically. Did he mean the government had actively abused him and his compatriots or simply ignored them? I asked. For the brother, it was a distinction without a difference: "Government do nothing," he repeated.

Some American veterans I met, regardless of their views on the war and its outcome, were troubled by this neglect and felt the United States owed its former comrades-in-arms stronger support in easing their circumstances. From what I saw of District 4's lost lives it was hard to disagree.

It was also hard for a reporter to resist going there, and I made several forays into the area's tangled alleyways. On one occasion another American and I were visiting after nightfall, and despite the presence of two trusty cyclo men, I wasn't thrilled about being in such a dicey neighborhood after hours. But the younger of the drivers had wanted to show us where he lived and introduce us to his wife, and I didn't feel right about turning down the invitation, so off we went.

On cyclo patrol, Saigon, 1994.

The cyclo man's house was a squashed rhombus on an alley crooked as a goat's hind leg. Inside, the one-room cavity was hot and dark, like stepping into a sauna box fully clothed and partially blindfolded. As my eyes adjusted to the gloom, I could see off to my left a low-slung bed swathed in mosquito netting behind which the driver's wife lay clutching to her chest a ball of some kind that, on closer inspection, turned out to be a baby. Mother and child appeared utterly drained of energy in the clammy heat.

I felt awkward as I stood there staring down at the woman while she smiled weakly at the big foreigner who had unaccountably materialized at her bedside. The cyclo man explained the baby, the couple's sixth, had been born the previous week. The woman looked brave and exhausted—and quite beautiful, I thought. I remember being struck by how the skin on her face and forearms gave off a sickly, phosphorescent sheen in that dark place. I felt sorry for her when I learned that she was only thirty-two years old, although I don't know whether it was because her best years, such as they might have been, were very likely gone or because you could sense what burdens lay ahead for her in a hut with a ceramic rain barrel as the only source of water for drinking, cooking, and bathing.

After we had traded clumsy pleasantries and the husband had filled us in on the challenges of their life together, I pulled from my shoulder bag a gift I'd brought for the lady of the house. It was a semi-fancy silk table-runner, and immediately I felt like a total fool. The couple may have had a table in that hut of theirs, but if they did I didn't put it down in my notes.

It not infrequently happens that a dead serious moment opens the door to farce, and as I continued to probe Saigon by cyclo, I detected an attitude shift among the Irregulars. Word seemed to be going around that the big foreign journalist had an odd but apparently harmless fascination with their domestic lives, one that might possibly be converted into cash subsidies in lieu of a table-runner. Whatever the motivation, the drivers entered into a not-so-subtle competition to impress on me how poor and mean their lives really were. Mr. Cua tried to lure me back to District 4 to meet his wife and children on the promise of a special souvenir photograph he said he was keeping for me there. Couldn't he bring it to the hotel? No, he said, it was something that, for reasons unclear, was necessarily at home.

It was a pretty transparent business, but how could you take offense? Such was the desperation of men trying to provide for their families in a place where the war continued by other means and the defeated, so close to their government and so far from American concerns, continued to pay a heavy price. Today, when I read about places like Afghanistan or Iraq, I think back to District 4 and wonder about how young mothers and fathers are getting along in America's newest spheres of influence.

6

In other parts of Saigon, on other days, the signs of a budding prosperity the Communists had not managed to stamp out were so visible the city's rebirth seemed a foregone conclusion. Then, inevitably, as I would point out in my *Geographic* story, something would happen to undercut my confidence.

We'll get to one such incident in a minute but first a little background. I was now splitting my days into threes—one part consisted of my peregrinations with Government Fixer Duan, another of my own enterprise reporting, and a third my after-hours cyclo explorations, which took on a familiar pattern. When the Irregulars had no more pedal left in them we broke for dinner, drivers going off to find a bowl of noodles after dropping me and whatever companions might be along at a foreigner-appropriate restaurant, like the street-side café where, one night, I discovered a bird had shat in my hair from an overhanging tree; having finished my dinner, I was left to ponder the metaphysical question of exactly what I had eaten.

After dinner the Irregulars would return and on occasion pedal over to a bar called Hein and Bob's Place not far from the Saigon Opera House in District 1. Every long-distance reporter needs a listening post, and this establishment, run by Bob Shibley, an American vet, was a good one.

Tall and laconic, Bob had served as an army captain during the war and afterward worked in midlevel corporate jobs in the States. He returned to Saigon in the early 1990s not to open a bar but because, like other war veterans, he missed the excitement of Vietnam. Having recently gone back to the States for a visit, he'd been spooked by the quiet suburban streets and couldn't wait to return to the manifest energy of Saigon. He also confessed to having acquired a case of what old Saigon hands called the *maladie jaune*, an attraction for Vietnam's ubiquitous population of bright, beautiful, and graceful women, one of whom was now his wife and business partner.

I asked Bob if it was hard to set up a business in Saigon. Not really, he said. You had to pay off the cops, of course. "We've got girls here and that's illegal," Bob told me. "We've got tables outside and that's illegal." Illegal in this case simply meant the authorities would do nothing to curb the "illegal" behavior as long as you paid up. And pity the foreigner who didn't. When another American running a bar up the street had refused to give the cops their payoff, his Vietnamese wife had been summarily jailed. "They really nailed him," Bob said.

"Cops make twenty dollars a month," he said at another point. Then, lo and behold, you'd suddenly see them riding around the neighborhood on fancy motorbikes that cost many months' salary. "We laugh when we see a cop on a bicycle," said Bob drily. "We know he's an honest cop."

Talking to Bob's employees, I was able to learn a little more about the younger generation's lives and dreams. A pleasant toothy woman told me she'd come from the Mekong Delta to study English. "American English," she stressed—so "I can get a good job!" I asked her if she wanted to work for a foreign company. "Of course!" she said, stunned at my dimness. Her winsome friend, Phuong, who hailed from Dalat in the Central Highlands, attended "airlines school" during the day and worked every night till one in the morning, "seven days a week."

"All day long" and "seven days a week" were phrases that cropped up so often in impromptu English conversations I suspected everybody was using the same English-language textbook that nonetheless spoke to the reality of their lives. Pulling a long face, poor Phuong said she'd flunked a recent interview for a job with Vietnam Airlines "because of my poor English," but she was determined to keep plugging way. One of the reasons she worked at Hein and Bob's, she said—and I believed her—was to practice English with foreigners. As far as I could tell, Bob and his wife maintained a wholesome work environment, meaning the girls weren't expected to sell themselves. And there was none of the malevolent snickering from the staff that greeted foreign arrivals in the

more infamous tourist traps like the one down the street that resembled a constrictive intrauterine chamber done up in red and
black leatherette.

One evening the conversation was floating along agreeably
when, as I later wrote:

> . . . a violent commotion erupted outside. About a dozen young
> Vietnamese filled the picture window like extras in a B movie.
> They brandished bottles and shouted angrily, stopping just beyond
> our view. Minutes later they sauntered back, nonchalantly adjust-
> ing their hair and clothes. In the brawl—which was rumored to
> have had political overtones—a young man had been left lying on
> the pavement in a pool of blood. Later, word came: The man had
> died en route to a local hospital.

Running a bar on Saigon's mean streets wasn't for the fainthear-
ed. After the ambulance had pulled away, Bob confided that he,
too, had been savagely mugged. He was walking down the street
in broad daylight when a business rival had come out of nowhere,
stabbing him and puncturing a lung.

Bob was surprisingly philosophical, I thought, about the difficulties he faced in Saigon's sharp-elbowed street economy, and in
our several conversations wrote them off to prevailing cultural attitudes. He told me about a bright twelve-year-old girl who had
been working the area outside his bar into the wee hours. Bob offered her parents a deal. If they agreed to take her off the streets he
would pay for her education through high school and reimburse
the parents for the lost income. The parents accepted. A short time
later, however, the girl was back in front of Bob's bar. When he confronted the parents, they didn't understand the fuss. They wanted
both his money and what the girl was making on the streets, Bob
said, "and they couldn't see why the foreigner shouldn't pay," no
matter what the merits of the grievance.

Bob pointed to what he saw as the moral of the story: "When
Americans come here," he said, "their first instinct is to help. But

you can't help by giving people money. The only way you can help is by giving them a job."

I found Bob to be such sober and thoughtful company that I grew to admire him and trusted his opinion. Three years later, when I returned to Saigon, I asked my cyclo driver to drop me in front of Hein and Bob's so I could compare notes with him again. The place had undergone a serious facelift—there was a fancy new bamboo bar with matching stools and more attractive hostesses in greater numbers. There was no Phuong, though, and while I was wondering if her dream of working for an airline had ever come true, a sassy Saigonaise sat down next to me. She said her name was Ann: "I study eka-nom-ik."

I asked after Bob. Was he coming in? "He sick," Ann said. Suspecting the run-around, I told her, look, I was only in town for a short time and I wanted to say hello to my friend. After giving me a graceful third-degree, Ann said, "Okay, I help you."

She went behind the bar, made a phone call, and returned. "Bob's wife say you write on a paper who you are and we give to Bob." I pulled out a business card, scribbled a note, and attached a *National Geographic* tchotchke I'd brought him as a gift, which Ann promised to see into Bob's hands.

"You write very small," she chided as she took my note behind the counter, where a tough-talking drill-sergeant of a mama-san supervised several girls in parsing my message like an ancient rune.

Two nights later I returned for a progress report. Before I could make the door, I was stopped by a street tout who accosted me with his hilarious mile-a-minute patter:

"HeyyouJoelongtimenoseewhereyoubeensolonghowbouta-pieceofass?"

"Too old," I said, shaking my head and pushing past the man.

He guffawed: "Younotoooldyouhandsomeyoulooklikefucking-moviestar."

Inside, Ann approached with her pouty lips and perfect teeth and said bluntly, "He no remember you." Incongruously, she then gave me a number purportedly for Bob's cell phone, which didn't in fact connect to anything. I later heard a rumor that Bob had been murdered; maybe somebody had put a contract out on him, but like other rumors that swirled around Saigon it proved impossible to substantiate. Saigon remained confusing that way.

The question of Bob nagged at me off and on for years, and only after further recent sleuthing did I uncover a more reliable story: Visa problems had barred Bob from Vietnam in the mid-nineties. He spent roughly a year in Laos trying to get back in and then, in 1997, returned to the States where, the following year, he died from injuries suffered in a traffic accident in Minneapolis.

On the night of Ann and "He no remember you" it appeared he hadn't been in Saigon for some time.

7

I was lucky in Vietnam. For somebody who went into his work there not having a single in-country guru to rely on, I had done rather well; the priests and magicians and their apprentices had come out of the woodwork to help me do my job, as if on cue. And no one was more memorable or helpful than Pham Xuan An. Like the correspondents who had known him in the old wartime days, I'd been totally charmed by his charismatic brain, intricate personality, and canny insider's knowledge. He always seemed to have an impossibly fascinating set of facts or figures at his finger-tips—about who was sinking money into what condominium purchases abroad in case history threw them a curveball, for example. Because of his fact-oriented reportage and corrosive wit, it wasn't hard to understand why the country's ruling hierarchy would play it safe and deny him a travel visa.

An's approach to sizing up the world reminded me of something I'd first learned years before from my British uncles at the *Far Eastern Economic Review*. Stated simply, there is no such thing as a "country," at least in the monolithic sense, or as envisioned in the dreams of its nativists or nationalists. For an inquiring observer, a country—any community, really—is best thought of as a set of test tubes, each one containing discrete elements that, when mixed with others, not infrequently produce volatile, often unpredictable results, and therefore the chemicals and their mixing need to be closely watched. What was uniquely true of Vietnam, as An and others described it, has also been true, mutatis mutandis, for every other complicated place I've ever encountered.

In 2006, Pham Xuan An, ex-*Time* magazine correspondent and army general, secret agent and People's Army Hero, died of emphysema at a military hospital in Saigon. By then, Vietnam had continued to fight out its contradictions, its new sources of light illuminating the dark corners of its historical drama but the darkness fading too as the country slowly reconciled its past with its present. The process has moved ahead in fits and starts in the years since. But for all that, and perhaps oddly, the first thing that comes to mind when I think of my encounters with An was something that occurred during my visit to his house in 1997.

Taking a break in a conversation that lasted several hours, I stood up, stretched my legs, and then somehow managed to lock myself in An's cramped under-stairs toilet. When I didn't return to the parlor, the old spy tracked me down, discovered his large, disappeared interlocutor struggling with the door latch in the tiny compartment, and liberated me with a flat, mirthless smile.

I was also left with the kind of questions that don't easily go away: What so thoroughly fascinates us about the life of a double agent? Why do such figures become the shadowy heroes or antiheroes of so many of our movies and novels? Is it because we human beings are such natural double agents ourselves, so often saying one thing and doing another, as we wend our contradictory way through what the literary types call the heart's dark forest? Does that explain why we hold in awe somebody who plays a deadly game so flawlessly for so long and at such high stakes—an Olympic gold medalist in the deceptathlon, if you will?

An's unofficial biographer Thomas Bass is probably right in one respect: We won't know the full scope of An's activities until Vietnam's intelligence archives disgorge the voluminous dispatches he wrote for his spymasters in Hanoi.

Yet even then I suspect we won't really know. Documents, however detailed, rarely contain the whole story, and An surely will remain one of the great enigmatic figures of the war. Our mutual friend David Halberstam (who was killed in an automobile accident in Menlo Park, California, just seven months after An's death) had a great sixth sense about people—a bullshit detector, as it's sometimes known in the trade. He'd been as surprised as anybody about An's marathon deception but also respected his friend and, for the briefest of moments during that first trip to Saigon, I thought I knew why. It came when I was forced to cut my trip short because of a family emergency in Tokyo.

I had foolishly lost my exit permit and, based on stories I'd heard from reliable sources about authorities using the flimsiest of excuses to hold up and shake down foreigners trying to leave the country, I was afraid I'd miss my flight. Phoning An to say good-bye, I mentioned my predicament. Unbidden, he swung into action, dispatching an intermediary to accompany me to Tan Son Nhat airport in case there was trouble—a gesture, you might say, of *fraternité*.

My pulse was racing as I rode the terminal escalator up to the departure level and offered my passport to a balding, impassive immigration official in a rumpled uniform. Just in case my melodramatic capture narrative bore any semblance to reality, I had stored my transcribed notebooks on a computer disk, which I not so cleverly concealed in the pocket of my shirt. The man gave my travel documents a perfunctory look and then banged down his exit stamp. Smiling incandescently, he said, "Please come back to Vietnam!"

I'll say it one more time: I did not become a Vietnam expert by any stretch of the imagination. But I did manage to find intelligent, complex, and strong-minded sources that helped me establish the contrasting viewpoints necessary to "triangulate" a rudimentary snapshot of Saigon at that interesting point in its history.

When you think about it, I suppose, our guides are always there, moving through the background of our stories and our lives, helpful or capricious, as fortune allows. As reporters, we pride ourselves on working hard to dig out our sources and hear what they have to say, and we certainly deserve some of the credit. On the other hand, I've always been struck by the undeniable mystery of field-work, and speaking personally, I can never wait to see what un-known personalities will step forward to shape a story's fate.

My final thought on the matter is this: For those who seek to observe the world in a serious way, the music may change, but the waltz is nearly always exactly as Robert Frost describes it in his poem, "The Secret Sits":

We dance round in a ring and suppose,
But the Secret sits in the middle and knows.

LIVING
(SEMI-)DANGEROUSLY
IN INDONESIA

1

My late mother was as cool as they come in a crisis. I was nine or ten, playing army with my pals in a big wooded lot down the street from our house when, creeping through sticker bushes to spy on the enemy camp, I accidentally squashed a hornet's nest underfoot. In no time the avenging insects had carpeted my head, neck, and arms with dozens of stinging welts. Having read somewhere about bee-sting victims suddenly dropping dead from anaphylactic shock, and betraying the incipient storyteller's weakness for drama, I furiously pedaled my bicycle home to say good-bye to my mother.

But my mother, the tall, strawberry-blonde grocer's daughter who had lived through economic depression and war, wasn't buying it. "You're not going to die," she said, with just enough mockery in her voice to make me believe her. She then bundled me into the car for a trip up to Hillman City to see Dr. Leary, just in case. The laconic, silver-haired physician concurred with my mom's diagnosis, adding with a flinty smile, "You read too much!"

My mother found Dr. Leary's punch line hilarious for the way, I suppose, it poked fun at the obsession among her generation of Depression-era moms and dads with their kids riding the escalator of education to success and higher social status. On the other hand, no good mother wanted to see her son or daughter turn into a clueless egghead. And so, "You read too much," capturing the irony of the age, became an inside joke she would remind me of all the years I was growing up.

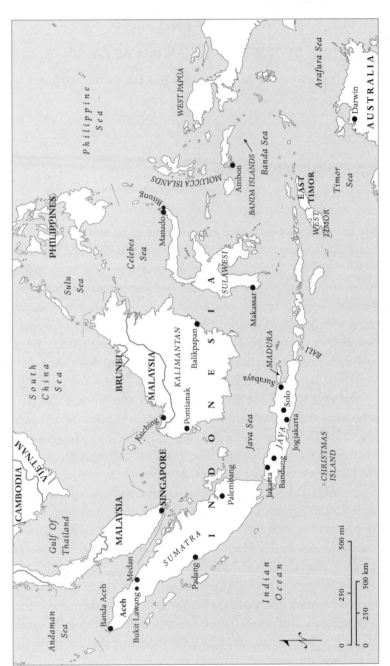

Indonesia.

It took me forty years, but I eventually turned the tables. In 1999, Bob Poole green-lighted my proposal for a story entitled "Indonesia: Living Dangerously," a first-class adventure that would clock in at five thousand words and contain one, possibly two, lucky escapes. Heaven knows it was a delicate time in Indonesia.

The previous May Suharto, the country's longtime dictator, had fallen from power after student dissidents occupied the area around the national parliament and lined its expansive roof to call for his ouster. Although the wily strongman survived the tumult, ordinary Indonesians weren't so lucky; hundreds of people died in the riots and looting that followed reports the police had shot and killed a number of young protestors, and Jakarta's morgues overflowed with body bags.

My mother had been reading about the mess in Indonesia, and was on the phone to me in New York. "I think you should tell them you're not going," she said.

"I beg your pardon?"

"You heard me, Mister," she said, her tough-guy tone faltering just a bit at age seventy-nine. "Indonesia is *too* dangerous. I don't think you should go."

"Okay," I said, "I'll give the editors of *National Geographic* a call and tell them my mommy doesn't want me to take the job."

My mother burst out laughing. "Well, now that you put it that way, it does sound pretty silly," she confessed. You had to hand it to the old gal: She had a good sense of humor and knew, in any event, she was arguing a lost cause. Nonetheless, our conversation contained a small revelation. After all those years, I finally sensed the anxiety she must have felt but had kept so well hidden on the afternoon of the angry hornets.

So just to cheer her up, I added, "You read too much!" And we both had a good laugh. But mothers sense things that kids, however old, don't, and mine wasn't wrong to worry about Indonesia.

Indonesia wasn't *not* dangerous. With Suharto gone the country was lighting up from stem to stern with violent clashes between and among forces he had long kept under wraps—Muslim and Christian fundamentalists, ethnic and communal rioters, and people simply out to settle deadly scores over money or politics.

In spite of all its turmoil, however, Indonesia was a place I'd yearned to visit for many years. Part of it was its sheer mystery. Flung across the floorboards of Southeast Asia, it was the region's biggest country, and arguably the hardest for an American to see into. For years, the Suharto government had denied visas to foreign correspondents, summarily booted out those who got in, and meanwhile terrorized local journalists to keep them from spilling its shenanigans to the wider world.

Now that the lid was off, the question arose: How does a naturally risk-averse reporter like me handicap the risks of reporting in such an unsettled situation? The answer of course is to read too much—or I should say to read as much as humanly possible. Redmond O'Hanlon spoke to the common neurosis of many a long-distance reporter when he noted, in his travel classic *Into the Heart of Borneo*, ". . . I was astonished to discover, on being threatened with a two-month exile to the primary jungles of Borneo, just how fast a man can read."

Here's my typical modus operandi for reading my way into a story: consult news clips, quality long-form articles, and books, and get to know the ins and outs of your story as quickly as you can. Figure out why you're going to a particular point on the map and what you can reasonably hope to achieve there. Once the sketchy outlines of the story and its players emerge, seek out other reporters, diplomats, scholars, and businesspeople who've recently traveled the same territory. In short, know what you're getting into.

Reading too much, in and of itself, is never enough, of course. And therein lies the epistemological problem that stems from having to deal with the contradictions buried at the heart of all learning, a condition pithily summed up by Madame Laoutaro, a character in Robertson Davies's novel *The Rebel Angels*: "Every big thing is a secret, even when you know it, because you never know all of it."

So you need a plan, a hook, that all-important metaphor I've mentioned before, to explain what needs to be explained. In

Indonesia's case, the country was far too big, complicated, churning, and diverse to cover as a whole. I'd have to be highly selective in my choice of venues while still trying to capture the essence of the place overall. Once again, Bob Poole delivered the goods, helpfully asking what, if anything, would hold this sprawling pressure-cooker of a nation together now that Suharto was no longer sitting on the lid.

To answer that central question, it seemed to me, you would have to travel to the country's various hotspots to measure the levels of religious, communal, economic, and political tension that were buckling the society's tectonic plates and ramming them into one another with such unpleasant consequences. Strung together, I thought, these "seismic" snapshots just might give readers a comprehensive sense of what troubled the country and where it was headed. To help pave the way, I managed to find through the friend of a friend a local fixer named Norman Wibowo, and soon we were out testing my plan in Indonesia's volatile islands.

Norman and I had been on the story a couple of weeks when we bumped into veteran journalist Aristides Katoppo at the Jakarta airport. A thoughtful, bewhiskered man of scholarly bearing, Tides had just flown in from Sulawesi, the big island that always looks to me like a jigsaw-puzzle piece on growth hormones, and specifically from a mainly Christian area on the island's northeast corner. Something, it wasn't clear exactly what, had stirred the pot in eastern Indonesia's remote Molucca Islands, and Christian refugees were pouring into the harbor town of Bitung fearing for their lives.

Tides said the Indonesian media didn't yet have the story in hand—it was that fresh. He suggested Norman and I get on a plane and go have a look for ourselves. So the very next day we flew to Sulawesi, where in time we walked into a cramped enclosure and what seemed like most of the 1,113 people housed there moved forward to tell me their story, which is precisely where I started mine for *Geographic* readers:

*Night fell fast over the harbor at Bitung on the far northeastern tip
of Sulawesi, and the refugee camp, an old rattan factory, was hot
and steamy as a terrarium. A group of shell-shocked Christians,
gathered in the glare of a hanging bulb, were telling how they'd lost
their homes on Ternate in the nearby Moluccas.*

*"The Muslims burned our houses!" said a retired army ser-
geant. "They destroyed our churches!" the village English teacher
chimed in. "We were massacred!"*

*Such commotion was new to this sweet-smelling hillside town
of neat homes and manicured yards but part of a larger malady
racing through the watery gut of eastern Indonesia. For decades the
area, also called the Spice Islands, had touted its mixed communities of Muslims and Christians as models of interfaith neighbor-
liness. Then, in January 1999, it plunged into primeval war, and
now thousands were dead, a half million uprooted, and nobody
could say exactly why.*

*The ex-army man, Anton Letsoin, said that Ternate's trou-
bles began when a letter on faked church stationery was circulated
among the island's Muslims. Convinced that a "cadre of Christ"
was forming up to attack them, they rallied at the local mosque.
There, a witness said he overheard his neighbors raise a chilling
cry: "Seek out the Obets"—slang for Christians—"and destroy!"*

*Who had manufactured the letter? The refugees blamed local
political schemers, rogue military units, or maybe gangsters from
Jakarta, who sought profit by sowing discord. Nobody wanted to
believe it was religion. "We were living in peace," cried the teacher.
"We never experienced religious hatred before!"*

I ultimately chose to open that way because it allowed me to touch
on what was then the central mystery of Indonesia: Who, in this
newly liberated but still troubled land, was doing what to whom
and why? There were outbreaks of violence between Muslims and
non-Muslims, some but by no means all provoked by Islamic radi-
cals who had been suppressed by Suharto and were determined to

define post-Suharto Indonesia on their terms. But that was only part of it. Indonesia was so diverse, with its three hundred separate ethnic groups and its various religions, mainly Muslim, Christian, Hindu, and Buddhist—and so big and sprawling, with its six thousand inhabited islands and 225 million people—there were many moving parts that had to be looked at. Digging into my fieldwork, I tried to develop the story, one snapshot at a time, mindful of how history had helped frame Bob's question about whether the country could keep from flying apart:

Bottling up Indonesia's volcanic intensities has never been easy. The Dutch began creating the basic geographic container 400 years ago when visions of cornering a lucrative market in nutmeg and cloves inspired them to join bits of geology belonging to Australia, Asia, and the Indies. Using superior technology (i.e., musket and cannon) and divide-and-conquer tactics, they kept the area's Muslim sultans and tribal chieftains off balance and under control.

After independence in 1949 the republic's founders pressed a national slogan of "Unity in Diversity" but relied on a blend of charm, cunning, and military muscle to keep the country's feral forces in check. And no one ordered the chaos better than Suharto. As a rising young army officer he fought to expel the Dutch. When Indonesia's first authoritarian president, Sukarno, lost control in the mid-1960s—a scalding time remembered by Indonesians as the Year of Living Dangerously—Suharto corked the bottle with a crackdown that cost as many as 500,000 lives.

Suharto went on to translate two oil booms into impressive economic and social gains, fueling aspirations among ordinary Indonesians for the democratic voice he was determined to deny. But with no strongman to keep order and only wobbly new institutions to guide them, Indonesians are living dangerously once again. Can they make their unwieldy union work?

2

Grappling with that question would have been impossible without Norman Wibowo, my inimitable fixer and friend. Norman grew up watching Hollywood Westerns on Jakarta TV and spoke perfect idiomatic American English, if a little John Wayneish at times. On top of that, he was loyal, brave, and true, as well as switched on and plugged into the local gossip—the perfect guide, as I said in my 2005 book, *Allah's Torch: A Report from Behind the Scenes in Asia's War on Terror.* But if I had to choose, I'd say his most remarkable asset was his ironic sense of humor, which would come in very handy considering the essentially unfunny nature of our assignment.

It was Norman, it bears repeating, who taught me in a way I hadn't realized before that humor is often the means by which people in tough circumstances—Indonesian people in this particular case—cope with a precarious world. Leaving the city of Solo by train late one afternoon after driving through a riot-demolished neighborhood, I settled into my seat on the train and was watching the sun set behind the blue volcanoes when—*Kah-thud!*—a rock spider-webbed the window inches from my head.

Norman Wibowo in the field, Jogjakarta, 1999.

"Don't take it personally," Norman advised, after I'd jumped a foot from the sudden concussion. It was just some kids letting off a little steam in a time of crisis. Indonesia was a place, he counseled wisely, where you should never, ever, misplace your sense of humor or risk falling into despair—a tall order at times, even for Norman.

When it came to organizing our trip to restive Aceh Province, for example, Norman struggled against deep misgivings. One of Indonesia's hottest hotspots, Aceh was known to be tough, byzantine, and unpredictable. It was also unavoidable if I was going to make good on my plan to present reporterly snapshots from some of the country's troubled neighborhoods. But Norman, a Jakarta boy, knew zip-all about Aceh, and neither did I. And despite best efforts to study the Indonesian press for clues, and to consult with the cognoscenti in Jakarta, we never achieved "fingertips," that feel for a place beyond and below the headlines that tells a reporter how to get the story while avoiding its potential for presenting nasty snags.

So we did what came naturally—we tried to avoid going to Aceh for as long as we possibly could, based on the magical thinking, I suppose, that somehow our logistical and epistemological problems would solve themselves. When that didn't happen we nonetheless found ourselves landing in . . .

Indonesia's westernmost Aceh Province, where the big island of Sumatra jabs a thumb into the Andaman Sea. In the capital, Banda Aceh, a bomb had ripped through the police chief's home the night before, and the city was deathly quiet, its imposing Baiturrahman Grand Mosque white as a china teacup in the noonday heat.

Indeed, no sooner had we arrived at the airport than we became bit players in a low-quality farce. For starters, our driver, a nervous, birdlike young man in a heartbreakingly clean white shirt ironed, I was willing to bet, by his mother, seemed determined to get us killed. On the way in from the airport, he was barreling down the empty highway as if the brake were a foreign object when Norman yelled, "Whoa!"

I looked up from my notebook just in time to see a large brown-and-white cow come hurtling toward us. The driver swerved, missing the beast by inches, as one very large, frightened eye shot past my window and then quickly sank behind us. Out of morbid fascination I asked Norman how somebody almost hits a cow on a completely empty highway, to which he replied with corresponding gloom, "It isn't easy, Boss."

In the city, on the way to our first interview, Norman turned to look out the back window and caught his breath. "We're being followed," he said. He was referring to a small van hugging our tail that was filled with ill-shaven, angry-looking men. While Norman and I were transfixed by our pursuers, the driver lost his way, shot past the address Norman had given him, and then proceeded to stop in the middle of the main thoroughfare and back up.

"Stop!" Norman shouted and the driver stopped—within a few inches of smashing into the trailing car. The men glared through their windshield as if they wanted to rip off the driver's head. When nothing happened, I got out of our van and walked into the Harvard English School to take up my conversation with its owner, Muhammad Ilyas. Meanwhile, Norman spotted two men with short haircuts observing him from an unmarked car in the parking lot:

> "In this situation," said Ilyas, squinting into the violent sunshine but ignoring the men, "anybody can do anything they want." A wave of bombings had escalated a decades-long struggle between the military and separatists vowing an independent Islamic state. "In class the other night we heard an explosion a hundred meters from here," said Ilyas, a vigorous 35-year old with bushy hair and a tense, baked-on smile. "We didn't know what to do!"
>
> Aceh's volatile spirit is rooted in its history as a fiercely independent sultanate, not put under Dutch administration until 1918. Resentment was amplified in recent decades as "Suharto Inc.," the dictator's cabal of associates, skimmed the province's wealth, which includes 40 percent of Indonesia's LNG production, a leading export. Since the late 1980s a stark increase in murder, rape, and other human rights abuses allegedly tied to the military has only deepened the wounds.

That Aceh's four million people are living dangerously was high-lighted by the gumshoes lurking outside Ilyas's door. I didn't want to get my host into hot water, but I had to know: Why had a pious Muslim named his school for a 17th-century Puritan minister from New England? Simple, Ilyas said: While at college in Connecticut he had been inspired by John Harvard's example of "promoting education." Before I left, I gave him a few mementos—a crimson Harvard ball cap that drooped over his brow and a cassette tape with the Mormon Tabernacle Choir singing "Fair Harvard."

Ilyas insisted on playing the tape, but I punched the wrong button and the football song, "On, Wisconsin" blared out. Nearby storekeepers glared in our direction. Norman rolled his eyeballs at the men in the car.

When we located the Harvard anthem, Ilyas broke into a boyish grin, and we stood at mock attention, warbling lyrics. But when our cracked notes faded, his smile hardened again. Like many educated, enterprising young Acehnese, he distrusted Jakarta but had grown weary of living in an undeclared war zone.

"I thought we'd make a contribution here," he said. But with uneasy truces leading to more violence, "right now it's hard to concentrate."

3

Aceh was a nail-biting ordeal from beginning to end. In my room at the Kuala Tripa Hotel, Norman phoned a human rights activist who had promised to welcome us with open arms. Now the man was saying he couldn't see us at all. How about tomorrow? No. Saturday? No. Shaken, Norman put down the receiver. "Boss, it was like somebody was holding a gun to his head," he said.

Our plans, such as they were, continued to implode, and thus we arrived at that moment when your ignorance as a reporter can get you into deep trouble. Without people to help you triangulate reality, you're rudderless in unpredictable seas. It was time to retreat and recalibrate. At the local airlines office, we tried to move up our flight reservations from the Monday to the Sunday. No soap. The flights were full with long waiting lists. Everybody, it seemed, wanted to get out of Aceh. We were cursing our luck when a friendly ticket agent tipped us that the airlines had just added a flight leaving in about an hour for the regional hub at Medan. He put us on the passenger list.

Norman and I rushed back to the hotel to pick up our gear and head for the airport when our driving-challenged driver killed the battery in the van. A security guard, the bellman, and I pitched in to push the vehicle across the parking lot to get it started. As soon as we'd gathered any momentum, however, the driver inexplicably stomped on the brakes and stalled out the engine. When he accidentally threw things into reverse and sent me flying backward into the flowerbed, Norman, who had been observing the scene from the checkout counter, swung into action. He opened the door, told the driver to get out immediately, and nipped in behind the wheel. Within a few seconds, he had the engine purring like a Sumatran tiger.

The world can change quickly for the long-distance reporter, and in the space of a couple hours Norman and I found ourselves in the relatively quiescent north Sumatran city of Medan, with a new van, a competent, sweet-tempered driver named Iwan, and headed for our next stop, the orangutan rehabilitation center at Bukit Lawang. Norman had arranged for us to talk with the European activists who helped rescue orangs from the illegal logging operations that had driven them to the edge of extinction in the wild. After the stresses and strains of Aceh, I must say, I was very much looking forward to chilling with the orang lords of the tropical rainforest.

It was dark by the time Norman and I crossed a bridge over the rushing, tea-green waters of the Bahorok River and hiked in the lee of the jungled hillside to the place of the Europeans. Our hosts appeared to be excited and a little nervous over a visitation from representatives of the world-famous *National Geographic*. Possibly they had mistaken us for members of the Society's wildlife team. In any event, a fit, elderly Swiss gentleman started the conversation, memorably, by establishing an unsettling degree of eye contact with me. "Orangutans are my life," he declared earnestly.

Still stressed by our escape from Aceh, I was momentarily at a loss for words, when an earnest young Brit named Andy Blair spoke up. He asked me how people in Aceh assessed the local threat to *their* orangutans. I could feel the steam building to dangerous levels inside my cranium. It had been a while, and my mental cork was getting ready to blow. Fixing Andy in what Norman called my "Viking look," meaning icy and predatory, I said, like a total smart ass, "I think the people in Aceh are more concerned with preserving the human population right now than they are with other species." Bad of me, I know, but I hadn't adjusted to my new circumstances yet.

The orangutans got their revenge the next day when Andy led us up a steep mountain path to meet Akbar, king of this particular hill. I had never encountered an orangutan outside a zoo before and was about to learn two memorable things. First, Akbar had excellent eyesight. Sitting in his tree house about fifty yards into the jungle, he spotted me holding my brand-new travel computer, which was about the size of a hardcover book. Making a beeline, he swung forward on a succession of ropey vines until he was standing in front of me, feet planted firmly on the dusty trail and staring covetously at my treasured laptop. It was at that point I received the second lesson: Orangutans are much stronger than humans. Akbar unceremoniously ripped the computer from my hands as if I wasn't even holding on, and then swung back to his platform to acquaint himself with the new technology.

Andy, excellent man, saved the day. Fluent in orang, he persuaded Akbar to return to the trail where he somehow wrestled my computer from the ape's superhuman grip. But Akbar was ready to rumble, and he and Andy rolled round and round on the ground demonstrating a variety of impressive holds. It was quite the show. As a token of thanks, I later sent Andy a sequence of still photos I'd shot of the skirmish with, if memory serves, a risqué title dealing with interspecies relations. I'd recovered my sense of humor such as it was and is, but I must say, I never really forgave Akbar, against whom I still harbor a powerful grudge.

Norman and I quickly moved on to investigate other issues, but a few years later, at the tail-end of 2004, I was watching TV in my apartment in New York when I heard the news that the massive Indian Ocean tsunami had hit Aceh Province. (Estimates vary, but it's likely that 150,000 or more people died in Aceh alone.) I looked aghast at footage showing the area near Banda Aceh's grand mosque, where those thugs had once considered dismantling our poor driver. The streets were now a roaring, flotsam-choked river, flushing houses, motorcars, and people, who knows where? The shock of the tragedy did eventually help prompt the Indonesian government and rebels to come to terms, but all I could think about was poor Ilyas and his star-crossed attempts to bring the light of English grammar to a hard, dark place.

4

To properly cover the Indonesia story, I also had to come to grips with a big, crosscutting issue that helped explain the sense of hurt and injustice then endemic to large parts of the country—the main island of Java's chokehold on political and economic power. In my article I framed it this way:

> *Overconcentration of power and wealth in Java is one thing many Indonesians can agree on. Roughly the size of Alabama, the island has two-thirds of the country's population, and Jakarta, its premier city, is the unrivaled center of politics, finance, urban culture, and communications. Resentment of such dominance fuels separatist fires all over the map, including oil-rich Riau Province in east central Sumatra and remote Irian Jaya [today, West Papua], with its gold and copper.*
>
> *But such rumblings unsettled most people I met. In Bandung, a tree-lined college town 120 miles southeast of Jakarta, where Indonesian nationalists proclaimed the anti-Dutch movement in the*

1920s, I spoke with students on "Jeans Street," a discount shopping area known for its looming plaster-of-paris replicas of Batman, Superman, and other action heroes.

"We sympathize with the Acehnese people," said a bluff handsome young man, a computer science major, "but I worry what will happen if Aceh leaves." Eavesdropping, a truck driver paused his munching on a sticky bun to protest. "What if East Java wants to leave too?" he said, truculently. "I guess it's okay for Indonesia to become a pip-squeak country?"

Averting that fate may hinge on what Indonesians call refor-masi, or democratic reform. High on the official agenda is cleaning up the country's notoriously corrupt law courts and scandal-tainted banking system.

At that point in the writing, I looked to bring forward a source from among the dozens of people I'd interviewed who could speak to the issue with authority:

"You can't run a modern country like Indonesia by tradition," said His Highness Hamengku Buwono X, the 53-year-old sultan of Yogyakarta, when I caught up with him at a fish farm in the ancient Javanese capital. The sultan, who serves as local governor, was calmly puffing on a cigar, advising rapt villagers on how to use the Internet to be competitive in the global marketplace. A man from one of the country's oldest ruling families (whose name means "he who carries the universe on his lap"), he is considered one of its most progressive leaders.

"If decisions are based on the Javanese way," said the sultan, "people outside Java call it injustice." Furthering Jakarta's tentative efforts to decentralize political power and share the country's wealth more evenly, he said, was the best way to preserve the union. "In the past the central government always thought they knew better. We have to come up with a new approach . . . but there's a long way to go."

5

Having set out one possible solution for Indonesia's woes, I then introduced another of my seismic snapshots, this one stark in a distinctly haunting way, to show the extent of the challenge involved:

> *Others were convinced that moving forward meant recapturing the past, even if it led to bloodshed. In West Kalimantan Province, on Borneo's western shoulder, Dayak tribesmen had recently battled settlers from Madura, an austere little island east of Java, prompting reports of hundreds of deaths, some "spectacular beheadings," and Dayak magicians invoking warrior spirits to spook the police and army.*

The big trouble in Borneo started in December 1996 when, according to a Human Rights Watch report, Madurese boys were accused of "bothering" a Dayak girl at a pop concert up country from Pontianak, the capital of West Kalimantan. That led to angry words and, later that same month, to the Madurese knifing of two Dayak youths. That, in turn, brought a counterattack in which the Dayaks reprised their headhunting traditions. According to the report, ". . . the Dayaks waged what appeared to be a ritual war against Madurese communities, burning houses, killing inhabitants, and in some cases severing the heads and eating the livers of those killed." A grim business.

According to various accounts, the Madurese set up roadblocks, dragging victims from cars and buses and killing them on the spot. The Dayaks did the same. Ultimately, the Madurese proved a weak match for the Dayaks, who were said to have stacked Madurese heads along the roadside like so many cannonballs. The army sent in troops to quell the rioting, and in no time a pocket-sized civil war spread through provincial jungles and along West Kalimantan's normally serene back roads. The fighting raged on for the better part of four months.

The wholesale bloodletting had long since stopped by the time Norman and I flew into Pontianak to take our snapshot. I'd heard that the local Dayak chiefs, angered over Jakarta's failure to protect their interests, were threatening to secede from the Republic of Indonesia and set up their own country, the Federasi Dayak Raya or the Republic of Federated Dayak States, and I was eager to ask after their plans. From the air Borneo was a gorgeous treat. The island's big green meniscus resembled an endless ocean of trees, filled as it was with voluptuous swirls of emeralds and limes and sages flashing in sunlight that collected in a corona of gold at the horizon. It was my first good look at the island's wild interior parts, and I have to say it was one of the most beautiful things I've ever seen.

Norman was less enthusiastic. Normally as brave as they come, he sat on the plane nervously tapping his armrests and staring silently ahead. His problem wasn't hard to fathom: He'd been reading too much, in his case too many lurid accounts of Dayak misbehavior in Jakarta's tabloid press. To cheer him up, I drew his attention to the fact that a fellow passenger appeared to be fetching souvenir boxes of Dunkin' Donuts back to Pontianak. The boxes were stacked in tiers and trussed up with string for easier carrying. I said something to the effect that a donut gift for family and friends must be the in-thing this season, but Norman was in no mood for my lame jokes. He chuckled grimly, with the resignation of a man headed for the chopping block. Poor guy.

I sympathized, but not that much. Personally, I had nothing to fear from the Dayaks. They did not see America as the Great Satan, unlike some of the militant Muslim groups raising a ruckus elsewhere in Indonesia. Quite the contrary. They took a much less charitable view of "Javanese imperialism," however, and Norman, descendant of Javanese royalty, was as Javanese as you could get. His fears were confirmed when we got to our hotel, a rambling, shambolic affair stretched along a muddy riverbank, and he phoned a local Dayak activist. Unaccountably miffed at our late arrival, over which we had no control, the man said we could find our own way to the chiefs' council meeting that night.

Ringing off, Norman said, "Jeez, what a huffy guy," but I knew what he was thinking. Being Javanese, and therefore considering himself to be clairvoyant, he interpreted Dayak pique, even in its mildest form, as a fatal sign. I wanted to be sympathetic, as I say, but I figured our contact, a family man, probably had to look after his kids, or something, and nothing more. Frankly, I was more concerned about my room at the hotel, which appeared to be haunted. Twisting a tap in my bathroom produced roily water the color of blood. The carpet was methodically tattooed with cigarette burns, as if ritual torture had been conducted there. When Norman produced a van and driver to fetch us to the chiefs that evening, I was relieved to have someplace to go.

It was only when I caught a glimpse of our chauffeur that I started having second thoughts. Gaunt-cheeked and uncommunicative, he hunched over the wheel, staring fixedly ahead as he piloted us over a couple of big bridges as if on a delivery run to the River Styx. In the suburbs, dark squat buildings gave way to tin-roofed shanties. Soon we were zipping cluelessly along in near-total darkness, which I distilled into my *Geographic* article as follows:

> *So it was with trepidation that I drove through the port of Pontianak, its rivers gleaming darkly in the moonlight, to the deserted edge of town . . .*

Trepidation was the right word for it. "Any thoughts on where we might be headed?" I asked Norman, who was staring out his window into the encompassing blackness.

"You're asking me?" replied the master fixer, drily.

I was about to order the driver to turn back when he veered off the road, skidded to a stop in a patch of gravel in front of a nondescript two-story wooden shack, and motioned for us to get out. I was going sweaty-palmed, when a man stepped from the shadows and instructed us to follow him through the door and up a creaking staircase. It is precisely at such moments of weakness that our embedded stereotypes do our thinking for us, and suddenly, shamefully, early childhood images of men with sharp teeth and bones through their noses I could have seen in vintage copies of *National Geographic* began dancing in my head . . .

But when the door swung back, I found a light-filled room with a conference table and a cluster of smiling, distinguished-looking men. Dressed in batik shirts and slacks, they glided across the floor to shake my hand.

I was both relieved and immediately captivated. Not only did the Dayak chieftains have the look of sociable conference delegates, they crossed the floor to greet me with the grace of ballroom dancers. There were a half-dozen of them, all short in stature ("Seventy-five percent of Viking height," as Norman observed) and powerfully built. Their faces were creased like fine old leather. But it was their eyes that made the deepest impression—gleaming under heavy brows they betrayed a combination of boyish enthusiasm and deep cleverness. I was totally hooked.

I was also becoming annoyed by Norman's escalating case of the heebie-jeebies. Invited to sit at the head of the table, the two of us took our seats while Norman squirmed around and stiffly interpreted the preliminary chitchat, as if still weighing the risks of ritual decapitation. Ignoring him, I asked the men why they wanted independence?

"I used to love Indonesia very much, but everybody wants to separate now!" a young activist blurted out before the chiefs could say a word.

Reddening with frustration, he ticked off local grievances: Big farming and timber interests had driven the Dayak, semi-nomadic farmers, from traditional haunts along Borneo's complex river network and into squalid towns. There the Dayak, now mostly Christian, had encountered enterprising, hard-nosed Muslim Madurese, who ran the shops and worked in the factories. The Dayak were chagrined by Madurese custom that allows men to carry the carok, a big curved knife, in public—a violation of Dayak adat, or customary law.

"They show they are the brave men," said the young man. "They think the Dayak are cowards!"

The elders' reaction was swift, elegant and memorable:

One of the chiefs lifted a bushy brow and silenced him with a glance
that might have paralyzed a small animal, and then spoke up softly.
  The Dayak felt very Indonesian and didn't want to leave the
union, he said. "But there is rampant injustice against our commu-
nity"—in jobs, education, and particularly in sharing the proceeds
from the exploitation of Borneo's natural resources. Unless Jakarta
offered a solid plan to even the score, the Dayak had no choice but
to go their own way.

The speaker's name was Acong. Above a fine Dayak mustache he
sported eyeglasses with stylish gold-wire frames; below, his smile
was missing his front teeth. I asked, generally, if the men didn't
think it was tricky for West Kalimantan, a place so relatively small
in size, to survive as an independent nation.

The elders traded probing looks, and then I got a little clairvoyant myself, thinking "Of course!" These shrewd characters weren't
about to precipitously yank themselves from the Indonesian union.
What they were after, it seemed obvious to me, was to create a
bargaining chip they could use in negotiations with the central
government, now that Suharto's departure had put the future up
for grabs. A man named Maran, not a chief but a medical doctor,
spoke to the subtlety of the thing: "If we are oppressed further," he
said, "then we want our independence."

That sounded reasonable to me, but how to resolve their lethal dif-
ferences with the Madurese? A chief named Miden said that con-
flicts had to be adjudicated according to adat. If one Madurese
harms another, try them by Indonesian law—but if a Dayak is
victimized, tribal elders must decide.
  Many Indonesians I talked with felt the country's haphazard
justice system gave ordinary people little recourse in the law. Yet to
allow rival ethnic groups to judge one another by conflicting, home-
grown rules struck me as a recipe for disaster.

"We don't have to kill the Madurese," said Miden. "We're civilized people."

The chiefs *were* exquisitely civilized, and that's a fact. Even Norman was impressed. "These guys are very articulate," he observed in a heartfelt whisper, as the men held forth in Bahasa Indonesia, which was not their native tongue. "They sound like they're talking at the United Nations," he marveled.

When I pressed the chiefs on their bloody skirmishes with the Madurese, however, they dug in. "When the conflict occurred, the Dayak were portrayed as violent, uncivilized wild men," Maran said. "But when the Madurese fight they aren't portrayed that way."

The chiefs nodded their agreement. The Dayaks had fought as hard as anybody to free the country from Indonesia's Dutch colonial masters after World War II. But after independence in 1949, it became clear that independence belonged only to the Javanese. The Dayak were treated worse than hunting dogs, Maran said, speaking graphically: "When the quarry was killed, we weren't even allowed to lick the blood."

Under Suharto, the men agreed, the military got its hooks into Kalimantan and now they wanted the army to go away and let them do their own policing. The military worked security for the big logging companies, said Miden, and that was a clear violation of its role. "When a truck loaded with logs passes by, it's always guarded by military troops. . . . If we protest, suddenly we're not dealing with the corporation anymore, we're dealing with the military."

As the elders saw it, the military was behind gambling, prostitution, and the area's ubiquitous karaoke parlors. "The troops come into villages, take our girls and make them pregnant without any responsibility," Maran said.

When their set-to with the Madurese occurred, the younger, red-faced man, who called himself Albert, said hotly, that the military "couldn't control the situation," so they told the Dayak to "kill all the Madurese." No sooner had the Dayaks done their best to comply, however, than the army stepped in and "claimed success for making the peace!"

The increasingly edgy words filled the torpid air with electricity as insects buzzed frenetically around the room's bare lightbulbs. Suddenly one of the other chiefs, a man named Ajung, jumped to his feet. "Oh-oh, Boss," said Norman under his breath, eyes darting apprehensively. "Mood swing coming."

He wasn't wrong. Ajung stood behind his chair, eyes dancing, and said he wished to tell us a story illustrating the Dayak relationship to authority. During the disturbances, the police had arrested a young man from his village and Ajung had gone to the stationhouse to find the officers standing around the poor fellow aiming their guns at him. "Why do you need all these guns?" he asked.

The police replied they were worried because they thought the young man was about to go into a trance. "Then you don't need guns," Ajung said. "You need me!"

By this point, reports of Dayak black magic had scared the pants off both the police and the army, and the cops were worried the warrior dead might suddenly start popping out of the woodwork, craving a bloody fight.

Ajung's eyes flashed and narrowed as he pantomimed how he'd rescued the young man from jail—or maybe the police had just thought better of it and let him go. In any event, we had come to the emotional pivot of the evening. Ajung acted out threats and counter-threats, as his voice vibrated in his chest, and his fellow chiefs rocked ever so slightly in their chairs, rolling their eyes and stroking fine mustaches. When Ajung raised an arm and shook it menacingly, as if brandishing a spear, approving murmurs seemed to hold the group in a kind of sway. This was storytelling in its original form, I thought, and how lucky I was to witness it firsthand. All that was missing was the campfire, with its ring of light, and the forest darkness looming all around.

Then suddenly it was over. Ajung sat down and blinked his eyes, his colleagues shifted in their seats, and the men went back to smoking their luxury brand cigarettes and discussing matters of state.

At one point during our discussion, Ajung indicated that the chieftains were developing a foreign policy. "The Dayak support the opening of relations with Israel," he wanted me to know.

6

Bedlam would break out again the following year, this time a few hundred miles southeast of Pontianak, in a town called Sampit, in Central Kalimantan Province, and hundreds more Madurese and Dayak would succumb. Once again the Dayaks were portrayed as the villains or, as a *New York Times* reporter, writing under a Jakarta dateline, called them, "vicious headhunters." The violence was ghoulish indeed. On the other hand, few Americans took notice of such remote goings-on; only a relative handful of foreign-policy pros worried that the pockets of unrest scattered throughout the Indonesian archipelago might ready the ground for Al Qaeda–related terrorist groups, and you can't fault them. Concern about the potential for spillover from such unhappy conditions is rarely unreasonable.

The morning after our meeting with the chiefs, Norman and I drove north over the Equator and into the heart of Dayak country:

The highway shot through sunny patches of jungle along a river where small fat pigs ran for cover and women in sarongs dried streaming hair. [T]his was the same area where Dayak had reportedly retaliated for earlier attacks on their tribesmen by pulling Madurese from their cars.

A local journalist broadly confirmed the mayhem—four Madurese had died for every Dayak. A Dayak herself, she was convinced the Madurese had started it. "They don't like the Dayak people," she said. I wanted to ask the Madurese about that but many had fled, and the rest proved hard to find.

When all was said and done, I guess you could say the Dayak had succeeded in casting a spell on me because I was now so deeply interested in their story. Realizing I had only scratched its surface, I cooked up a plan to return to Borneo to do a documentary film. But that takes money, and to raise it you must find a way to attract an audience. Back in New York, I asked a producer acquaintance working at a big network news program for advice.

"Tell me," he asked, "how many of these Dayaks speak English?"

Well, not that many, I guessed, but so what—that's what subtitles were for, right?

He looked at me with infinite pity. I had to realize, he said, "The only way we could do a story like that for our audience is if the Dayak had kidnapped Britney Spears."

He was right of course. Television in the age of reality TV wasn't ready for reality. At about the same time, the *Economist* magazine completed the circle, running a commentary entitled "Orang-utans on the brink," properly discussing man's inhumanity to ape in the Borneo jungles but glancing over the human-on-human toll.

7

In a country of unavoidably thorny issues, the most comprehensively worrisome to many Indonesians was the swift, head-spinning emergence of Islamic fundamentalism in the wake of law-and-order Suharto's demise.

As I observed in *Allah's Torch*, "the overwhelming majority of Indonesia's Muslims," who make up the overwhelming majority of the country's population, "are decent, even-keeled people, and generally about as warlike as Ohio Presbyterians at a church picnic." At the time of my reporting for the *Geographic*, however, it wasn't at all clear how the future was going to unfold. I quoted Mochtar Buchori, a veteran parliamentarian, who put the problem very well, I thought:

> "What kind of Islam are we going to have as the mainstream?" said Buchori. "If we're heading for a hard-line Islamic civilization, this country is really going to disintegrate."

Events in certain parts of the country were already making Buchori look like a prophet. The mother of all nuisance conflicts was raging far to the east in the Molucca Islands where the main city, Ambon, had descended into a bona fide war zone split between Christian and Muslim enclaves. Accordingly, Norman and I headed for the Moluccas for a look at the country's melt-down scenario in a place with historical resonance, particularly for American readers:

I got a glimpse of what such chaos might be like in the old trading port of Makassar at the southwestern tip of Sulawesi the night I boarded a passenger ship called the Bukit Siguntang, *bound for the remote Banda Islands. Under floodlights police armed with automatic weapons prodded travelers up the packed gangway or pulled them aside to search their luggage for guns or knives. Security was tight because the ship would first stop in Ambon, the city in the southern Moluccas where the worst of the fighting between Christians and Muslims had taken place.*

Not thrilled about traveling such treacherous waters, I was nonetheless determined to see the Bandas because of their central role in shaping early Indonesia. In the seventeenth century this tiny subset of the Spice Islands was the center of European efforts to monopolize the trade in nutmeg, prized in pre-refrigeration Europe for preserving meats and wrongly thought to ward off plague. Most intriguing was an obscure 1667 treaty that capped off a "spice war" with a novel arrangement: England would swap its piece of the Bandas for an isolated Dutch trading post, the island where I live—Manhattan.

So to prove to myself that even in middle age curiosity can trump raw fear (and because airports were closed), I elbowed my way on board. There I made an unsettling discovery: My friend Norman Wibowo and I would be sharing the ride with 600 members of a militant Islamic group called the Laskar Jihad. Reports I had seen in which the Jihad allegedly had vowed to defend Muslims in Ambon by cleansing the area of Christians flickered through my mind. Since all bule—white people—were automatically

*"Christian" hereabouts, and Norman was in fact one, I was now
truly worried.*

*The dim companionway was clogged with the Jihad, young
men with prayer caps and scraggly chin whiskers, looking hollow-
eyed and severe. Locked in my tiny cabin, I entertained unmanly
thoughts of jumping ship.*

8

Blessings come in strange disguises. The thing that kept me from
chewing off a paw in anguish on the benighted *Bukit Siguntang*, in
the first instance, had a lot to do with the fundamental creepiness
of our cabin. German-built, the ship had started life as a trim, tasteful passenger liner with trim, tasteful staterooms. As things now
stood, however, our cabin was hot, airless, and filthy. Always one
to count his blessings, Norman made the indisputable point that it
was far better to be on our side of our ridiculously delicate door
than on the side with all the dour jihadis.

I expanded on this misadventure in *Allah's Torch* but was un-
able to fit in one memorable episode. It began when I lay back on
my bunk, doggedly trying to maintain my aplomb while Norman
picked up a story he'd started telling me earlier in the day about his
infatuation with a *bule* woman who worked at one of the European
embassies in Jakarta. Unfortunately she already had a boyfriend, an
Indian, Norman said, but he interpreted that as a good sign. Why?
"She likes the dark-skinned men, Boss," he said, smiling and arching a devilish eyebrow.

I was chuckling at Norman's tale in spite of myself when the
hull creaked and stuttered and the good ship *Bukit Siguntang* heaved
forward into the night sea. When Norman suddenly stopped in
midsentence and cried out, "Oh, shit!," I glanced over to see him
jabbing his finger at the wall flanking his bunk where three large
cockroaches, brown-black flares, shot up the wall. Reaching the top
of their arcs, they stopped and hung there like synchronized swim-
mers waiting for the music to start.

Norman screeched, "Aiiiyeee," or words to that effect, and sprung to his feet. Mimicking one of his gung-fu fighting heroes from the movies, he grabbed a rubber sandal and started smacking at the wall, somehow managing to miss all three roaches, which vanished into a crack near the ceiling. During our travels together, Norman had repeatedly and, in my view, unfairly chastised me for my failure to appreciate the sacrifices and discomfort required to experience what he called the "real" Indonesia. I'd been looking for a way to exact revenge on him and now I had my chance.

"Welcome to the real Indonesia," I said, smiling smugly as I lay on my back staring at the ceiling, my head pillowed on my open palms. I was savoring the turnabout when I felt a tickling sensation on my left forearm and looked down to see a thumb-sized cockroach waggling his antennae, aggressively, I thought, as if signaling some kind of territorial challenge.

"Aaggh!" I cried, as I shook the creature loose and leapt to my feet. Both Norman and I were now crouched in defensive postures in the middle of our seagoing telephone booth. Then came the deluge. Mouths agape, we watched as roaches seemed to pour from every crack, crevice, and seam. There were sprinting, torpedo-shaped cruisers and fat mother roaches spewing something that looked like wet coffee grounds as they ran. Many—dozens? hundreds?—of cockroach babies, no bigger than pencil jots, soon joined the adults, swarming the walls, moving in crazy little circles all over the place. "Norman, we're under attack," I whimpered.

But the long-distance reporter must always keep his wits about him, and I had a plan. I reached into my duffel bag for a spray can of heavy-duty mosquito repellent and started firing wild bursts at the roaches, the theory being that chemicals designed for mosquitoes might not kill cockroaches but it would slow them down long enough for Norman to whack them with his flip-flop. The tactic, though messy, worked well enough. When I had spritzed a bulky female about to slip under the fluorescent light casing, Norman brought the hammer down, splattering the wall—and himself—with coffee grounds and custard.

"Eeeeiiuuuueee!" Norman cried, fastidiously wiping his hands with a tissue but clearly inspired.

"Time for the heavy artillery," I said.

Reaching into my bag again, I produced a bottle of a highly concentrated chemical disinfectant called Dettol. I make it a habit to carry this miracle product in my travel kit wherever I go in case I'm called on (and luckily the call has yet to come) to disinfect a large wound, sanitize surgical tools, or deliver a baby—but it's good for routine jobs too. At the moment, I was determined to scrub down every square inch of our cabin in order to deny the enemy territory by putting it hygienically off limits.

When we'd mixed up a batch of Dettol in the stopper-less toilet sink, plugging it with a piece of cardboard from a box of chocolate chip cookies we'd been sharing when the roaches attacked, Norman and I scrubbed and scrubbed and scrubbed, occasionally stopping to gingerly deposit the larger bits of detritus in a plastic bag Norman held at arm's length.

At one point, Norman grabbed his mattress by a corner and lifted it to expose a steel bedframe where a roach patrol ran for cover, traversing an uneven delta of wizened grapefruit seeds, ancient candy wrappers, and rivulets of unidentifiable brown goo. Norman seconded my feelings by making some strange, involuntary gagging noises but the worst had passed.

It took us an hour or more but the cabin cleaned up nicely. It was now possible to appreciate the underlying Teutonic character of the ship that was visible in bucolic scenes of the Rhineland, or whatever they were, bolted to the walls over the bunks. Deprived of their microscopic smorgasbord, the roaches had mostly disappeared. Operation Cleanup had been, well, a smashing success. Best of all, it took our minds off darker visions of getting our throats slit by the jihadis camped out in the passageway.

Our labors completed, Norman and I collapsed onto our bunks, and I thanked my lucky stars for the diversion. I also prayed that I could somehow avoid leaving our cabin for the duration of our three-day voyage to the Bandas. That was not possible of course.

Yet venturing out into the corridor the following morning to get some breakfast in the dining room, my perspective changed:

> *In the morning light, as I picked my way along the corridor, the Jihad looked like kids away from home for the first time, awkward, a little malnourished, and slightly less dangerous than teenagers waiting in line for a rock concert.*

That discovery, while not entirely liberating, was enough to embolden me to explore the ship and engage the officers and crew in a way that would inform *Allah's Torch* and, in the first instance, my *National Geographic* story:

> *From the bridge the Banda Sea, broad and inky blue, combed along in luminous sunshine, but a dispute was brewing on board. Chief Officer Andre Pontoh said Jihad leaders had accused him of a grave error—posting the wrong times for the five daily prayers when devout Muslims are required to bend toward Mecca. They were wrong—the veteran seaman had carefully calculated the schedule according to the ship's position. That didn't matter. On a recent trip a minor dispute had sparked a shipboard riot, and angry young men had lined up at the bridge windows to jeer at Christian crew members and run fingers across their throats.*

Pontoh followed up on this unwelcome newsflash by confirming:

> *[The] Moluccas were now so tense that* habis, *slang for annihilation, awaited Muslims caught in Christian strongholds and vice versa. The flood of refugees fleeing the turmoil had further complicated travel in a country that is largely water. All the ships were overcrowded and worked to the point of breakdown, but, said Pontoh, "If we don't sell tickets, people burn our ticket offices down!"*
>
> *Yet I marveled at how most of the ship's passengers went quietly about their routines, taking the risks in stride. That afternoon Pontoh and I visited the cabin of a pearl trader, a snaggletoothed man*

in a checkered sarong who presided over a box of plastic baggies bulging with pearls from the Arafura Sea.

"Bagus—excellent," he said, holding aloft a lustrous black pearl the size of a pea. As a boy I'd read tales of wild, seagoing corsairs and smugglers of tropical islands, and for a moment I was caught up in the romance—until the door opened. In shot a pair of heads, two rough-looking characters who surveyed the scene with sharklike smiles. The trader slammed the door in their faces and locked it.

"So I don't get murdered," he said.

9

Our destination in the Banda Islands turned out, but for the added elbow room, to be nearly as isolating and scary as the ship:

The next day at noon we sailed into Bandanaira, the main harbor, gliding under the towering green cone of its sentinel volcano. I was relieved to finally be there but disheartened that the rage sweeping other parts of Indonesia had found this remote spot too, as Tanya Alwi, an environmental activist, was quick to point out. Tanya, whose family ran the local hotel, said an argument between a village headman, a Christian, and a teenager, a Muslim, had unspooled, and 28 Christian homes went up in flame in a single night. A charcoal shell was all that remained of the town's Catholic church. Other structures had been reduced to thick stone walls of Dutch construction.

"One thug said to me, 'Be grateful we purified your island,'" said Tanya, with a mirthless giggle. A Muslim hajja, who had made several pilgrimages to Mecca, Tanya abhorred the violence. And it hadn't been good for business: I was the first guest to stay at her Dutch colonial-style hotel in two years.

Most Bandanese Christians had been evacuated to camps near Ambon to be replaced on the islands by Muslim refugees from the beleaguered city.

"It's blind hate now," said Ramon Alwi, Tanya's brother, as we sat near a banyan tree at the hotel drinking good, dark coffee from the Indonesian hills. For both Muslims and Christians the disputes had taken on fatalistic overtones, said Ramon, "but basically it's more cultural than religious."

The Spice Islands harbored countless local clashes over land boundaries or scarce resources that were old when spice-seeking Europeans arrived to amplify the tensions. In the Bandas the Dutch won local princes over to Christianity by giving them cannon to fuel bloody sibling rivalries. "Those fights are still remembered in the villages" and are easy to rekindle, Ramon said.

Who had provided the spark this time? Many suspected that forces loyal to Suharto wanted to touch off a chain reaction of violence in the islands that would destabilize the government in Jakarta. "There had to be an emcee," said Ramon, but basically it was the old, complicated story of Indonesia: too many fighting for too little.

In the corner of the patio a giant TV screen flickered with images of a scantily clad rock diva gyrating on MTV. "People in Jakarta talk about 'globalization,'" said Ramon, and how the new consumer culture would pull Indonesians together by sandpapering rough edges off parochial customs, "but here," he added wryly, "we're two centuries away."

10

"Brilliant, Dahlby." That was how one Western diplomat sarcastically summed it up when I met him in Jakarta and told him where I'd been. He apparently thought I might have been in some danger. Very likely he knew something I didn't. By the same token, however, I must say that not everyone in the diplomatic community had developed exquisitely sensitive fingertips for Indonesia's trouble spots. While bumping around the country, taking my seismic word pictures, I had intermittently phoned Jakarta trying to set up interviews, and I recall one friendly press attaché in particular who routinely asked, "Where are you now?" The question, I thought, signaled a sense of wonder at someone quaintly beating the bushes for live journalistic specimens.

At the risk of putting too fine a point on it, the value in collecting data the old-fashioned way is precisely this: In a situation like the one pertaining in Indonesia at the time, meaning chaos unfurling remotely and sporadically, close to the ground and not infrequently in areas without cell phone transmission or Internet access, all the world's intel satellites, hoovering up their terabytes of information, couldn't substitute for reporterly eyes and ears focused on the immediate scene. Don't get me wrong: The great sky-sweepers can be very good at counting the coconuts in the trees (or imaging the deployment of troops and weapons), as my standard mantra goes, but they're not much help in telling what folks sitting under the trees are actually thinking or planning. What the spooks call reliable human source intelligence is as important in intelligence work as it is in journalism.

The problem with relying too heavily on the nonclassified Internet, as the alert reporter will know, is roughly similar. The digital revolution has done wonders for our efforts to see the world more clearly, right its wrongs, and challenge its stupidities. At the same time, it's helped amplify the nincompoop's illusion that we can know the world at arm's length, without getting our sneakers dirty or delving into the specific circumstances that take us beyond and below the chatter. In "A Scandal in Bohemia," no less an authority on reliable reporting than the great Sherlock Holmes said it well: "It is a capital mistake to theorize before one has data. Insensibly one begins to twist facts to suit theories, instead of theories to suit fact."

In short, you have to wonder about the extent to which our growing dependence on digital tools reduces reliance on ourselves—on our direct observation of people and events, our tenacity and deep attention to figuring out what we see and hear, and the acquisition of the street smarts that allow us to negotiate a tricky neighborhood or read deception or reliability in the eyes of a bureaucrat, priest, or gangster. Without the application of what the old-timers called "rat-like cunning," what kind of reality do we end up with? Think about it for thirty seconds and you'll see what I mean: The digital age has at once legitimately blown our minds and blinded us into the bargain.

When all is said and done, to *go* really is to *know*, deeply and in context.

11

Because collecting reporterly snapshots requires us to move around from place to place, permit me a final word about travel. Advanced planning is an absolute necessity for reporting from the field, I repeat. In the end, however, success not infrequently boils down to a matter of faith, or, depending on your view of the infinite workings of the cosmos, an individual's willingness to be lucky. No matter how much you study or plan, the bigger the event or process the less likely it is to cooperate with even the most sophisticated efforts at control.

Take airline travel, for instance. I was comparing notes on travel challenges in Indonesia with an intrepid *National Geographic* photographer one day when, after hearing my random horror story, she said, "Flying is the most dangerous thing we do."

How could I argue? Despite the news media's predilection for drawing our attention to blood and tragedy, most people who report internationally don't actually cover wars or rebellions when the bullets are flying or tramp natural disaster sites while the ground is shaking or the water is rising. (Hats off to those who do, of course.) The majority of us travel to the globe's medium and far corners to assess events that are neither inordinately risky nor overtly warlike—the big business deal, the pivotal election or the economic meltdown, for example. Yet even ho-hum assignments take us places where airline equipment is fragile with age and maintenance an afterthought—and suddenly we find ourselves on a trip to White Knuckle City in the Land of Broken Seats and Armrests.

That was where Norman and I found ourselves one cloudless, sun-fractured morning as we flew up Java's green spine from Bali's Denpasar airport on our *Geographic* assignment. Halfway through the flight, I began to notice certain irregularities in the behavior of our vintage DC-10. For one thing, the air-conditioning system had mysteriously shut down and the economy cabin grew humid as a sauna. Much more ominous, the plane's big jet engines slowed to idling in midair and we began, albeit very gently, to lose altitude. When the pilot unleashed a burst of Indonesian over the intercom, there was a sharp intake of breath among the Indonesian passengers followed by worried but incomprehensible murmurs.

Norman, who was dozing in the seat next to me, woke up briefly to remark, "Oh, shit!" and fell back to sleep. I gave him an elbow. "For chrissakes, Norman," I said, "what gives?"

"Nothing, Boss," he replied, groggily. The pilot had just said there was some trouble with the hydraulic system or something. No big deal. In fact, and not to get too technical about it, a failing hydraulic system made it impossible to maintain an altitude sufficient to clear the mountains separating the capital from the central Java plain. That was the thrust of the news item that made the *Jakarta Post* the following day—as well as the reason we made a wide, slow turn and limped back to Bali.

Three years later, Norman and I were on a subsequent reporting trip to Bali, this time on an evening flight out of Jakarta to look into the terrorist attacks that had killed 202 people a few months earlier in October of 2002. Once again, we found ourselves occupying seats in the front row of a weathered DC-10's midsection. The plane was rattling and dipping, unnervingly, when I looked over at the big, humpy-looking exit door to my right. I couldn't help but notice how the paint was rubbed away in a familiar pattern resembling the continent of Africa. I froze.

"Norman," I whispered hoarsely, clutching my armrests. "This is the same plane we took coming back from Bali three years ago!" I pointed to "Africa."

As if to underscore my discovery, the plane hit an air pocket, dropped sharply, and a poor flight attendant went flying head-first into the humpy door. After she had been led away, bleeding, Norman distracted himself by yucking it up with the rest of the passengers at the in-flight entertainment, a Dutch version of *Candid Camera* in which indignant *bule* did obnoxious things. Of all the trials we faced in Indonesia, this one, for some reason, still gets to me. The plane continued to buck and shudder all the way to Bali, but at least we didn't die.

<h2 style="text-align:center">12</h2>

In putting this book together, I've realized, to my chagrin, that a number of the kickers in my *Geographic* stories, those inevitable sign-off paragraphs, inadvertently carry similarly hopeful messages that the countries and people under the microscope will overcome their challenges, figure out how to conduct their affairs in a more productive, cordial fashion, and realize their dreams. I would be willing to revise all that now, and find a better way to leave readers thinking about the particular story they've just read. At the same time, I guess I still feel that formula of hope holds true for most people I've met, at most times, and in most countries. It was certainly true of Indonesia:

> *On my last day in Indonesia, I sat on the top floor of one of Jakarta's high-rise hotels, watching the city's dizzying, thistle-like skyscrapers push up through the sunbaked smog. Having glimpsed some of its darker corners, however briefly, I wondered whether the country's centrifugal urges could ever be peacefully—or democratically—contained.*
>
> *"If we're holding together after five years," said my friend Sabam Siagian, who had joined me in a cup of tea, "that's the miracle!" A spirited man in a crisp batik shirt, Sabam, a veteran journalist and a former ambassador to Australia, had a tart, incisive way of speaking, and I enjoyed his blunt honesty. Indonesia would have to make big changes in politics, the economy, law,*

education—whatever was required to create a new culture, based on respect for human rights regardless of ethnicity, culture, or religion. In short, he suggested, Indonesians would stick together because they wanted to, not, as in Suharto days, because they had to.

As we sat in the photochemical gloaming, I wondered whether they could do it. "There will be hot spots here and there," said Sabam, with the confidence of a man who knows dealing with the future occasionally requires climbing out on a limb. Indonesia might even lose a renegade part or two. "But the country will hold together and muddle through."

That was an appealing article of faith, and for this strange, beautiful, and scattered country and its people the hope for a scattered, if peaceable future struck me as a reasonable prayer.

Indonesia did hold together and things eventually improved. Terrorist attacks continued, including grisly hotel bombings in Jakarta in 2003 and 2009, but generally were sporadic and smaller in scale. Separatist urges, if not completely stifled, were gradually muted too. Quixotic leadership at the top was replaced when a competent ex-general with democratic instincts, Susilo Bambang Yudhoyono, was elected president in 2004. The country began to right itself, and while religious intolerance remained a worrisome issue, in key areas of the economy, governance, and efforts to root out corruption, things got better. Nonetheless it has remained a muddling-through kind of place, though muddling at a demonstrably greater level of efficiency. I'm glad I got to see it when the future was by no means assured in spite of the fact my mother was dead-set against it.

And speaking of my mother . . .

The first of my two trips to Indonesia for the *Geographic* was drawing to a close in December 1999 when over my omelet and toast one morning I unfurled my newspaper and was surprised to see Seattle splashed across the front page. The story dealt with how street protests against a meeting of the World Trade Organization in the city had turned violent as activists decried the forces of corporate globalization. A big color picture showed a young street warrior dressed like a ninja against a backdrop of flames and smoke. I carefully folded the paper and mailed it to my mother in Seattle with a note expressing my concern about her safety in such a dangerous place. "Ha, ha, very funny," she said later when we talked on the phone. But I could tell she liked the joke. I realized, and not for the first time, that my mother (and father too) had given me the most practical of gifts for a man pursuing the correspondent's trade of peeping into the alternately curious, painful, uplifting business of the world—a durable sense of humor.

I also thank my lucky stars for another unqualified blessing—the opportunities I've had, even in this age of ever-unfolding digital marvels, to leave the gadgets behind once in a while and venture into the real world, if only to see what's going on there, for myself and anybody who isn't lucky enough to go see for themselves.

REPORTER'S
LOG

ASSIGNMENT	WORD BUDGET	FIELD REPORTING DATES	PUBLICATION DATE
"Kyushu: Japan's Southern Gateway" Photographer: Michael Yamashita	6,000	March–April 1993	January 1994
"The New Saigon" Photographer: Karen Kasmauski	5,000	July–August 1994	April 1995
"South China Sea: Crossroads of Asia" Photographer: Michael Yamashita	6,000	June–September 1997	December 1998
"Indonesia: Living Dangerously" Photographer: Alexandra Boulat	5,000	November– December 1999 May 2000	March 2001
"Fuji: Japan's Sacred Summit" Photographer: Karen Kasmauski	2,500	May–June 2001 July–August 2001	August 2002
"Tokyo Bay" Photographer: Michael Yamashita	3,500	May–June 2001 July–August 2001	October 2002

PARACHUTING IN: TIPS FOR THE LONG-DISTANCE REPORTER

———————◆———————

1. Do your homework while still at home. Read broadly to familiarize yourself with the depth of field in which each new story necessarily sits.

2. Talk with at least three "gurus" in your area of focus—experts who can provide a tour of the territory from contrasting points of view.

3. Establish "horizontal context"—i.e., map out all the various issues the topic implies to get a comprehensive sense of what ground needs to be covered. Think about the basic questions: Why this story, why now? Why is it important? What is it really about? How would I explain it to an editor or producer in a single sentence?

4. While still piecing together the "big picture," start zeroing in on specific story elements—the "vertical context." Talk to people who are directly involved in these narrower slices of the larger story.

5. Identify "lenses" (e.g., history, psychology, political science, economics, art and literature) through which to examine the corner of the world under your microscope and think about how to apply them directly to your story.

6. In gathering material, go both broad and deep, looking for points of conflict, tension, and contradiction. Getting to the bottom of such discrepancies will lead you deeper into your story.

7. After learning as much as you can about the story without being on scene, map your reporting plans. Think about *who* you want to interview in the field about *what* and *where* you need to go. Gather contact information and, wherever possible, make arrangements in advance.

8. In taking the field, test your ideas and expand your grasp of the story by talking to people who can give you their "aerial view" of the territory in real time—diplomats, scholars, business people, and professionals. Ask them for suggestions about whom to talk to about specific issues.

9. Throughout your fieldwork use your time efficiently and keep in mind the big ideas and events that underlay your story, refocusing and refining as you go.

10. No matter what the story, challenge the conventional wisdom and static points of view. Hold stereotypes up to the light of day and methodically dissect them in view of real circumstances.

11. Look for the "internal logic" in people, systems, and cultures as a way to understand them. You don't have to like what people say—just try to understand why they say it.

12. Be hungry for knowledge, not just information.

13. Learn to listen.

ACKNOWLEDGMENTS

The independence of the long-distance reporter, traveling the world, free to follow his or her nose to adventure, is a charming, if necessary, illusion that makes the hard parts of the job more tolerable. The truth is that in our assignments as in our lives we depend on friends, fixers, family, and mentors to guide us every step of the way. I'd like to thank a few of them right now.

I am grateful to the editors and staff I worked with at the *National Geographic*, particularly Bob Poole and the late Bill Graves, who invited me to contribute to that remarkable institution and trusted me with the assignments that anchor this book. The magazine's photographers are among the world's best, and I was lucky enough to work with three of the finest: Mike Yamashita, who became a friend and partner in storytelling; Karen Kasmauski, who expertly documented the Saigon and Mount Fuji stories; and the late Alexandra Boulat, who produced such superb images for our assignment in Indonesia, and then left us too soon.

While I am solely responsible for errors of fact, memory, or interpretation, I'm indebted to colleagues and friends who generously read the manuscript in whole or part and offered their advice: John Burnett, Gerry Curtis, Robert Delfs, Christina Greco, Gerry Herman, Tomosuke Noda, Bob Poole, Ko Shioya, and Hideko Takayama. For their thoughtful answers to my reporterly queries, I thank Glenn Frankel, Richard Shibley, and Brittany Deputy. My gratitude to the fixers and sources that have helped me with my assignments over the years, including the few mentioned in this book and the many who are not, is big and deep.

I am exceedingly lucky to belong to a community of supportive colleagues at the School of Journalism at the University of Texas at Austin, and I thank them for their friendship and guidance. Special thanks go to Bill Minutaglio, who introduced me to Allison Faust at the University of Texas Press. Allison helped me turn an e-mail memo into the blueprint for this book, and the talented Casey Kittrell and the UT Press team—Lynne Chapman, John Brenner, and Nancy Bryan, among others—worked to see it into print. And Molly O'Halloran produced some wonderful maps. They are all highly professional, painstaking, and patient people, and I thank them.

Becoming a foreign correspondent in the first place would have remained an impossible dream without the tutelage of my gallant and comradely colleagues at the *Far Eastern Economic Review*, and I especially thank Susumu Awanohara, Philip Bowring, Anthony Rowley and the late Derek Davies, Russell Spurr, David Bonavia, and Donald Wise, for the inspiration and opportunities. From my Tokyo days, I am thankful to friends and mentors alike: Bill Chapman, Roy Essoyan, David Livdahl, Andy Malcolm, Ted Marks, Brad Martin, Arthur Mitchell, Mike Tharp, Geoff Tudor, Richard Hanson, and Ayako Doi and Kim Willenson. No list of mentors would be complete without including David Halberstam and B. H. Kean, MD, who showed me that incurable curiosity and a thirst for intellectual adventure are traits that great doctors and great reporters have in common.

In writing a book dedicated to students, I am reminded of what exceptional teachers I've had and how much I owe them, and I'd like to particularly thank Don Iverson, Frank Fujii, Roberto Maestas, Ben Yorita, and Terry Weston. They said the world was a demanding, idiosyncratic, and endlessly fascinating place—and it turns out they were right.

I'm grateful to my agent Philip Spitzer, a man of true generosity and heart, and his colleagues at the Philip G. Spitzer Literary Agency, Lukas Ortiz and Lucas Hunt. On a personal note, I'm indebted to Tom and Kathy Dahlby, my brother and sister-in-law, for their many kindnesses over the years, and to my eldest brother, Dave Dahlby, whose stories I miss.

Last but surely first, I wish to thank my wife, Toshiko, for putting up with my absences when I was reporting from the field, my states of distraction when putting together my assignments at home, and for patiently reading the story behind the stories in this book. Without her encouragement and advice, there would be no book to publish, few adventures to write about, and no one to remind me, in moments of doubt, to pull up my socks and get on with it.